HOW TO BUILD YOUR OWN
LOG HOME
FOR LESS THAN $15,000
by
Robert L. Williams

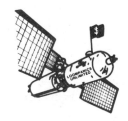

Loompanics Unlimited
Port Townsend, Washington

How To Build Your Own Log Home For Less Than $15,000

© 1996 by Robert L. Williams

Published by:
Loompanics Unlimited
PO Box 1197
Port Townsend, WA 98368
Loompanics Unlimited is a division of Loompanics Enterprises, Inc.

Cover photo by Elizabeth Williams

ISBN 1-55950-141-3
Library of Congress Card Catalog 96-77720

Contents

Introduction

Several months ago an article in a major Southern newspaper stated that an "average" house in the Charlotte, North Carolina, area would cost the buyer $400,000 for a 4,000-square-foot home. A house in the "above average" market would cost $739,000 for a dwelling of 4,000 to 5,000 square feet.

The houses described above were built on .7-acre plots with "impressive" views. Interiors included built-in range and oven, cabinets, wood floors, and seven to ten spacious rooms.

The house we completed at about the same time that the article appeared consists of 4,300 square feet, a 10′ x 50′ patio, a 10′ x 50′ elevated deck, a back deck, three levels of finished space, a workshop, dark room, second den, four bedrooms, and a total floor space equivalent to 25 rooms. The house sits in the center of a 40-acre tract of land with 2,500 feet of highway frontage and offers a commanding view of the South Mountains, Blue Ridge Mountains, and the Black or Unaka Mountains.

The total package — house, furniture, well pump, highly sophisticated alarm system, all 40 acres of land — cost us less than $33,000. The house itself, valued at more than $200,000, cost only $20,000 to build. If I had not been recovering from a badly broken leg at the time we could have built the house for $15,000 or less.

The "space equivalent to 25 rooms" requires explanation. My family and I enjoy lots of space around us, and we chose to have large rooms, some as long as 38 feet and 32 feet wide. We also chose to leave the exposed beams in the cathedral ceiling as part of the house, rather than floor the area and partition it in order to add more rooms.

Our cost per square foot was about $5.

This information is not intended as boasting; it is simply telling you what you can have for the same price or even cheaper. The entire point of this book is to show and tell readers how they can build a second

or vacation home or, for that matter, a primary and only home, for a tiny fraction of the cost of a new house.

And you can do so without the burden of large mortgage payments over a period of 20 to 30 years. You can pay cash for the house, and the day you move in, the house will be free and clear of all indebtedness.

In the bargain you can earn more money than you ever dreamed possible, if you are willing to accept Benjamin Franklin's dictum that a penny saved is a penny earned.

When we presented our plans to a builder, he informed us that the house would cost $150,000 to build. A housing-authority spokesman explained to us that if we qualified for a four percent interest rate, our mortgage payments would be either three equal payments of $50,000 each, plus interest, over a three-year period, or monthly payments of $1,300 for 30 years.

Simple math calculations showed us that monthly mortgage payments for one year would total $15,600. For 30 years the total payoff would be an incredible $468,000 — almost half a million dollars!

Of that sum, interest charges accounted for $318,000. But because we did not borrow any money, and because we built the house ourselves for $20,000, give or take a few dollars, we actually saved $448,000.

It took us 18 months, working in whatever spare time we could find after earning a living, to complete the house. There is no way that I could have earned $448,000 in 18 months, but if I saved that much money, then in a very real sense I did in fact earn that much money.

But, you could argue, my family and I had been professional builders for years, and had access to special price breaks from lumber and supply companies. Or, at worst, we were skilled wood-workers who could perform magic with hammer and saw. One of our very close friends suggested that building such a house for such a price, would out of necessity, involve large amounts of donated lumber and other materials.

This is very far from the truth. At the time we started on the house, I was sixty years old. My wife was 50, and our son was 14. For the past thirty years I had taught English on the high school, college and university levels; my wife had been a church organist, newspaper editor, and housewife and mother. Our son had been a child and a student.

None of us had ever undertaken such a challenge. In truth, we knew very little about building anything. We had done some minor repair work about the old house, but in no way were we carpenters or craftspeople.

And we qualified only as rank amateurs in the type of house-building we had undertaken. We had never even built a doghouse.

A quick word of explanation: a devastating tornado destroyed our former house and, left homeless and owning only what we could salvage from the wreckage, we could only stare in disbelief and frustration at the acres of beautiful trees uprooted by the storm.

So, borrowing from the trite adage that says if life gives you lemons, make lemonade, we decided that if the storm left us with only logs, we'd make a log house.

Not a log house in the tradition of what modern log houses are, you must understand. We priced some of the log-house kits and found that the kit alone for the house we wanted would cost us about $87,000, which left us with the task of buying materials and building foundation walls, installing plumbing and wiring and roofing, in addition to assembling the logs once we were ready to use them.

We built our house with a chain saw as our primary piece of equipment. We did not own and had no access to fork lifts, cranes, tractors, or any other heavy equipment. We owned an old and battered pickup truck, two chain saws, and basic carpentry tools such as hammers, screwdrivers, and the like. We also owned a small garden tractor that was 15 years old and barely mobile, but it served its purpose well. We found that we had to buy some tools as our work progressed, but these expenditures were fairly minor and easily affordable.

Incidentally, we counted the tools, including the chain saws, as part of the cost of building the house, even though we still have the chain saws and other equipment. We even counted the cost of gas used to drive to the supply houses for equipment or supplies. So this book does not include only part of the cost of building. If we decided to buy a sandwich for lunch, we included that expense as part of the cost of the house. In brief, we tried to include every cent of money we spent relative to the building of the house. That even includes minor and major repairs to the vehicles and chain saws we used for the house construction.

There are several great advantages we had over many people: we had lots of spare — or at least free — time; we had highly flexible hours; we already owned land, and we had the well and septic tank already installed.

We also had lots of fallen trees!

But, armed only with hope, need and determination, and in the faces of literally hundreds of people who said we could not possibly achieve what we were setting out to do, we built the house we had always wanted.

Some time ago *Mother Earth News* featured my family and our house on the cover. The captions accompanying the photo stated that we had built a 12-room "palace." I should point out that what we built was a log house, nothing more or less. But we could not be any more pleased with a palace. That's because our house represents what many millions of people desire: to beat the system, to prove to ourselves and others that dreams are attainable, and to glow in the satisfaction of having achieved a high level of self-reliance.

A quick note about donated materials: the building materials that went into our house were purchased by us. Nothing that we used was "donated," except in the sense that the folks at the building supply stores "gave" us the materials after we gave them our money.

What we did, many people have told us, was possible because of our desperate circumstances and our courage and ingenuity. They point out that most other people do not have such qualities. To this I say: RUBBISH! Everyone who faces an expense of half a million dollars (that he or she does not have or have ready access to!) is also in desperate circumstances. Other people all over the nation and world have the same ingenuity and courage that we have. To me it takes courage simply to face another day of teaching the middle-school kids, to hit the road and try to sell a product to people who want to keep their money, or to face the emotional problems that are common to nearly everyone.

I feel that simply living and surviving in the modern world requires courage and ingenuity. More to the point: Can you or the typical man — or woman — on the street do what we did? Of course you can, if you meet a few basic requirements. You must be in reasonably good health, for the work is hot and exhausting, the hours are long, and there is abundant frustration in the early days of the challenge. You must have some knowledge of the operation of a chain saw and enough common sense to help you deal with a few minor problems that will be special only to your particular needs and circumstances.

You must not be easily defeated or disappointed. Or, if you are quickly depressed, you must be able to bounce back with a renewed determination and resolution.

You must have access to a building lot and some trees, and you should realize that from time to time you will need someone to help you with some of the more difficult processes. Husbands and wives working together should be able to handle reasonable challenges. Children 12 years of age or older can do a great deal of the work.

You will need ready cash or credit for the items that you cannot cut with a chain saw or obtain free of charge. These items include roofing, wiring, light fixtures, plumbing, tiles, cement blocks, bricks, and similar other materials.

You must be able to follow simple and basic instructions.

And you must have the patience of Job at times. There will be days when everything seems to go wrong. It will seem that the work is moving with infuriating slowness, particularly in the early stages, and you may experience heat and cold weather, bites from insects, and scrapes, scratches, and bruises.

But these problems are common to nearly all major endeavors you tackle outdoors. For every problem, however, there are the realizations of short-range dreams and goals. For every setback there are compensating rewards. And for every ruined length of timber there are the joys of seeing your house taking shape.

Perhaps above all, there is the glowing satisfaction that comes from knowing that you have challenged the system and won a devastating victory.

This book does not presuppose any skills or knowledge on the part of the reader, except for elementary aspects of hammering and sawing and measuring. The approach is very simple and down-to-earth. Specific directions and suggestions are provided in clear and easy-to-follow language.

Photos and drawings clarify written instructions.

Sample (and simple) house plans are included. You do not need complicated blueprints, unless your local building code requires them. You can also modify any plans to meet your own needs or desires. The house described in this book is smaller than the one we built, primarily because of our awareness that most people do not want or need to tackle such an ambitious project. But any dimensions can be expanded or reduced. If you prefer a house twice the size of the one described, simply double all appropriate lengths and other specifications, or enlarge the house proportionately according to your needs.

In these pages you will see my suggestions on how to handle specific types of work. These are only suggestions. If you have a better way, or even if you *think* you have a better way of doing the job, use your own creativity and ingenuity. Don't sit back and accept one man's advice when your own judgments are equally good and perhaps much better.

I should point out that nothing in this book is theoretical. There are no syllogistic arguments proving on paper that certain techniques are workable. I know that every step in this book works, because I have done everything that is described in these pages. In most cases I have done these things more times than I care to remember.

Even today I am still doing these kinds of projects. I have no reason or intention to do otherwise. I love outdoor work, and after having built (with incredible help from my wife Elizabeth and our son, Robert III) a house, tractor barn, equipment shed and tool house, and three-car garage, I plan to continue working on chain-saw buildings and projects until I no longer have the strength, time, interest, or reasons to keep on.

And I am not being unduly modest when I say that what we have done, you can do. You can do it as well and perhaps much better than we did. And I want to hear from you when you succeed beyond your highest expectations.

Now, good luck and good building!

Chapter One:
Basic Considerations

Some people should not build a chain-sawed log house, or any other kind of house. Just as some people should not own dogs, cats, parrots, or Arabian stallions, not all people possess the emotional attitude needed for the hard work and the occasional — or frequent — frustrations you may encounter.

Five basic types of people should only glance at this book, put it down, and move on to the more interesting areas of the mall. These five are: those who are in poor health or are at such an advanced age or chronic state of debilitation that the stress and strain of the work could be dangerous to their health; those who are highly mobile and might feel the need to pull up stakes and move at a whim or at a moment's notice; those who simply dislike physical work to the point that they refuse to do it at all or do it only under duress; those who are so impatient that they cannot stick with a project from beginning to end; and those who are wealthy enough that they do not worry about paying the high prices needed to purchase a house on the modern market.

There are other types of people, of course, who should not attempt this sort of work, and it might be easier to list the types who should undertake this level of challenge.

First, there are those who simply cannot afford traditional housing. We have all read the horror stories of people who see the house of their dreams, manage to come up with a down payment and closing costs, and then find that they are saddled for the next thirty years with gigantic mortgage payments. And if you are among those who cannot afford to give away four dollars every time you pay one dollar on your mortgage, you should perhaps give serious consideration to building a log house such as the one described in this book. (A friend recently confided to me that by the time he pays off his mortgage, he will have spent five times the cost of the house itself. In our own case, we would have paid more than three times the cost of our

house — and we were offered a four percent interest rate!)

There are others who love the excitement, challenge, and reward of doing things for themselves. They like to get their hands dirty; they revel in long-range projects that offer them the chance to show what they can do.

Some want a second home in the mountains or at the lake, while others prefer a hunting lodge or wilderness get-away home. Still others enjoy working with their hands and using their imagination and judgment to solve problems and take charge of their own lives.

In short, if it is sensible or meaningful for you to take on this challenge, then read on. If you are serious about the task facing you, make certain before you get too involved that you will have (a) enough spare time to work in blocks of several hours, (b) adequate funds to pay for the basic tools needed or contacts who can arrange for you to have at least temporary use of them, (c) access to land on which to build the house (close enough to the trees for you to eliminate hauling the logs long distances), (d) an understanding mate or partner who will enter into the challenge with a willing heart and back (or at least stay off your back while you are hard at work on your dream log house), and (e) a good chain saw and a supply of sharp chains.

The ideal location for a log house, chain-sawed or not, is obviously in a wooded area and preferably along the shores of a stream or lake. But well-designed and soundly constructed log houses fit into virtually any environment. I was surprised to learn very recently that more than half the log houses being built in the United States are constructed inside city or town limits.

To expand on the ideal location, the perfect setting is within a grove of thick trees so that you can clear a space for the house and then use the logs cut from the clearing as walls of the house. If you don't have ready access to logs and must haul the logs to the work site, you will have to prepare yourself to spend extra money, because you will need, first, equipment that can load the logs onto trucks and, second, trucks to haul the logs to the building site.

Our logs were essentially 200 to 800 feet from the house site. We found that we were able to transport them this short distance by hoisting the large or butt end into the back of a pickup truck and then dragging the log behind the truck. If you can possibly do so, buy land with a good stand of usable trees on it. When possible, use trees that need to be thinned or harvested so that you are not ravaging the countryside but actually helping ecologically.

When we cut our logs, every tree that we used was already on the ground or had been uprooted to the extent that it remained standing only because it didn't have room to fall. After we had cut the fallen but sound trees, we trimmed up the usable limbs and tops for firewood. The sawdust was, after it rotted, used as compost for our gardens, as were the ashes after the firewood had been burned. We left the smaller limbs in small piles to serve as nesting places and homes for birds and small animals.

One question that arises almost invariably is that of which kinds of trees make the best logs for a house. The answer is that straight, large, and tall trees are needed. Beyond that, it really doesn't matter greatly. Some wood decays much faster than others, and some is so hard or knotty that it is difficult to work with. You will never find a sufficient supply of perfect trees, so choose from the best that you have available.

It should be stated at the outset that nearly all kinds of trees will rot quickly if allowed to remain wet for prolonged periods of time. Oak, one of the hardest woods in the East, will rot instantly if used as fence posts or in other ways that leave the wood in contact with the soil. Wild cherry or fire cherry is a good and hard wood that will last a fairly long time in wet conditions or in contact with the soil. Hickory rots immediately if allowed to remain wet for long periods of time.

Locust is an excellent wood in terms of its durability, as is cedar, but there is not an abundance of these trees in large enough sizes to consider building a log house from them. Good trees for log houses include poplars, in addition to firs, pines, spruce, and similar conifers.

There are obvious advantages and disadvantages of the basic types or varieties of trees. Pines, particularly loblolly and other slender and long varieties, serve wonderfully. Some prefer spruce or balsam or fir, but poplar is my choice for the best tree, especially if you can cut it when the sap is down.

Some argue that poplar is a soft wood that rots almost as soon as it contacts the ground, but you should realize that in some of the rainiest sections of the United States there are poplar-tree log houses that have stood soundly for more than two hundred years. Yes, poplar rots when it stays moist for long periods of time, but so does oak, pine, hickory, and most other trees.

Years before we ever realized that we'd need to build a log house, I cut boards from sound oak, pine, and poplar trees and stored one group of boards, including samples from the three trees mentioned above, in a dry environment; in an outdoor area I stored other samples; then I laid samples of all three types of boards on the ground.

The results were interesting to me. The boards on the ground all rotted quickly, with poplar decaying first, then the pine, and finally the oak. When stored off the ground but exposed to rain and sun and wind, the pine decayed first, then the oak, and then the poplar. Of the woods stored in dry conditions, the pine tended to soften fairly early, but the oak and poplar remained sound and firm for years. The poplar seemed to become harder and harder, until it was difficult to drive a nail into the wood. The same was true of the oak.

One major advantage of poplar is that the trees grow so tall and straight that you can cut logs 60 feet long which are knot-free and virtually arrow-true. Poplars are also very soft when green, and you can rip or mill the logs fairly easily; yet a dried poplar log becomes extremely hard and durable, and at the same time the weight is manageable.

A common problem with poplars is that they tend to check or crack when they dry, particularly if they were cut during summer months when they were in full leaf. You can reduce the amount of checking by applying a sealer before the log is completely dried. This checking is also common with oaks, firs, and pines.

Pines and similar trees are as a rule soft enough to cut very easily, and such trees are durable when handled properly. One disadvantage of such trees is that many pines are quite large at the bottom but taper so rapidly that it is difficult to cut a very long log with any real size. Several exceptions are white pines, loblolly pines, and members of the spruce and fir families. If you cut pine logs but do not stack them so that weight is upon them at all times, the pines tend to curve or curl as they dry. A dried pine log remains soft and easy to work with, and at the same time the log is light and easy to haul.

The best logs in terms of size are those just slightly larger than you need them to be. For instance, if you plan to cut 8″ by 10″ logs (and I recommend this size heartily; reasons will be provided later), the small end of the log should be barely large enough for you to make the cut. You will need to rip or mill away only a small slab on each side. If the tree is much larger, you will be ripping through great thicknesses, which take longer to cut and result in greater waste on the butt ends.

How long should your logs be? As long as the distances they must span. In other words, some logs should span the entire width or length of the house, while others must span only the distance between windows, between windows and doors, or between windows or doors and the corner of the house. This means that, depending upon the size of the house, you may need some logs up to 60 feet or so long, and some as short as four or five feet.

Why not use oak or hickory trees for your logs? First, the wood is very hard and incredibly durable if kept dry, but such wood is also very slow sawing. Hickory tends to dull a chain quickly, and both trees are so heavy that they are difficult for one or two people to handle without heavy-duty equipment. And it is often difficult to locate enough of the trees in one stand to build an entire house. Poplars, on the other hand, are known for their reproductive capabilities and rapid growth. Cut a huge poplar and leave the stump in the ground, and within a few years there will be three, four, or even five large poplars that have sprung from the root system of the cut tree.

How many logs will you need for your home? Naturally, the answer depends again upon the size of the house. For our house we calculated that we would need 112 logs (including very long and very short ones), which turned out to be a correct estimate.

Figure it this way: assume that you will cut logs that are eight inches thick and ten inches high. For eight-foot ceilings or walls you will need ten logs (equal to 100 inches, rather than 96, so your walls and ceilings will be eight feet and four inches rather than

eight feet, unless you trim off an inch or so on four logs and reach an even eight feet) in each of the four walls, if all logs run the full length.

So you will need 40 full-length logs or their equivalent. Then, if you plan to use log girders inside, you will need a log girder every four feet, including one at each end. You can then estimate that you will need 50-60 logs for a modest-sized house.

What are the first steps in starting to build this get-away house or retreat? Or this permanent home? Start by selecting the proper building site, choosing the floor plans you want, and then beginning with the basement (optional), foundation walls, the floor framing, and subflooring. Keep in mind that you need not spend a great deal of money on blueprints or plans that you purchase from any of the many sources available. You need not hire architects or draftsmen to design your home.

It is assumed that you are reading this book because you want to save money. So start saving immediately. When we started to select house plans, we found that the cheapest we could find would cost us more than $400. We discovered at about that same time that we could draw our own plans and save the $400 for use on more meaningful areas of the house. Stock plans may save you plan-check fees with your local building officials. If you have access to a computer, home-design programs can be purchased for under $25. Generally, the plans you produce from such programs will satisfy local building officials.

You can buy simplified plans for much less than the figure given above, but even if you save only $20, that is enough to buy a chain for your chain saw. More importantly, the plans you draw for yourself will reflect the exact house that you want, rather than the generic preferences of some magazine staffer.

How long does it take to sketch out usable plans? You can do it in your spare time whenever you have an hour or so to work. In this amount of time you can sketch out nearly all the basic plans you need before you get started on the house itself.

Your first step, however, is to choose the location for your home. Draw plans later to suit the terrain of the land you elect to use as your house site.

The following chapter will discuss the site selection.

Chapter Two:
Selecting the Proper Site

Obviously, you must have land on which to build, if you plan to construct a log cabin or house. This land may well be inside city or town limits (Remember: there are now more log houses built in urban areas than in rural environments) or it might be in a wilderness area. The principles of building remain the same for either location; however, it is highly important that you build as close as possible to your tree or log supply.

If you do not own land but plan to launch a search for suitable land, you will quickly find that prices vary to a truly shocking degree. There are rural locations where you can buy land for as little as $17 (the actual price of land we visited on a trip to the West in 1992) and for as high as $10,000 or more per acre.

What you will pay depends largely upon where you plan to build your dwelling. If you envision a log house situated on a mountain hillside with a great trout stream running through the front yard and with deer, bears, elk, wild turkeys, and other highly desirable animals abounding, you will pay a premium price unless you can stumble or finesse your way into a better deal.

On the other hand, if you want a cabin in the woods close enough to town for you to drive to work, or if you plan to try homesteading, you may be able to work out a surprisingly low price per acre. While I do not recommend subterfuge, it often pays off if a person can visit in a rural area, get to know some of the local people, establish yourself as a desirable neighbor, and then casually mention that you are in the market for land.

This takes time, but it is often worth the effort. My family knows a man who did just this, and a retired farmer sold him a tract of land not long ago for $180 per acre. The landowner, who refused to accept a higher payment, explained that he was getting along in years and he and his wife preferred to have someone trustworthy living nearby. This land, incidentally, had several acres of open pasture land, a dozen or more acres of exceptional timber, a stream that originated from a series of springs on the property, and an abundance of wildlife.

Why sell so cheap? As the farmer said, having a good neighbor was now more important to him than having more money. The logical rider to this clause is that if you get land cheap because someone wants a good neighbor, then you are expected to *be* a good neighbor.

Talk with bankers, realtors and businessmen whom you know to own property in your preferred area. If the bank is forced to foreclose on a mortgage, you might be able to work out a deal to buy the land from the owner who is about to lose it. Do not feel that you are taking advantage of an unfortunate person; instead, realize that there is no question that the man will lose the land: the only question is whether the new owner will be you or some other person.

Approach the owner and explain to him that you will pay him adequately for him to regain some of the equity he has in the land and at the same time protect his credit rating. He might prefer selling the land to you than relinquishing it to the bank.

Read the want ads with dedication. Some months ago I saw an ad in which the owner agreed to sell 1,000 acres for $500 down and $100 monthly. I did not check to see how long the monthly payments would be in effect, but it really doesn't matter. Think of such a deal as renting 1,000 acres for $100 per month. Even if you never pay off the debt, you will have the exceptional opportunity to live on a rather large tract of land at a very low cost.

While some may consider it ghoulish, watch for legal notices appearing after the death of a local person or for public notice that land will be sold for delinquent taxes. At times an elderly person will turn over his land to the state in return for medical care for the remainder of his life. The state then offers to sell the land to anyone who will agree to be responsible for the medical expenses of the owner.

From a strictly financial viewpoint, you might want to take such an opportunity into consideration. But keep in mind that the owner may live for months, even years, and at the rate medical costs accelerate and accumulate, you could owe a king's ransom by the time the land is available to you.

If you learn of a large tract of land for sale, you might invite friends to agree to buy smaller tracts, so that while you do not own extensive acreage, you will at least be surrounded by friends with similar interests and concerns for the land. Years ago some college students, three sets of them in fact, formed an unofficial club, and together they bought more than 900 acres in a beautiful mountain area. Then, as some of the group grew tired of living in the mountains, the remaining students, who by this time had completed their studies and were earning a living, happily agreed to buy the land being vacated.

When the enterprise ended, one student owned nearly all of the original tract. But because he was able to buy the land in small amounts, he was never financially strapped or, as they say in rural areas, he was never "land poor."

One of the best ways to find land is simply to get in your car and drive around the countryside where you think you would like to build your home. When you see For Sale signs, call the realty office or check with the owner.

There are many ways to locate and obtain land. You may be able to trade urban or city property to a ruralite who is ready to move to the city. If someone leaves acreage to a local college or university, you should realize that the college may never be able to use the land as such but would benefit greatly from the money to be derived from the sale of the land. The same applies to churches and other social organizations.

But before you try too diligently, decide just why it is that you want to live in the country. While there are numerous advantages (and I, for one, would not dream of moving back into town), there are also a number of disadvantages.

Keep in mind that everyone who lives in the country has a reason for being there. Some are farmers, which means that they will be operating tractors and other farm implements; they will be plowing or harvesting late at night, early in the morning, and at times all night long. They will perhaps keep hogs, sheep, goats, turkeys, and chickens for food. They will also spray their crops with chemical pesticides and fertilizers. So if these and similar operations will bother you, think twice before buying land adjacent to a huge farming operation.

Some people love to hunt and fish, and if you live in the woodland areas you must learn to discourage or accept hunters as a fact of life. On the first morning after our first night of living in the country, I woke early and opened the front door to enjoy the beauty of the country dawn.

And was shot in the foot!

Standing on my own porch, with the door ajar, I was stung by shotgun pellets fired by a hunter who had tramped the woods for years and either did not know or care that someone now lived where he had hunted traditionally. And I spent many thoughts on the topic of what might have happened if the pellets had been six feet higher. Blind writers and photographers are often at a severe disadvantage.

If you work in town, there will be the commute to worry about. If you forget to pick up a loaf of bread on the way home, you may have to face the choice of having no bread until the next day or driving back to town to buy a loaf. Home insurance is often higher in the country because of the distance away from a fire department.

But, to me, for every disadvantage there are at least a dozen major advantages. Our taxes are much lower than they would be in the city (when we bought our 40 acres, the total taxes on the land that first year were $25 — this was in 1975), and we grow fruit and vegetables and nuts, thus considerably decreasing our cost of living. Our land is so situated that at night there are no mercury-vapor lights shining in our faces; in fact, the closest light visible to us is the moon.

Living in the country offers, in many instances, free fuel in the form of firewood. Stands of trees that need to be thinned offer a constant supply of rough-sawn lumber, thus lowering the cost of constructing outbuildings to nearly zero. By chain-sawing your own lumber and timbers (after completing your house!) you will find that you can build a three-car garage for about $300, thereby saving yourself thousands of dollars.

There is, in the country, the beauty of nature in the form of wild flowers, birds and animals of all sorts. Depending upon where you live you might see on any given day a small herd of deer, foxes, coyotes, bears, wild turkeys, grouse, partridges, pileated woodpeckers, several species of hawks and other birds of prey, and countless other animals that are delightful to watch or, for some people, to hunt.

During a span of less than one month we had a huge black bear and a mountain lion set up squatters' rights on our land space, and the latter animal had been declared totally extinct in our part of the nation. None had been sighted in the wild in several decades, and yet one visited us on a number of occasions. Such visitations are beyond price.

When you have come to terms with the problems and joys of country or backwoods living, you are ready to select the land for your cabin or house. Ideally, you would want to locate the cabin among a grove of trees. If you are really fortunate, you can clear some of the trees to make room for the house and deck or porch, and then you can use the cleared-away trees for the walls of your house.

Among the other items on your wish list are a small stream that is spring-fed and, if possible, originates on your land. Such a stream is not subject to the pollution that is common to streams that flow through the property of numerous people. You want enough trees so that you can cut those needed for the house without depleting the forest. The trees should be large enough in diameter and long enough that they will run along the entire length of a wall.

If you choose to build your log house in town, you can still cut and mill your own logs and then transport them to your city property. If you can locate (and this is not difficult at all) some landowner who will permit you to harvest trees, you can cut the trees and square them on the site. Then you can load a small number of them into a pickup truck (being careful to weigh down the ends of the logs near the cab of the truck so they will not fall out on the way to the building site) and haul them away. Or you can hire someone with a larger truck to haul them for you.

So the options are many. You can enjoy rustic living in a subdivision, or you can homestead miles from town. What remains is making decisions such as the final location choice.

The ideal site is one between country roads, so that you can control how close your neighbors, present and future, will be. Before you settle on a plot of land to buy, investigate to see who owns neighboring land. Try to determine what the future of the land will be.

If the land owner has, for instance, six or seven children, and if there is a strong likelihood that these children will grow up, marry, and build their own houses on the farm, you will be faced in the near future not by one neighbor but perhaps by dozens. If five children and their mates set up housekeeping near your property, you have 10 neighbors already. If these couples have three or four children each, you may find yourself yearning for the quiet life in the suburbs.

Rural living is filled with stories of people who buy their idyllic tract of land only to learn a few weeks or months later that the neighbors have sold their property and the county has obtained the land for a landfill. Or that the owner decided to give up farming and construct a trailer park on his property. Often the best that can happen, and this is not always good, is that the land is divided among children, and suddenly five or six new houses appear uncomfortably near your property.

Naturally, if you prefer community living, this can be very good news; otherwise, it can be deplorable. Check zoning rules and regulations before you buy. In short, do your homework before you start buying and building.

When you buy property, be very careful about selling any part of it to friends or relatives. A man may sell a tract to his daughter and son-in-law, and when divorce time comes, the land is the prize which is fought over. Or perhaps the daughter dies and the husband inherits the land. He then can sell it to total strangers.

One suggestion is that if you sell land, insist upon a sales agreement in which the land, should the buyer wish to sell in the future, must be offered to you at the selling price.

The location of a log house should be, in a strong sense, the same as the site of any other type of house. If you do not plan to include a basement, look for a well-drained area that is flat enough so that you will not need to have extensive grading done. If you do plan to have a basement, the best terrain is a sloped hillside where the basement can be dug so that three walls of the basement are underground and the other wall offers a daylight type of basement.

If the house will sit on the bank of a river or stream, give adequate consideration to the possibilities of flooding. If you need such information, the Department of Agriculture can provide you with a map of the acreage that makes up the watershed area affecting the house.

You may be shocked to learn how many acres actually make up the watershed terrain. The forest area, cultivated fields, and any other land higher than the stream and with a slant toward the stream all contribute to the watershed area. After a torrential rain or after a series of rainy days, even small streams can rise to alarming heights as flash flooding occurs.

Unless there is a superb reason for locating the house right on the bank of the stream, you might be wiser to move the house site back from the creek and higher. If there is a severe slant to the land down towards the stream, move the house site so that the stream would have to rise a significant number of feet from its normal level in order to cause any damage.

Think twice, too, before locating a house atop a hill. The general notion is that a hilltop house looks impressive and commands a superb view of the valley or hillside below. While all this is true, it is also true that a hilltop receives the most heat from the sun in summer and the sharpest winds in winter.

A house on a hilltop is also a target for lightning. Before making a hilltop choice, research the electrical storms in your area. You may be astounded to realize how many lightning bolts strike during one single storm. Hilltops are also prime targets for tornadoes and wind storms generally.

Avoid areas that are constantly damp. Termite and other insect damage, decay, mildew, fungus growth, and many other problems often occur when the air inside and surrounding the house is too moisture-laden.

The best location for a log house may well be a hillside that is on the side which is protected from the weather. This means that the house should generally be protected as much as possible from the north wind, if you live in a cold climate.

If you have a forest area, select a spot on a gentle slope midway up the hill, away from potential flash-flood damage and out of the direct path of wind storms and lightning. Be sure that you can slope the soil away from the house on all sides, if possible, or that water rushing down the hill can be diverted around the house so that you will not have to worry about under-cutting or erosion during heavy rain-storms.

In moderate climates, basements virtually assure you that the water lines inside your house will never freeze. During a recent winter our temperature dropped below zero degrees Fahrenheit every night for a full week, and daytime temperatures never rose higher than the 'teens.' People all around us were experiencing terrible problems with freezing water lines, but inside our log house we did not have a moment of difficulty.

Give serious consideration to the trees surrounding the house site. In summer the trees do a wonderful job of insulating your house against the sun's rays, and in winter these same trees provide wind protection.

But these trees are also lightning attractors, particularly if the trees around the house are the tallest in the area. The larger and taller the trees, the greater the danger from lightning, and the greater the threat that a wind-blown tree will fall across the house and damage it severely.

Investigate the depths of the rock layers under the soil. County Public Works Departments or the Department of Agriculture generally have soil reports which you can refer to. If these rock strata are very shallow, you can not excavate very deeply for a basement. On the other hand, if the rocks are at an ideal depth, the rock layer itself can provide an exceptional footing bottom. Huge rocks too near the surface may mean that a basement is not a real option.

You should give serious attention to septic-tank locations and the drain field. Will the drainage pollute a stream or become a threat to drinking water? Will it be a detriment in any way to the environment?

What about right-of-ways for electrical lines, telephone lines, and water lines, if any? Many electrical companies insist on a very wide access lane under the wires, and you may have to give permission for the company to slash their way through a superb forest in order to reach your house. Underground lines may be an impossibility.

Many times when the electrical right-of-way is established, the cut-away area quickly becomes infested with poison oak or poison ivy, honeysuckle, and other unwelcome floral guests. The thick vegetation also offers homes to many birds, which in turn will attract snakes and other predators. Be sure you want these, or be prepared to keep the right-of-way cleared. Incidentally, the cut-away swath can become a superb garden location, if you are able and prepared to fight the roots and sprouts from the trees that were cut.

If you have several acres, you can possibly work out a route for the power company to follow without destroying your forest.

The telephone company in many areas prefers to bury lines, but if the lines must be run through a forest, many root systems will be damaged and trees will be killed.

Water lines, with rare exceptions, must run underground to prevent freezing and for general protection. What will the line trenches do to your forest growth? Or how much more expensive will the lines be because of the tree factor?

You may be planning to have a vegetable garden, orchard or small vineyard near the house. If so, will the plants receive enough sunlight through the trees? The proximity of trees may mean that rabbits, woodchucks and other animals may ravage your garden at night.

Heating with wood is a great option for log-house dwellers, but you must give consideration to the dangers created by sparks falling onto dead leaves or other flammable materials. You must also think about the potential danger of falling limbs which might crash onto the roof of your house.

Your road is of vital importance, particularly if your house will be a considerable distance from a highway or secondary road. If your area is prone to having deep snowfalls or ice storms, can you get your vehicles out? Can emergency vehicles reach your house if necessary? Are there curving stretches of road that will make it impossible for concrete trucks or delivery trucks to reach your house site? In case of heavy rains, are there low places along the road that will become impassable?

These are only a sampling of the questions that must be answered effectively before you invest time, money and energy into the construction of your log house. This does not mean that you should have second thoughts about building a log house; it does mean, however, that you should spend time considering your decisions before it is too late for you to change your mind.

Whenever I stick my hand inside a hole in the ground, I think first of what might bite me; my hopes of finding a gold watch are far down the list of possibilities. The same is true of searching for a place to live. If you were looking for a house in the city, you'd investigate schools, churches, neighbors, zoning ordinances, nearby factories, the tax rate, and dozens

of other potential problems. Why not do the same before leaping into country living?

Once you have made the firm commitment to country living, or at least to log-house living, and once you have committed yourself to the double-edged task and joy of constructing your own cabin, essentially with a chain saw, there are questions to be considered concerning the type of log house you build.

In the first place, when I hear someone say that he or she has always wanted to live in a log house, it comes across to me as being the same as wishing to drive a car or eat a meal or see a movie. A log house differs from nearly all other houses, but so do brick houses, tri-levels, mobile homes, and palaces.

When we speak of a log house, we are not talking about some esoteric adventure that will alter the course of civilization or create a dynamic new life form. So when someone tells me how much he wants a log house, I ask questions like: Do you want a round- or squared- or milled-log house? Do you want palisade-log walls or one made of horizontal logs? Do you want a butt-and-pass corner style or a dovetail or perhaps a third style? Do you want interior walls of logs or just exterior walls? Do you want...?

The questions could be endless. But the point is that before you decide to build a log house, you need to have some pattern, or architectural plan, or more-than-vague notion about the house other than the fact that there will be logs in it.

Start with the most basic meanings of the term "log house." You can have a ranch-style house. Or a frontier-cabin-style. Or the Norwegian-style or any of a dozen or so other styles. You can have a one-floor plan, a two-story plan, or a tri-level log house.

This isn't meant to be argumentative. It is intended to suggest that you should select a house style that suits you and your family or others who will live in it. If there are persons with debilitating illnesses or physical infirmities who will live in the house, perhaps a one-floor cabin would be better. If the family consists of a husband and wife and seven children, the house should perhaps have a sleeping loft, at least, upstairs.

If the house is to contain a cottage industry or be the site of space-demanding hobbies or workshop pursuits, perhaps you should consider a basement for the electrical equipment. Is the house to be a weekend retreat? Or is it to be your only place of residence? Do you plan to live in it for many years, or is it some investment experiment?

Only you can answer these and the myriad of other questions which must inevitably be faced. If your family is likely to grow within a few years, choose a plan that will permit additions with few problems. If you are in your retirement years, you may be content with a small cabin that will accommodate you and your mate and, on special occasions, two or three guests.

Finally, consider how the cabin will blend with the land. If you are planning to set the cabin against a backdrop of trees or hills, almost any style will do. If it is to be built alongside a river or lake, almost any style is effective.

But if it is to be sandwiched inside a housing development or subdivision, you may prefer to attempt something dressier. For the purposes of this book, however, my assumption is that the cabin is to be rustic, roomy, open, and attractive enough to fit into almost any background short of a country club. And you may be surprised to learn that some log houses not only fit into the club environment but are often the envy of the other residents.

This chapter, then, assumes that you will be doing all or most or a significant amount of the work, and that you will be working alone or with one or two helpers. You will not, we shall assume, have access to heavy machinery to do the lifting for you, and you will want to save money everywhere you can, not by cutting corners on quality but by learning to do sound, strong work with less financial outlay than you would expect.

It is further assumed that you will want to draw your own rough plans, do your own masonry work, install cabinets, and in general be the builder, not the contractor, for the house.

Presumably, you have already had the discussion about the pros and cons of country living and log-house ownership. You have concluded, along with me and millions of others, that the benefits of country living are too numerous to list; they are simply to be enjoyed. As Shakespeare stated, in reference to the Forest of Arden, we can find "tongues in trees, books in the running brooks, sermons in stone, and good in everything. I would not change it."

The proper place to begin is with the adventure of drawing your own rough house plans. Chapter Three will offer you a number of suggestions.

Chapter Three:
Drawing House Plans

You can purchase complete blueprints and layouts for your log house, if you wish to take that approach. One of the best sources is the bevy of log-house magazines on the newsstands. Nearly every issue will offer not only detailed information but also costs and addresses so that you need only make the phone call or send your check to have the plans delivered to you.

Or you can take the more courageous route and draw your own plans.

The fact that you plan to build your own house, rather than buy one, suggests from the outset that you are either interested in saving money or asserting your own self-reliance. In either case, you can draw your own plans and save money while proving to yourself that you are able to handle the work yourself.

If you choose to draw your own plans, keep them simple — very simple — at first. Work only on the dimensions and locations of the various rooms in the house. Start with the outside width and length of the house.

The size of the house will depend, in part, upon the size and availability of logs. If you have trees that will produce logs 60 to 70 feet long, you have far more latitude than does the person whose longest logs will be 15-20 feet. While you can splice logs by using shiplap joints, the process takes a small amount of time, and there is always the risk of damaging the log so that part of it is useless. But with practice you can learn to join logs quite effectively in this manner.

If you merely want a hunting lodge or cabin to be used on weekends or a few days out of the year, you may wish to build only a small cabin. If you choose this route, you can build a 20 x 20-foot cabin with a sleeping loft. Such a cabin will take a short time to build and will cost very little.

Such a cabin could have a kitchen/eating area, a sitting room or den, and a bathroom. The sleeping loft could be located in the abbreviated upstairs or loft area. The basic cabin would consist of 400 square feet on the ground floor and perhaps 240 square feet in the sleeping loft.

Assuming that the cabin would have walls nine feet highs, you would need 11 logs in each wall (if each log is ten inches high and 20 feet long), for a total of 44 logs for all four walls. If you choose to use logs all the way to the roof peak, you will need ten more logs on each end. However, these eave logs will be much shorter than the wall logs. You will start with a log that is nearly 20 feet long, but each succeeding log becomes shorter and shorter until you will be measuring by inches rather than feet when you reach the top of the eave.

If you use a puncheon floor, you will need 30 eight-inch logs to cover the entire floor area, or 24 ten-inch logs. In this part of the house you can use shorter logs without problems, so you can make good use of log sections that were not long enough to be used in the house walls. You can also use traditional floor framing for considerable ease in construction, and at the same time you can save on the number of logs needed.

Assuming that you wish to cut your own joists and flooring, you will need 14 joists plus double headers, which would add eight more 20-foot joists, making a total of 22 joists. A huge tree trunk or log, about 16 inches in diameter, will yield about seven 2" x 12" joists. Thus, three logs will provide nearly all the joists needed for the floor.

With this basic approach, think in terms of a cabin with a front and back door, two windows on the front and back, two windows on the end away from the kitchen, and no windows on the fireplace side of the house. The kitchen can be located to the left of the fireplace or wood-stove area. The dining area is located adjacent to the kitchen. The middle of the room is the sitting area, and at the far end of the house you can locate the stairs leading to the sleeping loft.

In essence, that's about all you need to know as a starting point. Once foundation walls are built and the floor is framed, you are ready to cut and stack logs.

If your house is to be a little more ambitious, such as a two-bedroom house with one and one-half baths, kitchen, dining area, den, and two small guest bedrooms upstairs, you need to think in larger terms. Perhaps the house should be 40 feet long and 24 feet wide. You must also keep in mind that the $15,000 log home suggested in this book is a modest affair. If you enlarge greatly, you will add to the total cost. The more you enlarge, the greater the cost increments will be.

You can fairly easily find trees that will yield logs 40 feet long, so if you use 8" x 10" logs, you will need to cut the same number of logs as before. The only difference is that the logs must be a little longer.

If you decide to go for the huge house with all kinds of extra room, plan for a structure 52 feet long and 32 feet wide. Such a house will need the equivalent of 112 logs, plus two more for floor supports running the entire length of the house.

Here is a sample layout for such a house: Imagine that the house runs east and west, with the kitchen, fireplace, family room, and eating area in the west

end. On the north side you can have a huge family room/dining room with the fireplace in the west wall, and on the other side of the house you can have the kitchen sink, range, and part of the cabinets on the south wall. On part of the west wall you can have the refrigerator and the rest of the cabinets. Inside the L formed by the cabinets you can have a breakfast dinette (Figure 3-1).

As you face the south wall, the back door can be at your left and at the end of the cabinets. Also to your left can be the wall that separates the laundry room/-sewing room from the kitchen area.

As you face the north wall, in the center of the house is the front door. To the right of the front door is the stairway leading to the second floor. Under the stairway is a second set of steps leading to the basement.

As you stand in the center of the house and face east, a small hallway leads to a bathroom on the right. At the end of the hallway is a huge closet, with bedrooms on each side. In the master bedroom another bath is off to the right or toward the west. The wall on the west side of the bathroom separates the bath and the laundry/sewing room.

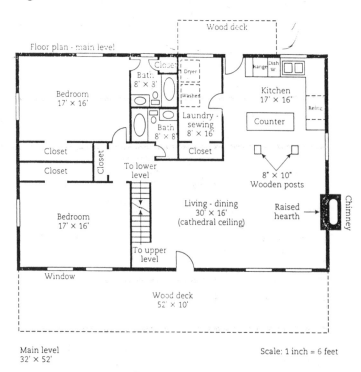

Figure 3-1
Floor plan for ground floor.

On the first floor, then, you can have kitchen/-dinette, family room, dining room, laundry/sewing room, two bathrooms, and two bedrooms. Upstairs, as soon as you reach the second floor and you stand facing the south wall, there can be an open sitting area that is surrounded by a continuation of the stairway railing. The sitting room overlooks the kitchen/dinette, dining room, and family room and fireplace (Figure 3-2).

A small alcove is to the east of the sitting room, and inside the alcove two doors lead to upstairs bedrooms or guest rooms. If you wish, you can convert either of those rooms to a den or library.

From the sitting area, if you face the west wall, there are twelve girders connected to the central girder that runs the length of the house. In this open space you could, if you wish, add four very large extra rooms or six average-sized rooms. Or you can leave the area open and enjoy the spacious element created by the cathedral ceiling.

Under the family room and in the basement there can be a second fireplace or wood stove and a downstairs or basement den. Under the kitchen is a recreation room. Under the bathrooms and part of the bedrooms are a workshop and a photo darkroom. Under the bedroom on the north side of the house there can be an office or similar space.

This is simply a basic plan that we worked out for our own house. It is very easy to diagram and provides an abundance of room. Nearly all of the rooms are multi-purpose, or could be.

If you have never diagrammed or sketched a house plan, start with a large sheet of white paper or graph paper. For your working schematic, let one-quarter inch equal one foot. This means that a 52-foot long house would be 13 inches long on the diagram. The 32-foot width would be eight inches.

If you want the kitchen to be 20 feet long and 16 feet wide, sketch a line at a right angle to the south wall. Measure from the southwest corner for five inches along the south wall. The right-angle line from the south wall will reach to the center of the house. The house is 32 feet wide, so the center of the house is at 16 feet. Thus, the line would be four inches long.

If you want the laundry/sewing room to be eight feet wide, draw a line parallel to the four-inch line and two inches from the laundry/ sewing-room line.

Assume that you want the second bath to be eight feet wide and six feet long. Draw a line parallel to the east wall of the laundry/sewing room. This line should also be two inches from the laundry wall and one and one-half inches long. The west wall of the bath is also the wall separating the bath from the bedroom, and this line should be continued from the 1.5-inch mark

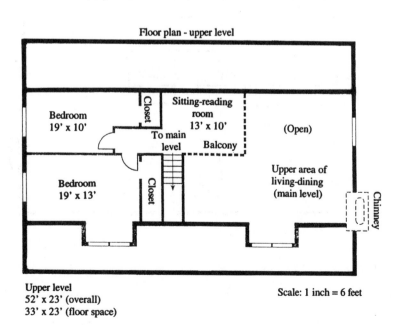

Floor plan - upper level

Bedroom
19' x 10'

Closet

Sitting-reading
room
13' x 10'

(Open)

To main
level

Balcony

Bedroom
19' x 13'

Closet

Upper area of
living-dining
(main level)

Chimney

Upper level
52' x 23' (overall)
33' x 23' (floor space)

Scale: 1 inch = 6 feet

Figure 3-2
Floor plan for upstairs section.

to a four-inch length, which means that the bedroom north wall, or a portion of it, is flush with the hallway wall.

The outside wall on the south provides one wall of the bedroom, and the bathroom walls provide the other boundary. You now need the north wall drawn in. Remember that the kitchen is 20 feet long, the laundry room is eight feet wide, the bathroom is eight feet wide, all along the south wall. This gives a total of 36 feet. If the house is 52 feet long, the remaining distance is the length of the bedroom, which means that the bedroom is 16 feet long along the south wall.

Return to the kitchen area and mentally place yourself at the corner of the kitchen's east wall and the laundry room. You are at the center of the house and facing east. Draw a line from the corner to represent the designated length or width (whichever you prefer) of the laundry room and bathrooms. The laundry is eight feet wide and the bathrooms are also eight feet wide, so the 16-foot line would be represented by a four-inch line from the exact center of the house from north to south. The line, of course, will be toward the east end of the house.

You now have the two bathrooms diagrammed, along with the entire south side of the ground floor. If you want a large closet at the end of the hallway, you need to draw a right-angle line off the center line toward the south wall. A half-inch line will represent two feet of closet space on the south side of the line.

Now draw a right angle line from the half-inch line toward the east end of the house. This line represents the north wall of the hallway bathroom and the north wall of the bedroom you have just sketched. This means that inside the bedroom you can have a long closet two feet deep along the north wall of the bedroom.

Now for the north side of the house. If the front door is to be in the center of the house, measure from the west end of the house a distance of 26 feet, to be represented by 6.5 inches. The width of the rough door opening is 36 inches, so the doorway opening on the front and back walls will be ¾ of an inch long.

Assume that the stairway is six feet east of the door opening. Measure off 1.5 inches for the wall separating the north-wall bedroom and the stairway. This wall does not reach all the way to the center of the house, because you need to allow two feet for the hallway. (You have already allowed two feet for the hallway when you diagrammed the south side of the

house, so the two distances will leave you with a hallway four feet wide.)

Your wall line will then be 14 feet rather than 16 feet. Mark a line at right angles to the north-side line. This line must represent 14 feet; therefore, it must be 3.5 inches long. The hall is six feet long, so you will need a line running east and west and 1.5 inches long.

Continue the hallway line all the way to the east wall. This will become your bedroom wall, with space allowed for a long closet two feet deep and backed against the closet in the other bedroom.

The ground floor is essentially planned. Remember that you have the option at this point (and for a considerable time from this point) to change any interior dimensions you desire.

You may now wish to sketch out the upper floor. On a new sheet of paper, draw the line representing the stairway, which will be three feet wide and will attach to the west wall of the second bedroom sketched. You will need a ¾-inch line to represent the stairway, which leads to the sitting area upstairs.

The stairway will be 13 feet long, so you will need a line three and one-fourth inches long. The stairway does not begin against the outside wall. You need to move the stairway out from the wall three feet, which means that you will have a ¾-inch space between the north wall and the base of the stairway.

The sitting area extends west to the kitchen/laundry room line, so you will need a line running west along the center line of the house for 12 feet, or three inches long. Because of the roof slope, the sitting area cannot extend to the south wall. It must stop four feet from the south wall, and the line represents 12 feet, so it must be three inches long.

A four-foot-wide alcove is at the east side of the sitting-area wall, so it will be represented by a one-inch line (half of it on each side of the center line) and the alcove will be three feet deep, so use ¾-inch lines to diagram the alcove.

Continue the center line from the sitting area to the east end of the house. This line represents where the two upstairs rooms will back against each other.

Now complete sketching the upstairs rooms, which, like the sitting area, will stop four feet shy of the outside wall. This means that each room will be 12 feet wide.

In the open area, draw in the positions of the girders, which will be ten inches high and eight inches thick and spaced four feet apart. Start at the chimney wall on the west side and measure out four feet (represented by a one-inch line) and draw a line from the north wall to the center line. Continue doing this all the way along the open area on the north side of the house.

Now you are ready to calculate and inscribe the basement dimensions. If you want a second kitchen (or canning kitchen, as some folks in the rural areas call them), the best place for it is directly under the formal kitchen. Such a location simplifies the wiring and plumbing later.

Before you plan on any basement water connections, however, you must first make sure that the kitchen sink and any restroom facilities in the basement are higher than the septic tank, if you plan to use it for drainage of these facilities. If you cannot have a gravity flow, you should change the plans at this point.

If you want a family room or recreation room downstairs, you can use the entire north side of the basement or, if you don't have immediate plans for the basement kitchen area, you can use the entire western half of the house for a recreation area. You will have room for ping-pong, a pool table, a home entertainment center, card tables, video games, and other interests (Figure3-3).

You will want a daylight side or wall of the basement, so that you can have a door to the outside. You can even have extra-wide doors which will enable you to bring autos into the basement, which then becomes a garage, if needed.

This suggestion is not without its flaws, however; you will have the vehicles inside a very small percentage of the time, if you are like many families, and you will be taking up a great deal of heated space. If you live in an extremely cold climate where a heated basement may be necessary for proper vehicle operation and maintenance, the garage idea might be a good one for you.

In fact, the idea of a basement or an upstairs area could be less than a perfect notion if you or family members have trouble with stairs. Naturally, any plans you make should be built around your particular needs. This is why you should, if possible, have a strong voice in tailoring the house to your needs rather than buying a set of plans created for a mass market.

If you have need for a conference room or office space that is far from the traffic pattern of the house, you may wish to do as we did and devote the 17 x 16-foot room on the north wall adjoining the basement den to office space for the family. Here expensive and necessary or desirable items around the house could be stored here. Temperatures are high enough in winter and cool enough in summer for the area to be comfortable for users and convenient for heat-sensitive computers and film.

I suggest that the final space on the south wall be set aside for a workshop where minor maintenance can be done and small projects completed. If you plan to install a table saw and other woodworking equipment, you will need an exhaust fan to carry the sawdust from the room.

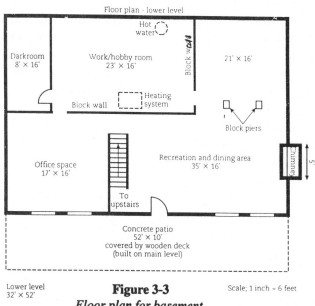

Figure 3-3
Floor plan for basement.

All that remains for the basic layout of the rooms is to determine whether you should have decks at the front and/or back of the house. Perhaps the best suggestion is to first determine how much use you will make of a deck, and then choose the side of the house where the deck will be most enjoyable.

If you have a beautiful view to the north, then locate the huge house-long deck on that side. If the south side of the house is shaded and you need relief from the summer sun, you may opt for the south side for the deck. If the winter weather makes the afternoon sun a delight, choose the north side.

Or, decide which side of the house serves best, and put a huge deck there. Later you can add a smaller deck to the less desirable side of the house. But before you do either, determine as well as you can whether you need a deck at all.

My opinion is that a log house needs a deck and that people who live in a bucolic setting should have a deck. And while no one person's opinion is any more than that — only a personal opinion — I am totally convinced that the perfect deck is one that can be reached only via the house: no steps leading to the ground and no other access to the deck.

There are several reasons for this belief. First, if you like to sit on the deck at night, there is always the possibility of intruders surprising you, whether the intruder is in the form of a mugger or a wild animal. Second, if you have outside pets that love to spend time with you and your guests, the deck offers a sanctuary that the pets cannot invade when their presence is not wanted.

But the best suggestion I can make is to please yourself and your family. Incidentally, when we asked for an estimate on the cost of building our deck, we were given three prices: $5,500, $6,300, and $7,500. We built the deck for about a tenth of any of the prices, and the result is highly pleasing to us.

Your house plans are, for the moment, complete. Later you will need to make minor adjustments and include wiring and plumbing details, as well as allow for cabinets and appointments of various natures.

The simple truth is that when you have determined your house site and the outside dimensions, you have made the proper start, and you now need to complete foundation walls, floor-framing, and then wall-building. But first, please take the time to read Chapter Four carefully. It deals with the basics of chain-sawing.

The major wish I have for you as you begin your project is that you build your dream house and have no negative experiences at all. The worst result would be for you to suffer an accident. So read, re-read, and then practice the safest chain-sawing methods.

The suggestions made here are not recommendations; they are only possibilities to consider. You should tailor your house, as I stated earlier, to your needs and bank account.

The house sketched out here was built for $20,000. Total work time on the house was 18 months, but because we had to earn a living while we worked, we could work only about four or five hours each day. So, reduced proportionately, the time for building the house was realistically about nine months.

Always keep the Ben Franklin adage in mind as you work: A penny saved is a penny earned. We saved $448,000 by paying for all our materials as we worked, so that we paid no interest charges at all. In fact, we actually earned a little interest on the money we left in the bank until we needed it.

Seen in the light of the money we saved, the house was a real bargain in our eyes. It is extremely unlikely that we could have earned $448,000 in the time it took us to build the house, as I have already stated elsewhere.

How much you save and what type of bargain you make will depend largely on how much of the total work you do, how much lumber you cut rather than buy, and how much, if any, you must pay others to work for you.

Study the drawings in this chapter, consider your options, and start to work. Chapter Four gets you started.

Chapter Four:
The Basics of Chain-sawing

A chain saw is a fantastic tool. It can accomplish wonders in the hands of an experienced and wise person. It can save you more money within a few weeks than you dreamed possible.

A chain saw is also a lethal weapon which can mutilate, maim, and kill within seconds. It can be deadlier than the bite of the king cobra, the krait, the bushmaster, or the coral snake.

Used properly, the chain saw is unparalleled; if it is used carelessly, it is equivalent to playing Russian roulette with a single-shot pistol.

So start with a basic assumption: The chain saw can be dangerous. So can cars, guns, bathtubs, and pocket knives. Do not begin your work while you are terrified of the best tool you have at your disposal. Instead, learn a few basics about chain-sawing, particularly the type of chain-sawing that is part of building a log house.

Begin with proper care and maintenance. Your owner's manual tells you what types of fuels and bar oils to use. Follow the manual's directions for mixing oil and gas, and use the kind of gas that the manufacturer recommends.

The manual also suggests that you clean or replace filters and cleaners on a regular basis. If you have a clogged air filter, the saw will be hard to start, difficult to keep running, and unsatisfactory in use. You will use too much gas, foul out plugs, cut less wood, and spend an inordinate time tugging at the starter cord.

A chain saw in good condition may be difficult to start when cold, but after it has been used for a few minutes, it should start after that with one swift pull on the starter cord. There is no really good reason for pulling 10 or 20 times on the cord and exhausting yourself before you start to work.

Keep a supply of fresh and uncontaminated gas on hand, with the proper oil mixture. If you are using two or three chain saws, and if each one needs a different

mixture, use cans that are clearly labeled. Do not use gasoline that does not have the oil mixed with it. You can ruin a chain saw within seconds if you do.

If the machine is in good condition and you have the proper fuels, turn your attention to the chain at this point. Always keep a chain in good condition on the saw, and when you are sawing, make certain that the chain is sharp and that it is installed properly.

A few words about sharpening: you can take the saw to a repair shop to have the chain sharpened; you can buy one of the electric sharpeners; you can get one of the rigs that attach to the chain-saw bar to guide your sharpening; or you can buy a round file and sharpen it yourself.

Figure 4-1
Using file bracket and holder.

If you take the chains to be sharpened, you have time and money invested as you drive to the shop and lose valuable work time and then pay $5 or so for the sharpening job. The electric sharpeners run off a car or truck battery, and if you cannot get the vehicle to the cutting site (if you are in the woods working on logs, for instance), you need to take the time to carry the saw back to the vehicle. The sharpeners also cost several dollars.

The rigs work satisfactorily, but require time to set up and use, and also cost a relatively small amount. If you use the file and sharpen the saw yourself, you may have some degree of difficulty in getting the hang of the job, but once you do, the result is a superior sharpening that costs little or nothing and is extremely fast and handy.

So I recommend that you sharpen your own chains and that you do it with a round file with a fifty-cent wooden handle attached. To use the file, you need to set the chain saw where it can be easily held in place while you work. One of the best locations is in a short chunk of log that will not be used for anything else but firewood later. Cut a kerf or groove deep enough so that the saw will remain stationary in the groove while you use the file on the teeth. See Figure 4-2.

Figure 4-2
Using round file to sharpen chain.

You should carefully note the condition of the teeth when the chain is new, and keep that picture in mind as you sharpen the chain when it has been well used. Notice that on the back of the tooth there is a diagonal mark provided by the factory. This mark is the angle of the cutting edge of the tooth when the tooth is correct.

With the saw in a stable position, hold the file with one hand on the handle and the other on the tip. Position the file so that it is "inside" the tooth area. That is, the file fits into the cut-out under the cutting edge. Notice that the underside of the tooth is where the actual cutting occurs.

With the file against the tooth, push the file gently forward and away from your body, in the direction of the hand holding the tip of the file. You should feel the file slide very gently along the underside of the tooth, and if you are doing the job well you will see tiny bright filings falling away.

An unsharpened tooth is dull in color or hue; a newly sharpened one is bright and shiny. The newly sharpened tooth is smooth across the cutting edge, while the old tooth may have tiny gaps or an uneven cutting edge on it.

Unless there has been unusual damage to a tooth, give each tooth a certain number of good strokes. Usually five light strokes will sharpen any tooth adequately.

To keep track of your progress, you can find (on most chains) two teeth in succession on the same side of the chain. Start filing here and continue to move from tooth to tooth until you are back at the starting point. If you don't find them, you can always locate the starting point because the tooth will be bright and shiny, rather than dull.

File all of the teeth on one side of the chain. Then shift to the other side of the saw and sharpen the teeth on that side as well. Do not skip any teeth and do not use more strokes than necessary on any tooth, unless it is damaged.

A well-sharpened chain will cut faster and smoother, and you will get a better cut on your logs or lumber, you will work less, and the saw will be less abused. A dull chain damages both work and saw, and exhausts the operator.

For the fastest and smoothest cut possible, you can file the teeth so that they are straight across rather than diagonal. You will cut out under the tooth to a slightly exaggerated extent. When you file in this way, you will have a ripping chain rather than a cross-cut chain. You can also buy factory-prepared ripping chains, but if you want to file your own, here's how to do it.

Use a flat file at first and file all the teeth until they are at right angles to the bar. Then use the correct size of file and push it smoothly and firmly across the underside of the tooth. Maintain a slight upward pressure so the bottom of the tooth, where the cutting occurs, receives the pressure.

Figure 4-3
Cutting notch in tree before felling.

Figure 4-4
Final cut in felling tree.

When you have completed this step, use a file one size smaller than the one you used for the first step. File out a fishhook shape behind the cutting edge. You will find that such a chain cuts almost twice as fast as a traditional chain. You will also find that the kerf or groove is slightly smaller, and that the cut is extremely smooth.

As you work, stop and sharpen the chain every few minutes, if the work is tough. You may find that after you square one long log (20 feet or more) the chain should be sharpened. If you file often, the job can be done in a few seconds; if you wait until the chain is really dull before filing, the job takes much longer.

Now, what kind of chain saw is best for the work? The worst mistake I have ever heard occurred when a person said that since he was not experienced with a chain saw he would buy a small saw and use it until he felt secure, after which he would buy a much larger saw.

Experienced operators of chain saws are far more likely to advise the man as I did: "Buy the biggest and best saw that you can handle. The larger the saw and the more powerful it is, the less chance of kickback and injury. The smaller the saw, the greater chance of kickback. The small saw bar hits an unseen snag or tree limb and the saw leaps into the air, perhaps injuring the operator. The more powerful saw hits the same snag, and rips through it without hesitation and without incident."

This advice still holds. The more powerful saws generate more revolutions per minute and exert greater force against the wood. They cut faster, work the chain and the operator less, and in general do a better job. Even some chain-saw manufacturers are guilty of advising customers to buy lightweight saws, which to me seems a dreadful mistake.

As far as brand names are concerned, there are many fine saws on the market today, and I have used a fair number of them. Consult with people who have used the saws or, if you know no one, contact me and I'll give you an honest, unbiased preference. The operative word here is preference. I am not qualified to state which saw is better or not as good, but I am entitled to my views and opinions.

When the saw is fueled and ready to go, you should already know several key facts about chain saws. This knowledge may well protect you from serious or even fatal injury.

1. Always keep the sawing area as clear as possible of logs, sticks, rocks, fuel cans, and other movable items. You cannot afford the risk of falling onto a running saw or having the saw fall upon you if you lose your footing.

2. Before you start to saw through a limb or tree trunk, always look behind the limb or log to see if the saw bar may hit something. The area should be clear. If there are small limbs and snags, clear these away before you start to saw.

3. When the day is windy, exert even greater care than normal. This is especially true if you are felling trees. A tree with a trunk cut three-fourths through is virtually at the mercy of the wind, and it can easily fall in any direction if the wind changes. One of those directions might be upon *you*.

4. When dropping a tree, whenever possible allow it to fall as gravity dictates. If a tree is leaning clearly to the west, it is often very difficult for inexperienced (and often experienced) sawyers to drop the tree toward the east.

5. Before you saw a tree down, notch the back side one-third of the way through the trunk. The back side is the side away from the saw on the final cut or, stated another way, it is on the side where the tree is supposed to fall. See Figure 4-3.

6. When the notch is cut, usually a foot or two above the ground, make the final cut on the opposite side from the notch and start very slightly above the notch and slant the cut only a small amount downward. This slant cut adds to the tendency of the tree to fall away from the chain saw operator.

Figure 4-5
Using wood wedge to keep cut from binding.

Figure 4-6
Using nearby tree as shield from kickback

7. If you must try to drop a tree against gravity, always be certain to have someone who can watch the tree to see that it goes the right way. Have a clear communication system. For example, if the tree is falling the wrong way (and sometimes the cutter cannot see clearly because he is too busy with his own work) the partner should rush up to the cutter, tap him smartly on the shoulder, and run toward safety. The chain-saw operator should, at the moment he feels the tap, drop the saw and follow the partner quickly. Do not stop to ask questions or try to save the chain-saw. They make other saws; there's only one of you.

8. When you are cutting down a tree, as soon as you have cut into the trunk (after sawing the notch), pause and drive in wood or plastic wedges (never a metal wedge). See Figure 4-5. Even if the tree leans slightly to the south, you can cause it to fall toward the north if you use notching and wedges wisely.

9. Keep children, pets, and other persons and valuables as far from the work site as possible. Before you drop a tree, be sure that you know where everyone in your area is located.

10. Anytime you are using a chain-saw, always imagine the arc in which the chain-saw bar tip will travel if the saw should kick back. Then make certain that no part of your body is in that arc. Keep in mind that when the saw kicks back, you are not going to have the physical strength to stop the recoil. But neither will the saw change the direction of its arc unless the chain strikes some object which deflects the chain. So when you start to cut, keep your head and shoulders clear of the potential arc.

11. Here is a trick that I like very much: If you are sawing one tree which has another tree growing within a foot or so of it, saw from between the two trees whenever possible. That is, do not put your body between the trees, but insert the saw between the two trunks. If there should be a kickback, the chain will hit only the other tree, not you (Figure 4-6). I use the same approach when I am lopping limbs off standing trees. If the saw kicks back, it hits only the limb above. Now, I know that there are those who will scream that this is unsafe, but it works for me.

12. When the tree is on the ground, it will be partially supported by limbs. Other limbs will be sticking upward in several directions. Cut off the free limbs first — those that are not in contact with the ground. A good procedure is to stand so that the limb, when it falls, will not fall onto your feet or legs. Some huge trees have very large limbs that could cause painful injuries, and if your feet become entangled in the smaller limbs, you are likely to lose your footing.

When you start to cut the supporting limbs, you need to watch for several potential problems. First, when a limb gives way, sometimes the entire tree crashes to the ground. At other times the trunk will roll sideways before crashing, and if it rolls in your direction, you could be in trouble.

Have someone, if possible, drag away the cut limbs as soon as they are free from the tree. Do not work amidst a tangle of limbs and branches.

When you cut a supporting limb, you will notice that the limb bends under the weight of the tree. Never try to cut into the deep part of the bend. If you do, the weight of the tree will cause the groove or kerf to tighten, and even the most powerful saws can pinch and be held immobile by the force. Always saw on the back side of the curve, never inside of it. You will be astounded by the fact that a limb slightly larger than your middle finger can bind and hold fast even the most powerful chain saws.

13. Work uphill from the log. Never work below it. A green or sappy log 15 inches in diameter may weigh as much as 60 pounds per running foot. This means that a 60-foot log weighs hundreds of pounds, and if this weight should roll over on you, it could snap bones like twigs and crush your rib cage and skull.

14. If you are sawing between two points where a log is supported, bear in mind that as you saw, the log will start to sink at the point of the cut. Soon the saw will be caught and held tight. To alleviate or avoid this problem, there are two methods, assuming that you must cut at that point. The first is to under-cut the log. You may wish to top-cut it until you have a cut a third of the way through. Then under-cut so that the saw rises to meet the original kerf.

The second method is to use wedges. When the first cut is deep enough that you can drive in a wedge and still have room for the chain-saw bar, pound the wedge in tightly so that the kerf cannot close when the log starts to fall in two separate sections.

15. Never, never bore with the tip of the chain-saw bar. If you can hold the tip steadily in place, it will, of course, eat its way through the wood, but if you allow it to move only slightly, it can kick back severely. So don't try it. Here I must confess that I have used the tip of a saw to bore many holes in trees, but I urge you not to follow the foolish example I set.

16. Do not attempt to cut through a tree that is lying flat on the ground. The chain will pass through the wood and hit rocks, sticks, or other debris, all of which can cause problems, not the least of which is a badly damaged or ruined chain.

17. Never allow the chain to dig into the dirt. Nothing short of a rock or chunk of metal dulls a chain faster than dirt.

18. Never saw rotten wood. Even a very brief contact with rotted wood will dull a chain instantly.

19. Never cut in anything less than good light. When it is too dark to see the chain clearly, it is also too dark to see other problems which might arise in the area.

20. Beware of snakes, ticks, hornets and other types of bees, biting and stinging insects of all sorts, and rodents whose homes may be destroyed when a tree falls. Imagine the predicament if a falling tree contains a hornets' nest or beehive.

21. When the tree falls, watch for the butt to kick up or for the trunk to fall across a leaning tree. If this happens, the butt flying upward can deliver devastating power, and if the tree falls over another tree, the butt end can then swing through the air with terrifying speed and energy.

22. If a tree falls into another tree and hangs there, if possible bring a tractor to the site and hook a chain or cable around the butt of the tree and pull outward until the top of the tree slides downward to the earth. Do not get under the tree and try to rock it or shake it loose.

23. If there are rotted or weak limbs on the tree, watch carefully as the tree falls. These limbs could break loose and fly through the air a considerable distance.

24. Do not attempt to hook a vehicle to a tree that is leaning in the wrong direction and try to pull the tree over in violation of the laws of gravity. A small truck simply is not powerful or heavy enough to overcome the weight of the tree and the force of gravity. I know one man who tried this, and the tree fell in the direction of its incline, crashed onto a house, and jerked the entire rear end out of the vehicle he used in his attempt to pull the tree over.

25. Never tie the trigger of the chain saw in the open position. It may become tiring to keep squeezing the trigger for hours at a time, but tying the trigger is extremely hazardous. The man referred to above also tied the trigger of his saw as he attempted to prune a neighbor's tree. He lost his balance and fell from the tree, and the loose chain saw, hanging from a rope, hit limb after limb, kicked back only to hit other limbs, and virtually mangled the tree beyond worth.

There are numerous other precautions, but they cannot all be listed. At all times, it should go without saying, use the best judgment of which you are capable, and never take safety for granted.

In subsequent chapters there will be additional information provided for using the chain saw. Rather than attempting to present a complete manual in one chapter, this book will offer special techniques and guidelines for the specific tasks undertaken in the log-house construction process. Chapter 36 describes some projects you can undertake which will give you experience, and boost your confidence in using a chain-saw before you embark on the construction of your house.

Chapter Five:
Tools and Equipment

With virtually any building endeavor there are common or ordinary tools and then there are special tools that are either essential or highly desirable. With special tools and equipment, there are inevitably additional costs.

There are, fortunately, many homemade devices that work as well or nearly as well as the manuactured devices, and with a little patience and energy, plus a great deal of imagination and creativity, you can invent your own devices.

In this chapter some of the basic tools are recommended. In other chapters where special equipment is needed, there will be suggestions as to how you can make your own, when possible, and save the high cost of purchasing a tool that may not be used for more than two or three hours in all.

Start with the basics. You will need hammering tools. These include a regular peen hammer or claw hammer, preferably the 20-ounce weight, and a three-pound hammer. You will also need at least one heavy metal maul of the type commonly known as the go-devil, although in many parts of the country this term refers to a totally different tool. The tool referred to here is the eight-pound splitting maul with the sledge-hammer shape on the upper side, or end, of the blade.

For leveling, you will need a carpenter's or mason's level, along with a line level and some twine. You can use a two-foot or three-foot level if a four-foot variety is not available handily.

For sawing or cutting purposes you will need a heavy-duty (but not the professional bow-style) chain saw, a few files, and extra chains. If you plan to use more than one brand of chain saw, you will need a fuel container (clearly marked) for each of the saws. Two two-gallon metal or plastic cans work well.

A measuring tape or some device that enables you to get fairly accurate measurements is essential. If you buy a tape, get one at least 25 feet long. A 100-foot tape is highly useful or even essential.

A carpenter's square or a quick-square (or combination square) is needed. In your toolbox you may also find it useful to have large screwdrivers of both Phillips-head and slot-head varieties. An adjustable wrench or good socket set will come in handy.

A word about the carpenter's square. This is not just an instrument that will permit you to mark straight lines across a log or board for sawing purposes. This highly useful tool can be used to lay off stairway stringers, measure the length, angle, slope, and bird's-mouth cuts for rafters, and aid you in literally dozens of important ways.

Figure 5-1
Using C-clamp for chain-sawing.

One very small tool that is amazingly helpful is a C-clamp. While inexpensive and simple to use, it has more uses in carpentry and construction work than you can imagine until you come to crucial points in your work. The C-clamp can help you to saw boards of all thicknesses, lumber of virtually any dimensions, and even molding and modified tongue-and-groove dimension lumber. When you are in the building process, the C-clamp serves as a worker's assistant in many ways and is immensely helpful when it comes to doing work alone.

From an economic standpoint, any work that you can do by yourself represents a savings to you, and if you can cut the logs, saw lumber, and do the foundation walls, floor framing, and other necessary elements of house building, you can save anywhere from hundreds to thousands of dollars.

While labor isn't a part of tools and equipment, it may be appropriate to mention the topic here. If you must pay an assistant or helper at the rate of only $5 per hour, you are paying out $200 a week or $800 per month if the helper puts in a full 40-hour week. Double that figure if you must hire two helpers. And keep in mind that when you take a coffee break, or when a sudden storm halts the work, the helpers' pay continues just as it would if you were getting full results from them.

In this chapter and elsewhere there are items described that you can build for very little time and money but which will save you significant amounts in terms of work, time and money. A few items are listed in this chapter, but in other chapters, as they become important, other helpful homemade pieces of equipment will be described, along with instructions on how you can make your own.

As far as other equipment is concerned, be sure to have the following in good condition: an electric portable drill, a heavy-duty crowbar, a hacksaw, pliers with long handles, a come-along or power pull, a length (at least 16 feet) of chain, ear plugs for use during chain-sawing, and a five-gallon bucket to hold tools not in use and too big for the toolbox.

In Figure 5-2 the power pull or come-along is fastened to the bumper of the truck, and the other end encircles a log that must be pulled into alignment with the log wall. The power pull is operated by moving a ratchet type of handle back and forth. One person can generate the power of several people by use of this simple and inexpensive device. The power pulls we purchased cost less than $5 each.

If you plan to do your own masonry work, you will need a good trowel, a jointer tool, a mortar box or construction wheelbarrow, and some mortar boards. You will ultimately need a good wheelbarrow, so if you must decide whether to buy the mortar box or the wheelbarrow, go with the wheelbarrow. For cement and mortar mixing, you will need a shovel and a hoe, minimum.

Figure 5-2
Using power pull or come-along.

At this point you should decide whether to buy or rent the tools, unless you already have access to them. If you plan to mix a great deal of mortar or cement and use it rapidly, you may wish to investigate a gasoline-powered mixer. Such equipment at this writing costs about $25 per day to rent. You may get better rates if you wish to rent by the week.

You can buy the machine, used, for about $700. So if you are going to be renting it for a month or more, you will be better off from a financial standpoint to buy the machine. When you are finished with it you can sell it for at least $500 and regain all but $200 of your money. You may even get more than $500 for the mixer if you kept it in top-notch shape.

Even if you lose $200, over a period of a month, you can look at the loss in terms of renting the mixer for only $6.66 per day rather than $25. You can keep the machine and use it for future building projects. You can rent it to others, and in 30 days you will have your initial investment repaid. From that point on it's all profit.

You can also rent fully-equipped tool boxes. Again, think of the amount of use you will get from the tools before you decide to rent or buy. In the typical rental tool box you may find a rather large number of items that you will have no use for. If you buy only the tools you will need, you may save money and also have the tools at the end of the project.

If you rent, all you have left are receipts.

When you obtain a chain saw, if you must buy one, spend the extra money and get one with a good reputation among users. You will be using this saw for many, many hours, and you can shorten or lengthen your job significantly by using a superior or an inferior saw.

You will find that you can cut costs in nearly every direction when you get your work underway. For instance, if you have a short (two-foot or so) level but find that you really need a longer level, which will cost you about $40 more than the short level, there is a simple way that you can lengthen the short level to 12, 14, or even 20 feet. All you need to do is cut or buy a long 2″ x 4″ and, after you are certain that the edge is straight, place it upon the two points in question. Then set the level atop the 2″ x 4″. Your reading will be very accurate.

If you want to save even more money and not buy a level at all, you can use a two-foot length of clear plastic tubing and plug up one end. Fill the tube by placing a large drop of oil (old, black motor oil will work fine, or mineral oil, etc., will work equally well) in it, fill the tube with water, and plug up the other end. In the center of the tube make two clear marks with a ballpoint pen or tape. Then tape the tube flat across the top of a 2″ x 4″ and proceed to measure levelness as you normally would. The oil will act as the bubble in the level, and you can tell immediately if a surface is level or what is needed to make it level.

If you do not wish to invest in a straightedge, you can make your own by using a chalk line. Hold the end of the line where you need to mark first, then stretch the other end of the line to the end point, and snap the line. The straight edge is marked.

To make your own square and save several dollars, select two straight lengths of wood (about two to three feet each) and position them so that they form a rough right angle. Drive a nail or use a screw to connect the pieces where they lap. Then move the members until they form a perfect right angle.

If you are not sure how to get a right angle, measure out the outside edge of one member six inches and mark the point. Then measure out and mark eight inches on the other. Then measure across the distance between the points. If the result is ten inches, your assembly is perfectly square. If it isn't ten inches, move one arm or the other until you have exactly ten inches.

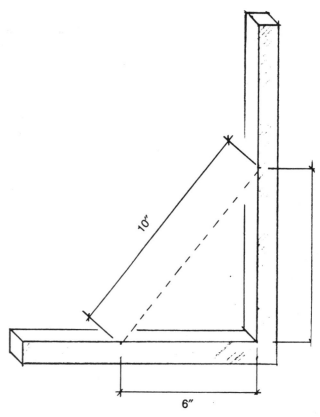

Figure 5-3
How to construct a perfect right angle for square.

If you use a small bolt and wing nut to connect the two members, you can tighten the wing nut and the square will be held stable. If you need to determine another angle, loosen the wing nut and set the angle at the desired point. Return the angle to the original point when you finish.

For heavy log work you will need a peavey or cant hook. These are astonishingly helpful, but they are also rather expensive. You can make your own very quickly and easily, if you really wish to continue saving money.

To make a peavey, cut a straight or nearly straight young wild-cherry sapling or shoot from a wild-cherry sprout. Other trees will work as well, but wild-cherry (or fire cherry) seems to be plentiful in many areas of the nation.

The pole needs to be six or seven feet long. A foot from the bottom or thicker end, attach a small chain or length of strong rope or cord. You can attach the chain by drilling a hole through the sapling and using a nut and bolt, or by cutting a shallow groove around the sapling and simply tying the rope into the groove. Leave the other end free for the moment.

Figure 5-4
Using homemade peavy to turn log.

When you are ready to use the makeshift peavey, position the sapling alongside the log to be turned and run the cord or rope or chain around the log and fasten it again to the peavey. Then by using the sapling as a lever, pull back on the sapling and you can turn the log quite easily.

For an even better variation, if you can attach a hook, no matter how makeshift, to the loose end of the cord or chain, use a hammer to drive the point of the hook into the bark of the log, and use the same leverage to turn the log.

There are several variations on this same bit of equipment, and you can try several of them that you may devise while at work. Necessity is truly the mother of invention, and after you have lifted logs or tried to pry them up with a lever and fulcrum for several hours, you will begin to see new and better methods of accomplishing your ends.

Getting the log to the top of chock or saw blocks is one of the key elements of the operation, and you will

need to find some way that accomplishes this end. If you do not have a better way, the following explains a method and a device that works wonders.

Figure 5-5
Driving in chain and spike for dragging log.

To build what I call a modified ring dog, you will need the same type of sapling or shoot that is described above, a length of chain, a long bolt (six inches long and 5/8-inch thick or thereabouts), and another long bolt or fluted (or spiraled) spike.

To make this little wonder, cut a short length of log (two feet or so) that is six to ten inches in diameter. Use your chain saw to cut two grooves in the surface of the log chunk, the grooves to be five inches apart and three inches deep. The grooves should be in the center of the log, equidistant from the ends. When the grooves are cut, use a chisel or ax to chip out the wood so that you have a wide gap in the log surface.

Now drill a hole through the end of the handle or sapling. The hole should be 5/8-inch or so in diameter (for a bolt, and only one-fourth inch for a fluted spike) four or five inches from the larger end of the handle. Drill the same size hole in the center of the gap you just made and through the rest of the chunk of log.

When both holes are drilled, run the bolt or fluted spike through the handle and down through the log chunk. The handle should be seated in the opening you made for it, and the spike or bolt will connect the handle to the chunk of log. If you use a bolt, turn over the log section and add a washer and nut. If you use a fluted spike, drive it through the handle and into the log segment. The spike should be slightly larger than the opening so that the spike remains tight inside the hole.

Figure 5-6
Chipping out for handle attachment.

Next, move up the handle two feet and drill another hole, this one parallel with the log section and through the center of the handle. Run a bolt through this hole after first running the bolt through the end hole in a chain link. The bolt need not be more than six or eight inches in length.

The modified ring dog is now complete, and you are ready to use it. Construction takes only 10 to 15

minutes at most, and the cost is negligible, particularly if you happen to have an old rusty bolt and length of chain lying about.

Figure 5-7
Installing spike through assembly.

To use the ring dog, push the handle and log section against the side of the log to be lifted. The log chunk now serves as a fulcrum and should be placed about two feet from the end of the log. Run the chain under the log and across the top and back to the other side of the bolt through the handle. Either slip a chain link over the bolt or wrap the chain so that you can hold it securely.

Now place one foot against the fulcrum and hold it tightly against the log. Pull back on the handle, and the log will rise easily until it rests atop the handle. Have someone place a saw block under and at right angles to the log, and then ease the log down gently so that it now rests on the chock block. Do the same at the other end of the log, and you now have the log off the ground and ready to saw.

If you wish to make your own straightedge rather than buy a commercial product, you can use a chalk line to mark two lines, the same distance apart (three inches is good) along the length of a board or similar piece of wood. Simply saw along the chalk lines, taking care to stay exactly on the lines so that the edges remain straight.

When the straightedge is cut (and you can make it anywhere from three or four feet up to 20 feet or more, the length to be limited only by the length of the timber or dimension lumber used) you can mark off six-inch gradations on the straightedge and use it later as a story pole (the use of the story pole to be described in a later chapter) or for cement-block alignment.

If you don't have a measuring tape or rule handy, simply use a one-dollar bill (or any other denomination that you have in paper money). Any time you are caught without a tape, you can use the one-dollar bill because it is exactly six and one-eighth inches long. That's close enough to count simply as six inches if you are making rough measurements. Or, for exact measurements, if you mark according to the dollar bill, the kerf or saw groove will use up the extra one-eighth inch.

Figure 5-8
Using the ring-dog to lift huge log.

If you are miles from a store or simply want to make your own tools when possible, you can make a maul by cutting a small straight limb from a fire cherry or similar tree (hickory and oak work

wonderfully) of manageable size. Bore a hole in the chunk of wood and trim the handle to fit. Then cut a tapered wedge to drive into the far end of the handle once the maul has been assembled. Figure 5-10 shows two completed mauls: one for heavier work and one for light work. The two tools combined cost less than ten cents to make. If you wish, you can make your own froe and maul for use in splitting shingles. Square two sections of wood, as shown in Figure 5-11, and shape a handle on each. Cut a groove into the small or froe part of the assembly and install a blade of your choice. In this instance I used an old lawn mower blade. It's cheap and crude, but I made shingles for a two-car garage and a work shed with it.

Figure 5-9
Maul head, handle, and wedge, ready to assemble.

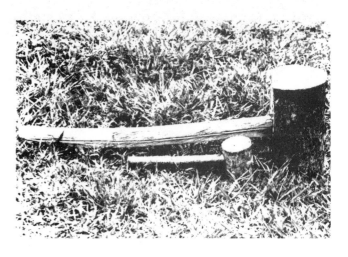

Figure 5-10
Large and small mauls, ready to use.

Figure 5-11
Homemade froe for shingle splitting and maul.

Figure 5-12
Homemade chain-saw miter box.

If you need to do some fairly precise fitting work, you may need to make a miter box, such as the one shown in Figure 5-12. You can make a smaller box by nailing three lengths of wood together as shown in the illustration and then using your own homemade square to lay out the straight-cut (at the left of the miter box) and the angle-cut grooves at the right of the illustration. To get the angles correct, lay out a square the width of the entire miter box (from outside edge to outside edge) and then saw diagonally from corner to corner in both directions.

There are several other devices that can make your work much easier. Among these are a rafter holder and spacer, a ridge-beam raiser, and special devices to hold wood while you saw logs or units of dimension lumber. These will be described in detail at the points where you need them.

Your first major use of these tools and other items of your equipment will be described in Chapter Six: Squaring or Milling Logs. This endeavor will be the first and certainly one of the most important of the steps in building a log house.

Chapter Six:
Squaring or Milling Logs

When you are ready to acquire your logs for the cabin or house, you have several basic options. These include buying a log cabin kit and building the house yourself, contracting a turnkey job and paying someone to do the work for you, hauling the logs to a sawmill to have them cut according to your needs, or using a chain saw to mill or square the logs yourself.

There are obvious advantages and disadvantages to each of the above methods. If you buy a kit, you will pay a fairly severe price for an above-average house or cabin. In 1989 when we began our house, we priced kits and found that we could buy a kit for a 3,175 square-foot house for $90,000; turnkey cost for the same house was $190,000.

Scaling down our costs (and our standards and desires), we could have 1,800 square feet for $25,000 (kit) to $90,000 (turnkey job). Settling for less and less, we could buy a kit for a house with 1,300 square feet for $22,000 or a turnkey job for $66,000.

All of these prices were out of our reach or unreasonable for what was offered, and since that time costs have gone higher and higher. We rejected the kit approach and considered hiring someone to haul the logs to the sawmill and then back to us, after they had been milled.

The problem here was that the cost of hauling was exorbitant, and we would also have to cut and drag the logs to the road and have equipment ready to load them. Then, after milling was completed, we'd have to pay to have the logs hauled back to us and unloaded.

Our goal was to get the best bargain in history for a log house, and the sawmill route was clearly out of reach. Not only were price and handling major problems, we found that we could haul only 20-foot logs and, even if we found a hauler for the longer logs, the sawmill could handle nothing longer than the magical 20-foot length.

So we rejected the sawmill idea.

At that point we decided to mill the logs ourselves by using a chain saw, a come-along (or power pull — the $3.25 variety), a chalk line, a 25-foot tape measure, a short (two-foot) level, a quick square, a nail (that's right — one nail of any size) and a pencil. Naturally we had a gas can and a jug of bar oil.

Thus equipped, we started to work, and what we did, you can do. There is no magic or mystery. You will, however, invest in sweat equity, time, energy, and some degree of frustration.

The first question was what sort of logs we could use, and the answer was simple: long, straight, and abundant. Nothing else really matters. You can use pine, fir, poplar, or whatever else is handy for you, if the logs meet the three characteristics listed above.

Here's what we learned, after trial and error. You can skip the mistakes by following a few simple instructions.

First, you must get the logs into a work area where you have room to do your work. A flat area is best, but if the logs are on a hillside, then you work on a hillside, unless you can somehow drag the logs to a better location.

Once the tree is down, your next jobs are to cut off the limbs, saw the log to the length you need, and then get the log off the ground so that it lies on chock or saw blocks. See Figure 6-1. It is far easier to position the saw blocks while the bulk of the log is still supported by a few limbs.

Saw off the top limbs first — those that are on the side of the tree facing upward. Then lop off the side limbs, leaving the bottom limbs until last. Cut a large sawing block from a tree you don't plan to use (12 inches in diameter and three to four feet long) and position the block under the stump end of the log.

Measure the log to get the length you need and then add, if the log size will permit, two extra feet, just in case you foul up one end while you are sawing, or in the event that you did not measure and mark accurately. The classic rule for such operations is to measure twice and cut once.

Figure 6-1
Setting the log on chock or saw blocks.

Cut off the top of the tree at the determined mark and then place a sawing block under the top or small end of the log. Now cut the bottom limbs so that when the final limb is removed, the log will fall upon the sawing block and you are ready to begin the rather challenging task of milling or squaring the log.

A word about cutting off limbs: you will notice that when you start to cut downward, the end of the limb may start to rise. This tells you that the outer reaches of the limb are resting upon the trunk of another tree or similar object, and the upward pressure will pinch or bind your saw bar and chain and you will spend the next few minutes trying to free your saw.

If binding starts, stop sawing instantly and begin to undercut the limb. As you do, the limb end will continue to rise and you can finish the cut with little if any difficulty. When all the limbs have been cut away and the area has been cleared of brush and debris, you can start milling.

The first step is to mark off the dimensions of the log you wish to cut. Assume that you want a log ten inches high and eight inches thick. Such a log will provide strength, insulation, and weight for your walls, yet it is small enough that you can find trees without trouble that will yield such logs and you can handle it when it is cut.

The ideal time to cut logs is when the sap is down — in the winter months. If you don't have a realistic choice, the next best time to cut them is when your chain is sharp. Green, sap-laden logs are naturally much heavier than logs cut when the sap is down, but you can handle cutting the logs at any time of year.

Mark the log-size on the small end of the log first. If you mark the large end first, you may find that the log tapers so much that the small end will not yield the proper dimensions.

Measure across the top of the small end of the log to see if you can in fact cut an 8″ by 10″ log from it. You can also choose to cut 10″ by 10″ logs, if you want two more inches of insulation and if you can handle the extra weight.

Figure 6-2
Marking the dimensions of the log cut on the small end of the log.

Once you are satisfied that the log is large enough, hold a level across the top portion of the cut surface and, making certain that the reading is a true horizontal, mark along the upper side of the level. Let the mark continue across the entire width of the end of the log.

Next, use a quick square (the longer squares will be too cumbersome to use in limited space) to make the side marks of the square or rectangle. See Figure 6-2. If you do not have a quick square, measure ten inches along the center of the first line and then use the level to complete the square. Hold the level so that you have a plumb or vertical reading, and then mark from the ten-inch mark downward to the bottom of the log end.

Do this on both sides. Then measure down eight or ten inches on both lines and mark the points clearly. Use the level again to get a true horizontal or level reading and mark along the level. The finished work, which takes only a few seconds, leaves you with your first cut clearly outlined.

Repeat: it is crucial for the rectangle to be perfectly true vertically and horizontally. The reasons for this importance will be made clear later.

Go to the large or butt end of the log and repeat the process so that you have a square or rectangle on each end of the log, and both rectangles are level or true.

Drive the nail into the end of the log at either of the upper corners. Loop the end of the chalk line over the nail. (See Figure 6-3.) and stretch the chalk line (blue chalk is much easier to see than any other color we could find) to the other end of the log. Hold the line taut so that it rests at the upper corner of the second square or rectangle.

With your free hand, lift the line and snap it along the length of the log. You will now have a chalk line reaching from one upper corner to the corresponding other upper corner. You are now ready to make the first slab cut with the chain saw — after you remove the nail!

Start at either end and lower the tip of the bar gently to the end of the log so that the chain cuts into the chalk line. Walk backward and pull so that the tip of the bar remains in contact with the chalk line. Cut a groove one or two inches deep along the entire length of the log. Figure 6-4 shows the groove cut.

Figure 6-3
Starting the chalk line. Note the nail in the upper right hand corner of the rectangle.

Figure 6-4
Making the groove cut along the chalk line.

Take care that the cut line does not leave the chalk line at any point. Try to hold the saw so that the chain and bar remain at all times parallel with the chalk line and perfectly aligned with it. If you allow the saw to tilt or lean, your groove cut, which is crucially important, will be slanted.

After you complete the groove cut, return to the starting point and rest the body of the chain saw on the top surface of the log. Let the bar and chain slip into the groove you have just cut. With the saw fully revved, start the next cut by tilting the saw bar toward the four o'clock position or to a point about two feet in front of the end of the log.

As you cut, keep your head well back out of the saw line so that if the saw kicks back, your head and torso will not be in line with the out-of-control chain. Lean forward at the very beginning of the cut to see that as you cut deeper and deeper the cut line follows the chalk line at the end of the log.

If you see that you are off the line, stop and make the necessary corrections. Once you cut through the end of the log it is almost impossible to make satisfactory corrections.

Once satisfied that your cut line is good, tilt the saw forward until the chain cuts all the way through the end of the log. Raise the saw and let the tip of the bar rest in the groove and pull the saw toward you so that the groove cut is made much deeper. When it is four or five inches deep, again rest the body of the saw on the top of the log and begin to tilt forward again until the bar is nearly vertical.

Keep repeating this process and work your way slowly and carefully along the entire length of the log. Concentrate on keeping the saw from leaning to the left or right, and always keep the entire bar and chain aligned with the groove cut.

Use the spikes on the chain saw to help you to cut faster. Let the spikes dig into the bark so they will hold the saw in place and keep its body from sliding forward when you lift the body and push the bar deeper.

When you are in the early stages of learning how to make the slab cut, you will be very slow, disappointingly so at times, but the entire slab cut along a 60-foot log should take only 20 minutes or so. As you gain confidence, you will also gain speed.

When you reach the end of the log, stand so that your feet are clear of the slab, which will be fairly heavy, when it falls free of the log. See Figure 6-5.

You are now ready to make the second cut, which can be done in one of two easy ways.

Figure 6-5
Completing the first slab cut. Note that on this cut saw marks were omitted.

The first way is to mark the second slab cut and make the first groove cut, then the slab cut with the log resting in the same position it was in when you made the first cut. To make this cut, drive the nail again into the upper corner of the rectangle you marked on the end of the log.

You may wish to create saw marks along the surface of the log in order to give more of the rustic patina. You can do so by raising and lowering the tip of the saw bar as you work your way along the log. The saw marks will occur about every two feet.

Again, loop the chalk line over the nail and pull the line to the corresponding upper corner on the other end. Snap the line and then make the second cut exactly as you did the first cut.

Sometimes the body of the saw has a tendency to slide down the bark, and you may have difficulty in achieving the leverage needed from the spikes. You can solve this problem by rolling the log one-quarter turn so that the cut surface of the log is now facing upward. See Figure 6-6.

Figure 6-6
With the flat surface turned upward, you can measure and mark off for the next two groove cuts.

You can now mark from corner to corner with the chalk line as before, and the chalk line is much easier to see on the freshly cut surface. You also have a flat surface for the saw body to rest upon while you are making the deep cuts.

The flat surface will help you to saw both faster and more accurately because the saw itself does not have the tendency to angle downward. Cutting time is decreased in part by the fact that you have less wood to saw through (because the slab section is now removed).

Mark and cut both slabs from the sides of the log. When this is done, you have three flat surfaces. See Figure 6-7. Only the bottom part of the log needs to be slabbed.

You will need to roll the log one-quarter turn so that the slab cut is in cutting position. Again, chalk the line, make the groove cut, and then slice away the slab. When the final slab falls away, you have a log with four flat sides.

If at any time you notice that the log tends to roll as you are sawing, slip a small wedge under one end (or both ends, if you need to do so to stabilize the log) until the log remains firmly in place as you mark and saw.

Figure 6-7
Completing the final slab cut. The result is a log that is almost perfectly straight and true.

You need to determine that the upper surface of the log is level before you make any cuts. If the log is tilted, you will either have to compensate by tilting the saw slightly, or you will have an inferior cut on that side.

When the log is finished, write down in a notebook the length of the log. As you cut others, note the lengths and keep track of the number.

Before you started to cut, you needed to have a general idea of how many logs you would need for the exterior walls. In our house we knew that we would need 100 logs for the outside walls, and we knew how long they needed to be. So in our notebook we had an accurate listing of the number of logs and their lengths, and when we had the logs for a specific part of the wall ready, we marked off that section of logs.

For example, if you have a door opening on the front of the cabin, you will not need full-length logs for that area. You need to measure from the corner to the rough opening of the door and note the distance. If it is 20 feet, and if the rough opening is 80 inches high, and if the window rough openings are 40 inches from the floor, you will need four logs 20 feet long for that part of the house.

Consult your plans and note the height of the windows and the distance between windows or from window to door or from window to corner. If the distance between windows is five feet and if the windows are 60 inches high, you will need either six logs five feet long or the equivalent.

"The equivalent" refers to two logs ten feet long and two five-foot logs, rather than to one 30-foot log. If you have a good log of that length, save it for long expanses of walls; do not waste it by cutting it into short sections.

Remember that when you are measuring from windows or doors to corners, always add one foot to the measurement. The house you are building, if you follow the suggestions here, will use what is called the butt-and-pass corner system, and you will need the extra foot on each log that ends at a corner.

As you complete each log, leave it on the sawing blocks to air-dry while you saw other logs. You may be astonished at how much lighter the logs will be after they have had a few days or weeks to dry.

You can start stacking logs into the walls before they have dried completely. They can continue to dry in the walls as well as they can while lying on the sawing blocks.

Continue to cut logs until you have all that you will need. This is a pay-as-you-go house that, if you budget time and money carefully, will be paid for by the time you are ready to move in. You do not, for instance, need to buy other building materials until the logs are ready to use.

If you need 60 logs, or 100, put yourself on a work schedule that is reasonable. If you can slab-cut four logs each day, in 25 working days you will have your hundred logs.

And for 25 days, or longer, you can leave your money in the checking or savings account, in your pocket, or wherever it will serve you best. Let it accumulate interest, no matter how small, until you need it. If you buy building materials far in advance, you are not only letting the supplies dealer draw the interest on your money, but you are also exposing the materials to theft or damage by weather or vandals.

Several tips for better cutting may benefit you. Here is part of the education I picked up while I was sawing our logs.

First, keep the saw's chain sharp. A dull chain takes far more time, energy, and fuel. It also causes greater wear and tear on the chain saw and results in inferior cutting.

You can buy the electric sharpener that connects to the battery of your car or truck. These work well and with one you can sharpen a chain within five minutes or so.

If you don't want to invest in the electric sharpeners, use the traditional file. Check with your dealer to be sure you have the proper file for the type of chain you use. Buy a 50-cent wood handle for the file so you won't be scraping your fingers every time you file a saw tooth.

Second, wear protective clothing and eye protection all the time you are sawing or filing chain teeth. The tiny filings from the sharpening process can cause devastating damage if you should get one of these in your eye. Wear boots with metal protection built into the toe sections. This metal can prevent painful and severe injuries and save the cost of medical treatment.

If you wear long-sleeved shirts, you will prevent many bites and stings from insects. Head covering protects you from injuries and from the sun's rays.

Third, when you are sawing, keep the log between you and the saw. When you are cutting off a slab, for example, if you are on the slab side and the saw "cuts out" or leaps from the groove, your foot or leg may be the next point of contact for the chain. But if you are on the opposite side of the log, the chain would have to cut through the entire log before it can reach you.

Before it can do so, you can bring it back under control.

Fourth, beware of the danger of "kick-back" and take steps to prevent it. Kick-back occurs when the tip of the bar makes contact with a rock, limb, stump, or other foreign object while you are cutting. The power of the saw causes energy to be directed upward and the chain to leap upward and do serious, even fatal injury to the operator.

Before you begin sawing, clear out debris from underneath the log. Remove all limbs or other objects that could cause kick-back. As you saw, be sure that the tip of the bar extends through the log. If it doesn't, you might push the bar tip into uncut log area and cause a severe kick-back.

Fifth, keep your sawing space clear of vines, limbs, and other materials that might cause you to trip and fall. As you saw, you are constantly moving backward, which means that you cannot see where you are stepping. If you trip and fall, you might pull the saw with you and disaster could result.

Sixth, learn to feel with your feet as you work your way down the log. Don't lift your feet, but slide them instead, so that you can feel any problems. Remember that the sawing blocks will jut out into your path, and you must feel for them with your feet and step over them while you continue to saw.

Seventh, keep a supply of fresh water on hand and stop to drink even though you don't feel particularly thirsty. One great problem of working with a chain saw is that the wind, sun, and heat generated by the saw, along with energy expended by your own efforts, can cause dehydration to become a problem long before you are aware of your body's needs. Drink small amounts often, rather than large amounts infrequently.

Eighth, keep first-aid supplies nearby. Some home remedies work wonderfully well. If you are bitten or stung by a wasp or hornet, one of the best remedies is a small amount of table mustard, the kind you put on hot dogs, smeared immediately over the bite area. Dozens of persons to whom I have imparted this cure assure me that mustard works well for treatment of nearly all kinds of stings and for sunburn.

If you are bitten by a spider, thick mud works well if you have nothing more helpful. I know this for a fact, because one day while we were sawing I was bitten by a black widow spider. The pain was intense,

but I packed the reddest and wettest mud I could find on the wound and never went to see a doctor.

I do not recommend such Spartan tactics if help is readily available, but in our case there was no doctor within reasonable distance, and if mud or mustard is all you have, then it's the best you have.

For most insect bites, a smear of anything greasy or oily — anything that will cut off the oxygen to the skin surface — will usually alleviate the pain and itch.

Ninth, keep fuel and other flammable materials away from the chain saw. When the saw runs out of gas, do not fill the tank immediately. Mark the next cut or haul away brush or sharpen the chain while the engine cools before you re-fuel.

Tenth, buy extra chains. Your saw may last for the entire duration of the house-building, but you will need chains. These may break or suffer irreparable damage, and it is far easier to replace the chain than it is to stop work and drive to a supply store to purchase a new chain.

Eleventh, if you can do so without hardship, keep a small toolbox handy in case you need to adjust the tension of the chain, adjust the carburetor, or clean the filters.

After the major cutting is completed, you are ready to stack logs. It is assumed that at this point the foundation walls, floor framing, and subflooring work have been completed.

For a financial report, when the final logs are cut, you should have a total of about $75 invested in your work on the logs. This depends upon many variables, but in our house, which is 52′ x 32′, our wall logs cost a total of $132.64.

Chapter Seven:
Building Foundation Walls

If you decide to include a basement in your log house (and as a person who took refuge in a basement when a tornado ripped the upper part of the house into a million fragments, I strongly recommend one), you will find that it is possible (but difficult) to dig your own basement. In terms of time and energy, you are better off to hire someone to bring in heavy equipment and do the job in a matter of hours, rather than weeks. An experienced grader can have a hillside as smooth as a table in a remarkably short time. See Figure 7-1.

Figure 7-1
*Earth-moving equipment can dig
your basement in a few hours.*

We hand-mixed and poured our own basement and saved hundreds of dollars, but the work was strenuous. We also dug and poured our footings, but you may prefer to hire the work done in a hurry. If

you want to prepare the soil for the footings work, you can lay off the lines and mark them by using lime, fertilizer, or any other common substance that will not blow away. When the footings are dug, it is fast and easy to bring in the concrete truck and pour and smooth the footings in a matter of an hour or two of hard work.

Figure 7-2
Setting up batter boards.

After the basement (if any) has been dug and footings have been dug and poured, it is time to start construction on the foundation walls. If you have not poured footings or basement, it is time to start your concrete work.

The basic concrete mixture is a simple 1:3:5 combination of cement, sand, and gravel. Type S cement is generally recommended (This is a regional name. It is also known as "Type II.") and, in fact, some building inspectors and local codes require the Type S material. As always, check the local codes before you start any construction work.

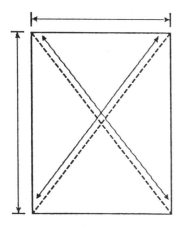

Figure 7-3
Measuring diagonaly in both directions for squareness.

You will hear the sand and gravel referred to as the fine and coarse aggregate. For mixing mortar, you will need masonry sand, which contains no tiny rocks or other detritus. For concrete you can use a coarser sand. If there are pebbles and fragments of rocks in the concrete, this is not nearly the problem that it would be if you were laying bricks or blocks.

When you are mixing concrete, use the same measurements and measuring equipment for each batch. Do not use guesswork. There may be times when, after a heavy rainfall, your sand is so moisture-laden that you do not need as much water as you normally would. Such adjustments are common in masonry work. If you measure cement by the shovel-ful, use the same shovel loaded to the same extent each time. If you use a bucket, fill the bucket to the same level for each batch. More about mixing later.

Before you mix anything, you need to set up your batter boards first. These are three posts connected by two horizontal pieces of board at each corner of the house (Figure 7-2). Each of the batter boards will form a right angle with one of the stakes exactly at the corner alignment and another stake two feet or so down each of the building lines. The boards or ledgers connecting the three stakes should be 1″ x 4″ up to 1″ x 6″ dimensions. If you have scraps of straight lumber

around, you can cut the ledgers from these scraps so that you need not buy any special lumber.

Think of the first stakes in terms of a baseball diamond. If one stake is directly behind the plate, the other and opposite stake should be directly behind second base. Similarly, the stake behind first base should be exactly aligned with the stake behind third base.

Still using the baseball diamond analogy, return to home plate (or, to be more accurate, two feet behind home plate). The next stake here should be two feet down the first-base line and two feet outside the line itself. The other should be down the third-base line in the same location.

Align all other stakes in precisely the same manner. When you are finished, there will be three stakes at each of the bases or corners. Now drive a small stake exactly where the corner of the house should be. You can drive an 8d nail into the top of the stake.

Next, align the batter board down the first-base line with its counterpart down the third-base line. Mark the exact point where the imaginary line that crosses the stake and nail would cross both batter boards. Saw a one-inch groove where the mark is made on the top of each board.

Now do the same with the boards running in the opposite (or first-base) line. Keep up the process until each of the batter board locations has the kerfs sawed in the boards. At this point you can stretch strong line (heavy cord that can be pulled taut without breaking). Masonry line works well. As you pull the cord very tight, you can tie a knot in it and slip the cord into the kerf already prepared. The knot will keep the cord from pulling out, and you have the precise boundaries of the house laid out.

You can check for squareness in two simple ways. First, use the Pythagorean theorem (more commonly called the 6-8-10 method of squaring) to check each corner. Measure down one side of the house as it is laid out to a distance of six feet. Measure down eight feet on the other side of the corner. Mark each of these two points. You can mark the cord with chalk or tape, or you can use your own methods of spotting the location.

Now measure from the six-foot location to the eight-foot location. The distance should be exactly ten feet. Do not settle for less than an exact square measurement.

Do this on all four corners, just in case you have made a slight mistake in some of the earlier measurements. If all four corners work out exactly according to the 6-8-10 formula, you know the house layout is square.

But just to be certain, use the 100-foot tape measure, if you have one, and measure from first base to third base, or from one corner to another, diagonally. Then measure from home plate to second base. The two measurements should be exactly the same. See Figure 7-3.

In order to get the precise building line, drop a plumb bob from the point where the lines cross at each corner of the house. The plumb bob should rest an inch or so above the nail which has been driven into the corner stake. You can also use a level to get a perfect reading, as shown in Figure 7-4.

Figure 7-4
Using level to determine start of foundation wall.

When you excavate for the basement, go beyond the building line at least two to three feet, so that you will have work room outside the foundation wall, when the time comes. When the grading is done for the basement, additional digging for the footings can be done at the same time.

In most areas, the building code requires that the footings be below the frost line. In the South footings

generally need to be 18 inches deep. In colder parts of the country, the footings need to be deeper.

As with the basement area, dig the footings wider than the actual foundation wall will be. In other words, don't dig a 12-inch footing trench if you are planning to use 12-inch blocks. Allow for the concrete to spread sufficiently to provide a firm and solid base for the load that will be placed upon the blocks later. Keep in mind that the entire weight of the outside walls, plus part of the roof weight, and, in essence, the weight of the entire house will be distributed among the footings and piers. If the footings and piers are not deep enough, the footings can sink and allow the house to settle and shift.

When footing trenches are done, you can pour footing concrete, after you have installed the leveling stakes. You will want the footings to be exactly level around the entire house, so you will need to establish a method of guaranteeing a correct reading.

A word about the importance of level footings: If you allow discrepancies in the footing surface, you may find that from the corner of the house (think again of home plate) to second base or third base, there may be a drop or rise of an inch or more. When you are laying blocks, you will find that the inch or more of discrepancy will wreak havoc with your accuracy in each course of blocks.

One simple way to get the footings level is to drive in the corner stakes and then run a line level to another corner. If you are not familiar with the line level, it is a tiny instrument (about three to four inches long) that can be hung upon a strong string or cord. When the cord is stretched taut, the bubble in the center of the line level should be centered exactly between the marks.

For ease in setting stakes, you can attach the line level at a point near the stake. Hold the line across the top of the stake and check the bubble. If necessary, drive the stake a little deeper and then check again. Keep doing this until the bubble shows a perfect reading. Check to see that the line remains very taut while you are checking.

Do this all around the footing trenches. If the level is correct from Point A to Point B, then if Point C aligns correctly with Point B, then Point C must of necessity be correct also. Then if Point D aligns properly with Point C, then Point D is correct. But just to be sure, start at home plate, proceed to first base, second, and third, and then return to home plate, to ensure that you did not permit any problems to occur.

Now drive stakes two feet apart under the line and in line with the stakes at either end of the trench. The top of the stake should be in alignment with the line connecting the first and last stakes in the trench. Do this all the way around the entire trenches.

Now, when you are ready to pour concrete, smooth the surface of the concrete until the tops of the stakes are perfectly even with the concrete surface.

By doing so, you have guaranteed that your footings will be either totally correct or so close that you can lay blocks with equanimity. Now it is time to build the forms for the footings. The footing forms are only boards that are set up to create the exact boundary of the footing concrete.

If you have excavated the basement, you can pour the basement and the footings concrete at the same time. If you are pouring only footings, you can use the form boards set up to the desired width. Stakes are driven outside the forms, and the boards are sometimes nailed to the stakes to hold the boards in place.

Now mix your concrete, unless you plan to buy it. The decision is not an easy one. If you have access to a mixer, you will perhaps want to mix your own. If you must mix by hand, you may want to hire someone to pour the footings for you.

It's not simply a matter of money; it's also a matter of time and energy, which can often be translated into money. Look at it this way: if you will need to devote 40 hours to mixing concrete and pouring the footings, how much will it cost you? Assume that the price of having pre-mixed concrete poured for you is $X. If you pour the concrete yourself, the cost is likely to be $X-Y. What is the difference in terms of dollars in the two figures?

Now make another calculation. How much money can you earn working at your job or from part-time work during the 40 hours it would take you to pour the footings? If the cost of the footings concrete is still $X, but you could earn $X+Z, aren't you better off financially to hire the work done?

Let's put it into specific figures. I hired a man to do some minor excavating for me. He charged me $200. He worked for about three hours, and he chided me gently and hinted that if I had not been so lazy, I could have saved the $200. However, while he did the work, I wrote a magazine article and earned $700. So

actually I came out $500 ahead of the game by having the work done for me.

This is particularly true in light of the fact that it would have taken me at least 12-16 hours to do the work myself, and I could have written several articles during the time lost.

Now this logic can be carried to an extreme. What if I could hire someone to build the entire cabin and I could earn more money than the construction cost me during the period? Should I simply let someone else build the cabin?

One final way of looking at the problem is that if you work in an office or classroom where you get very little exercise, you may welcome the physical exertion. Or if you have time and energy to work after-hours, the money you save may be well worth the extra effort. I, for example, cannot write all the time, and when I am not at the keyboard, I can save myself money by doing the projects I write about.

So, assume you decided to mix and pour your own concrete. There are several schools of thought on the proper way to mix the concrete itself. Some builders prefer to mix the cement, sand, and gravel together, and then add the necessary water to create a plastic mixture. Use this method if you like it.

Others prefer to start with water, about four gallons of it, and then dump in the cement. Then they add the sand, and finally the gravel. Still others prefer to mix sand and cement thoroughly, and then add the water, and finally the gravel.

My personal preference is to start with the water, then add the sand. I mix the water and sand until I have a slushy mix, and then add the cement, a small amount at a time. I add a shovel or two of cement, then mix the cement into the sand and water until the cement is totally absorbed. Finally, I add the gravel.

If you put in all of the aggregate first, you will find that it is very difficult to mix the gravel and sand and cement at the same time, while it is rather easy to mix sand and cement. When I add the gravel, I scatter the shovelfuls of gravel across the surface of the mixture and then work the gravel in a little at a time.

The sequence is not highly important. What is important is that you do not content yourself with simply wetting the cement and gravel. You must mix all the materials thoroughly. If you wish a somewhat stronger mixture, you may want to use the 1:2:3 formula, of cement, sand, and gravel.

You should do the mixing work as near to the actual footing site as possible. A bag of cement weighs 94 pounds, and you do not want to carry this a long distance. Nor do you want to haul wheelbarrow loads of concrete farther than is necessary.

As you mix, use a hoe to push and pull the materials. Push downward and away from you, then pull upward and toward you. Be sure to shove the hoe blade deep into the mixture in order to get the sand or cement at the bottom mixed effectively into the concrete.

If you do not have a mortar box, use a construction wheelbarrow for mixing the concrete. Do not attempt to do the job with a garden wheelbarrow. And if you use a wheelbarrow at all, do not try to mix a complete batch. The wheelbarrow will not hold it. Work with half a batch at a time. For convenience, you can use a five-gallon bucket which, filled with cement, will make half a batch of concrete when all the other materials are added.

When the first batch is ready, shovel or pour it into the footing trench. Fill the trench up to the top of the stakes by starting at one corner, where a temporary barrier has been placed to keep the concrete from flowing in both directions. Block off one length of the trench at the corner and start filling the space. After each batch is emptied into the trench, stop and use a trowel or screed implement to push the concrete down tightly into the mass. Do not leave large air holes. If the trench is over-filled, use the tool to push the concrete toward the next area to be filled.

When darkness or the end of work time is near, plan to set up a barricade similar to the one used at the end of the trench. Fill in the trench to the barrier at a 45° angle. This will allow the next day's concrete placement to "grab" your already-completed work. See Figure 7-5. Always allow time to clean up the hoe, mortar box, trowel, and other tools and equipment.

Continue your progression around the entire footing trench until it is filled. Smooth as you go. Do not leave humps or corners of gravel protruding upward. These will create severe difficulties when you are laying blocks.

Note how far a batch of concrete will go in the trenches, and you will have a fairly accurate notion of how many batches you will need to mix.

If you start work in the afternoon and plan to have three hours of work time, plan to mix only two batches of concrete. You could hurry and mix more, but work slower, do a better job, and allow more time for clean-up.

Some cabin builders in years past did not even use footings of any sort, other than flat rocks placed at corners to serve as piers. In more recent years, builders dug small footings and laid cement-block piers, or used mortar to bond rocks together. If you have any such plans, be certain to check with code authorities before you invest a lot of time and work.

When the footings work is done, you are ready to lay the cement blocks, if your plans include the basic foundation wall. Chapter Eight deals with methods of laying the cement blocks.

TODAY'S   FUTURE

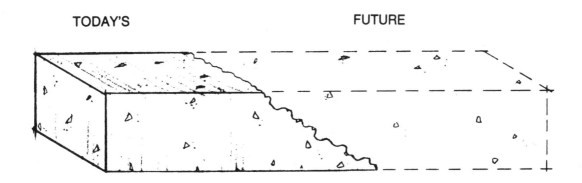

Figure 7-5
Always leave a rough edge on a day's concrete pour so that the next day's pour will adhere to it.

Chapter Eight:
Laying Concrete Blocks

When footings are poured and the concrete has set up so that it is very hard and the surface is completely dry, you can start laying concrete (or, as they are often called, cement) blocks. You have perhaps seen people, even experienced masons, begin laying blocks as soon as the footings are poured. This, no matter what anyone tells you, is not an accepted practice. If you cure the concrete properly, it will gain its optimum strength. After the initial hardening or "set up" of the footing, keep it moist for 72 hours.

Concrete, engineers tell us, begins to set up or harden as soon as it is poured, and within 72 hours the poured concrete is set up enough, assuming that the weather has been cooperative, so that you can do the block work. But the hardening process goes on for not only days but weeks and months and years. Some structural specialists insist that concrete continues to harden for at least a century.

Remember that the footing should be several inches wider than the concrete blocks you plan to use. And if all is ready and you are set to begin work, make one last-minute check to be sure that you have the width and length of footings needed.

A typical concrete block is about 15 inches long; however, when you add a mortar joint, the length is 16 inches. A block, when a mortar joint is included, is usually eight inches high. However, you can buy blocks in virtually any needed dimensions, from two inches high to up the eight-inch height. You can buy blocks that are solid, hollow or cored, with two cores, or three. Blocks come in several shapes as well, and in a number of thicknesses. Some are four inches (nominally) thick, while others are eight or 12 inches thick.

You can buy end blocks (which have square corners on each end), sash blocks (with grooves to admit window edges to slide down for installation of metal windows in a block wall), half blocks, header blocks (with cut-out areas for the headers to fit into the cutaway portion), and a wide variety of other styles.

You will probably wish to start work, if you plan to include a foundation wall as such rather than use a rubblestone wall or rock piers only, by using the more traditional "dished" block with "ears" on each end. The ears have a groove for mortar. Many building codes require 12-inch blocks for any part of any wall that is underground. Many builders switch to eight-inch blocks once the wall rises out of the ground.

Do you plan to do your own masonry work? If so, you will need to proceed slowly and be certain that you get off to a nearly perfect start. If you plan to hire masons, you will need to spend a substantial amount of money. And horror stories abound about a minority of unscrupulous block masons and brick masons.

It should go without saying that most masons are completely honest and proficient in their craft, but if you should have the misfortune to hire an untrustworthy one, you are in for a great deal of trouble and expense. A friend of mine hired brick masons to do the veneer work on his house, and he agreed to pay them by the thousands of bricks they laid. Months later, after he had moved into the house, the friend happened to go into the crawl space under the house, and to his shock he found stacks and heaps and piles of bricks — thousands of them.

The masons, of course, laid a dozen bricks and dumped two dozen or more under the house. The result was that the man was cheated badly on two major counts: he had agreed to buy bricks that he did not need — a sizable investment in itself — and he had paid the masons *not* to lay them — another huge cost.

This same principle and practice holds true in many areas of home building. One contractor whom I have known for years freely admits that he over-buys on all materials by at least 20 per cent on each house. The result is that when a house is completed, the builder has a surplus of 20 per cent of bricks, mortar, dimension lumber, sheet rock, paneling, shingles, and every other piece of material that goes into the house.

This means that every five houses will net the man a totally free house, from his point of view, and if the next house costs $100,000, half of which goes for materials, the contractor has cheated the previous five builders out of the total cost of one entire house.

And people wonder why it costs so much to hire a crew to build a house or do masonry or plumbing or electrical work!

If you must hire help, try to find someone who will agree to work alongside you. If you can work out such an arrangement, you can pay the mason to be in charge, while you mix mortar, keep blocks and bricks handy, and clean up at the end of the day. If you cannot work out such an arrangement, at least try to be on the premises when the work is done, unless the man you hire is completely reputable and has spotless integrity concerning his work performance.

Many masons work by the hour, while others are paid by the number of blocks laid. Cost per block varies from $1.50 and up. If you hire a man at $1.50 per block, and if he lays 500 blocks in a day, his work has cost you $750. If he charges more, you pay more. If you must pay a helper as well, your masonry work will cost you easily $1,000 per day.

So you can save a considerable amount of money by doing your own work, whenever possible. You may be slow at first, and your level of expertise can be highly discouraging. But if you persist, you can master the craft sufficiently to permit you to do the work you must do.

Start by mixing mortar. You will find many variations, but here is my method. Start by pouring five gallons of water into a mortar box (if you plan to lay lots of blocks, that is; if you plan to work only a short time, you can mix proportionately less), and then add eight shovelfuls of sand to the water. Mix the sand and water thoroughly, and then add a 70-pound bag of mortar mix to the sand and water.

Mix until the sand, water, and mortar mix are integrated fully and smoothly. Watch for lumps and foreign materials. Little by little, add 16 more shovelfuls of sand, mixing carefully and well as you do so. If needed, add more water to make the mixture more plastic. Only mix the amount of mortar you can use without adding additional water as you progress.

A good consistency test for mortar is that if you heap mortar on a mortar board and cut a V-shaped groove in it, the mortar should be stiff enough to hold its shape. At the same time it must be thin enough to be workable.

When the mortar is ready, go to the starting point for the first blocks. Always start at a corner, and, when feasible, build all of your corners before moving on to interior wall work.

Use the plumb bob (and if you don't have one, tie a nail to the end of a string and suspend the nail from the point on your batter board lines where the lines cross). Mark the spot on the footing where the outside corner of the first block must be placed.

If you don't have mortar boards, now is the time to make them. All you need is an 18-inch square of plywood or any other solid material. Underneath the plywood, nail two 2″ x 4″ lengths (other dimensions will do) standing on edge.

You need to set up stakes along the first footing. Tie some mason's cord to the first stake so that the cord is as high as the first block, including mortar bed, should be. Eight inches is a good standard height. At the other end of the footing, drive another stake and tie the cord again at eight inches.

For verification purposes, hang the line level on the cord to be sure that the two ends of the line are level. Then get ready to lay the first blocks.

Measure the length of the wall lines where you will be working. Then make certain that the distance in inches is divisible by 16. For example, if the wall line is 30 feet, that equals 360 inches, which, divided by 16 equals 22.5 blocks, which means 22 blocks and eight inches. You will need to use a half block to make the course come out right.

But on your second course, because you lapped the first block and "lost" eight inches, the wall will be not 360 inches but 352 inches, which is evenly divisible by 16. Make a similar check on all walls. If at all possible, shorten a wall an inch or two or lengthen the wall by a similar distance rather than trying later to fit broken blocks into the spaces left.

Your trowel, mortar box, mortar board, tape or other measurement device, and mason's cord should be at hand. Your first step in laying the block is to wet the mortar board and your trowel. Do not start with dry surfaces. The dry surfaces will absorb the water from the mortar and weaken it.

Hold the trowel with your fingers wrapped around the handle and your thumb laid along the handle. Scoop up a trowel-load of mortar and spread it in a gentle slinging motion along the line set up between the stakes. See Figure 8-1.

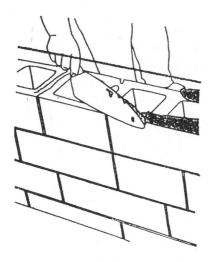

Figure 8-1
Buttering blocks in foundation wall.

Assume that you are going to lay the first course in a north-south direction. Lay the mortar bed at the north end of the footing and then gently lift the block and lower it into the mortar bed. The block should parallel the line you have set up. The outside of the block should come as close as possible to the block without actually touching it. See Figure 8-2.

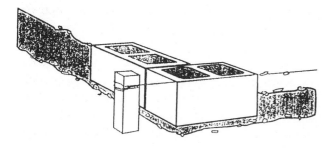

Figure 8-2
Using guide cords for block alignment.

When you lift a block, grasp the center of the block on the side with the thicker divider. With your other hand take the block by the front end. Lift until the block is level and lower it in that manner to the mortar bed.

Use your level instantly. Start by laying the level across the top of the block, lengthwise. The level bubble should be centered exactly. If it is not, tap one end of the block gently until the block is leveled. See Figure 8-3.

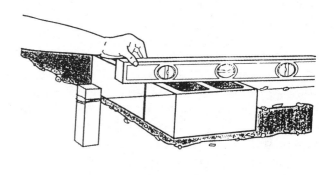

Figure 8-3
Use level in both directions on blocks.

Then lay the level across the block widthwise, and repeat the process of leveling it.

Now stand the next block on end and "butter" it by spreading mortar along the "ears." Scoop up a trowel-load of mortar and turn your hand sideways, so that your thumb is near your body. Let the point of the trowel slide down alongside the outer edge of the block and then pull the trowel downward and backward toward the other end of the block. As you do so you will spread the mortar uniformly along the block edge. Do the same to the other side by starting at the opposite side of the block and spreading the mortar in the opposite direction.

Before leaving the block, use the edge of the trowel to push mortar down into the groove at the "ears." This gentle pressure will cause the mortar to adhere to the block, and it will not fall off when you set the block.

When the block is mortared or buttered, lift the block as before and set it into the mortar bed. As you place the block, push it gently forward so that the buttered end of the block presses against the first block.

Use the level again in both directions, but first use the level or straightedge to ensure that the blocks are aligned as they should be. Hold the level flush against the side of the first block, and tap the second block into conformity with the first block. Then level the second block from both directions.

Do the third block in exactly the same manner. Each time, use the level to make sure that the blocks are staying in line, and make a visual inspection to verify that all the blocks are in line with the line you have set up. Make sure that none of the blocks actually comes in contact with the line.

After you have laid four or five blocks, go back to the start of the course and lay the blocks that butt at right angles into the side of the first block. When you lay a block, test to see that the two blocks form a perfect right angle. Check by using a square. You should also set up the block line and use the line level to ensure that everything is correct.

At the corner, after you have butted one block against the first one you've laid, lay the next block so that it laps the first one. This is the bonding that you will maintain throughout the entire course of blocks, and throughout the entire wall. Each block you lay should lap the block or the two blocks underneath it. See Figure 8-4.

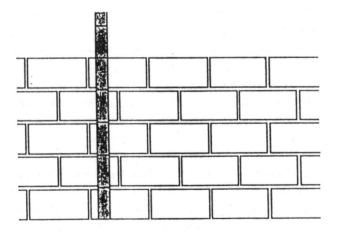

Figure 8-4
Using story pole to check course trueness.

Continue building the first corner. When you have laid five or six blocks in one direction, then lay blocks in the other direction, and each time lap the blocks at the corner and all blocks thereafter. Note that each block covers half of each of the two blocks under it and make certain that you keep this balance. If you permit the bonding pattern to drift, you will wind up at the end of the course with either too much or too little space for the final block.

When the first corner is as high as the wall will be, leave that spot and work at the next corner. Tentatively lay the blocks without mortar to make sure that you will have the spacing correct. Or you can position the first block and then use a measuring tape to measure from the outside edge of the first block to the inside edge of the closest block already laid.

Notice on your measuring tape that certain numbers are printed in red or a similarly noticeable color. These numbers will begin with 16 and, in progression, will include 32, 48, 64, 80, 96, 112, 128, 144, 160, etc. All these numbers represent an increment of 16 inches, which is the length of a block, plus the mortar joint.

As you build the second corner, continue to measure to be sure that you are not making mortar joints too wide or too narrow. If you find that you must do so, you can widen or tighten the joints slightly, and within the space of several blocks you can make up an inch or two without great difficulty.

Remember: when you measure the distance from inside edge to inside edge of blocks, that distance should end very near or on one of the marked 16-inch gradations, or it should be exactly eight inches away from one of the marks.

As you build the second corner, run a line level from the top of the first block in the first corner to the top of the first block in the second corner. If they are not level, you must make corrections. You can usually do so by thickening the mortar bed under the first block or by tapping the block downward until you have achieved a level reading.

When you lay the second block in the new corner, use the line level again to check for a proper reading. Do the same with all subsequent blocks. Professional masons need not check with such care, but if you are a beginner, it is much easier to devote time to checking than it is to devote time to tearing down part of a wall so that you can correct it.

As your new corner grows, keep checking the blocks along the length and across the width to ensure that the blocks are level. It takes very little to throw a block out of line: a tiny lump of unmixed mortar, a pebble, or a piece of debris can create difficulties that can upset the integrity of the wall.

As you work, as each corner reaches the desired height, move to another corner. Complete all the corners before you complete any full courses of blocks.

Keep the block line in place as you complete the first course between corners. When the course is done, raise the block line and finish the next course. Do this over and over until the entire foundation wall is completed.

You may also make a story pole that will be helpful to you. This, as mentioned earlier in another chapter, is made from a length of 2″ x 4″ or dimension lumber (for that matter you can use a long broomstick or anything else that is convenient). It can be constructed within a few minutes.

Start at the bottom end and measure up eight inches. Mark the spot clearly. Then continue to measure upward in eight-inch progressions until you have marks as high as the wall will be when completed.

You use the story pole by standing it beside the wall (and on the footing) and comparing the marks on the pole to the level of the top of the blocks. See Figure 8-4. Each block top should reach the exact height of the mark on the story pole.

You must remember, however, that the story pole measures only the height from the base of the wall. If the footing is not level, your wall will not be level, although the story pole indicates the proper height of each course of blocks.

In brief, check every way you can think of until you are totally certain that you are keeping the walls true. Spend the extra minute or two rather than devoting hours later to correcting walls.

It was mentioned earlier that you will need to break a block for every other course, or you can buy block halves. If you must break a regular block without the scored divider, move past the divider of the first core hole and, with the block lying on one side, use a hammer to tap gently along the side of the block. There will be a higher-pitched clinking sound at first, but when the block is ready to break, the sound will drop in tone to a dull thunking sound.

At this point turn the block over and repeat the process until the lower tone is heard again. Tap gently two or three more times, and the block will break along the line you have marked with the hammer. A masonry hammer works very well for this operation,

but if you have no such hammer, then a regular peen hammer will work.

When you find that one of the blocks you are laying simply will not come up to the desired and necessary level, there is a simple trick you can use. Raise the corner of the block slightly and insert in the space a tiny piece of gravel or rock chip. This extra support will keep the block at the right level, and when the mortar hardens the block will be very secure.

For a long time I felt that this step was cheating, but one day I watched professional masons laying blocks, and they used the gravel trick repeatedly. I have not felt guilty about it since that time.

Do not expect great progress the first few times you lay blocks. You may find that you are spending 15 minutes or longer on each block at first. Your speed will gradually rise until you are laying 10-15 blocks per hour, and after a little more practice you will be laying 50-75 blocks during a fairly long work period. At first, accuracy, not speed, is your goal.

If the weather looks at all threatening as you work, keep a tarp or sheet of plastic handy to drape over your recent work when the rain starts. Weight the plastic down to keep it from blowing off and exposing the new mortar to the rain, which will wash out the mortar and ruin all your recent work.

At the end of each day's work period, allot time to clean up the equipment. Leave your trowel as shiny at the end of the day as it was when you bought it. The mortar box should be clean and free from all mortar, which otherwise will dry during the night and adhere to the box worse than glue. Within a very short time, these accumulations will render the box heavy and unwieldy. Wash off the hoes, rakes, and other equipment.

When you are buying mortar, do not buy too much in advance. As a beginner you will not use more than one bag of mortar in a day's time, until your speed increases, and if you leave mortar lying around, it will absorb dampness and become impossible to mix well.

If you must leave mortar on the premises, wrap it in plastic; don't just cover it. Close out all dampness, if possible. And when you go to buy mortar, be wary of the dealer who allows his bags of mortar to sit outside for weeks and months at a time. His mortar will harden just as surely as yours will.

As you work, pause every hour or so to scratch out or joint the block work. You can buy a jointing tool, but you can just as easily use a brick or part of a brick. Hold the brick sideways so that one corner of the brick will reach part-way into the mortar joint. Rake the corner gently along the joints in all directions.

While the results will be appealing, prettiness is not the reason for jointing the work. When you rake out or scratch out a joint, you also push the mortar tightly into the joint and compress it so that it is forced into the pores of the block. As the mortar sets, or hydrates, moisture is sucked out of the mortar and into the block, along with fragments of mixed mortar. Thus a bond and seal are established.

When the walls are completed, this is the time for the parget work, if you plan to do it. This means that you will apply a layer of mortar, stucco fashion, over the outside of the walls. By doing so you cover the mortar joints and the blocks themselves and leave the wall looking more finished and attractive.

To parget a wall, mix mortar slightly thinner than you normally would. Then, before applying, wet the wall slightly. Spray water on it to enhance the bonding process. Then use the back of the trowel to scoop up a load of mortar. Start at the bottom of the wall and apply the mortar with a sweeping, upward motion, smearing the mortar thinly and evenly until you have covered the entire wall.

Later, if you plan to stick rocks onto the foundation walls for a more rustic look, the parget coat will help with the actual sticking by giving the cement-based mortar a good surface.

If you plan to pour a basement floor, Chapter Nine will be of help to you. Go to it next, if the basement is next in your order of work.

Chapter Nine:
Pouring the Basement Floor

It has been said many times that a basement is the greatest blessing or the worst curse connected with a house. If you have a good, light, dry basement, it is a wonderful place, as suggested earlier, for a second den, a canning kitchen, workshop, office, and literally dozens of other uses. But if the basement leaks, is too dark, remains so musty that mildew destroys everything that is vulnerable, and becomes a haven for insects and vermin, then that basement is worthless.

If you are going to have a truly useful basement, you must select the best possible terrain for the house and then take all the necessary steps to ensure that the basement does what you intended for it to do. There is very little, other than landscaping, that will affect the terrain, but there is a great deal you can do to help make the basement better.

As for grading and other landscaping work, one of the very best pieces of equipment you can find at a reasonable cost is a small tractor with a box blade. You can, in many parts of the country, rent such equipment, or, if you have a real use for it later, you can buy used equipment.

If you read want ads and trade papers, and if you are lucky, you might run across a superb buy. In our case, we visited a local tractor dealer and told him what we wanted and what our price limitations were. We concluded by telling him that if he found an older tractor in good condition and at a great price, we were definitely interested.

Only hours later a farmer traded in his ancient John Deere Series 40 tractor, along with a cultivator plow, turning plow, disk harrow, and other equipment. We were able to buy the entire outfit for $2,100. The first two weeks we owned the tractor we recouped our money's worth out of it, in that we were able to do some grading that would have cost us approximately the asking price for the tractor. The beauty is that after we did the work, we still owned the tractor.

The point of grading, with respect to the basement, is to slope the land away from the house. If you permit water to run toward the house, it is only a matter of time before some of it finds a way inside the basement. With very little earth-moving, you can drain your house area effectively. When it rains heavily, note where the water tends to collect. Then slope or terrace that area, and when it rains again watch to see if the problem has been corrected.

If the problem no longer exists, you have solved a major part of your difficulties; if the problem persists, you must keep on trying to divert water. Persistence, in this case, is one of the major keys to success.

When you lay your foundation walls, you can install drain tiles and a gravel field. The tiles cost very little, and if you will lay these around the outside of the foundation walls on the three highest sides, leaving the lowest area open, you can enable a sizable portion of the water to flow away from the house.

After the tile is in place, lay a level on top of and parallel with the tiles to see that drainage will result. You do not want the corners to be higher than the middle of the tiles. In such a case all you do is impound the water that should be draining away. Use a long timber, such as a 2″ x 4″ about 12 feet long, and lay the level on top of the 2″ x 4″, which in turn is laid on the drain tile. If you are outside the foundation wall and you are facing the house, and if the bubble in the level is outside or nearly outside the markings and to the left as you stand at the center of the wall, you need to raise the middle of the tiles by two or three inches. You can do so by placing flat stones, or any object that will not decay or move easily, underneath them.

If you are unsure of the level status, use a hose and funnel and run several gallons of water into the perforations on the sides and top of the drain tiles. If the water flows correctly, you have done all that is needed at this juncture.

When the drain tiles are correct, cover them with gravel so that sand and dirt cannot wash in and stop up the tiles. You can also apply waterproofing coatings to the outside and inside surfaces of the foundation walls. Ask your local dealer for his best product, and apply it generously. Remember that this is your best opportunity to correct your future basement problems, so take advantage of it and waterproof the basement.

The waterproofing should be applied as high as the highest blocks that will be underground. You need not cover the blocks above ground: you can parget these.

Once the foundation walls are completed, turn your attention to pouring concrete for the basement floor. You need not do this task at this time; you can pour the basement after you get some of the other work done, but if you plan to do it eventually, you might want to get started and be done with concrete work.

If you plan to have any interior cement block walls dividing the basement, this is the time to complete these. Dig footings and pour them, and then lay the blocks. In our house we laid a concrete block wall down the center of the house. The wall was as high as the foundation walls and 24 blocks long. This meant that the wall was 384 inches, or 32 feet long. At the 32-foot point, the wall made a left turn and connected with the foundation wall at the back of the house. This wall was 12 blocks long, or 192 inches, which is equal to 16 feet.

The purpose of this wall was to give great support to the entire east end of the house, which contains the downstairs bedrooms, upstairs bedrooms, and bathrooms. From the 32-foot point to the end of the house, which is another 19 feet, we installed a huge girder ten inches high and eight inches thick. The girder rested upon the western foundation wall and upon the interior concrete-block wall. Under the girder we installed oak posts that were also ten inches wide and eight inches thick. So the center of the house was supported well, and joists could then be run from the center wall and girder to the outside walls.

If you plan to mix your own concrete, this is the time to use the mixer, if you chose to buy one. You can purchase a used full-size mixer for about $600 at this writing. You can also buy a smaller model that will mix 3.5 cubic feet of concrete at one time. The cost of such a mixer at this writing is about $250 for the electric models.

However you decide to mix the concrete, there are certain chores that must be done before you can start. First, you must make a visual inspection of the entire basement area to determine whether the depth is adequate. If you plan to hang joists from the foundation walls rather than set the joists atop the walls, you will lose four to five inches of ceiling space. Your concrete will require another six inches of space, at least, by the time you install sand, gravel, and the concrete itself. If you run plumbing pipes and heat ducts under the floor, you will lose another foot of ceiling space.

Should you decide that you must have more ceiling room, you can still excavate by shovel, although this is hard and slow work. If you left a rough chimney opening in the foundation wall, you can drive a small garden tractor and trailer into the basement area and haul out the dirt. You can even plow the floor to loosen the dirt before shoveling it.

Once the floor level is satisfactory, the next step is to see that the level line for the floor is established. One easy way is to run a line level from wall to wall and mark the correct points on the wall. Run the level from several points to be sure that you have the proper readings.

For example, start from the outside foundation wall to the center block wall. Start at a point six inches up on the first block. Run the line level cord across the interior until you have marked the level line. You can then use a four-foot level or a shorter level with a long 2″ x 4″ or board under it and get a level reading on the straight-edged board, and then mark across the blocks at the top of the board until you have marked the entire wall. Mark both interior support walls as well as foundation walls. Then, when you pour, you should have a reasonably level floor and a uniformly deep bed of concrete.

Your floor will not be perfectly level. Even skilled professionals cannot always get a truly level floor. But you can come very close, and the floor will be perfectly usable.

Before you pour the floor, shovel in and spread a layer of sand (which can be regular creek sand) across the entire area your plan to pour. If you have small areas off by themselves, you might want to start here and cover only these smaller areas with sand. When this is done, add another two inches of gravel on top of the sand. Then cover the entire expanse with sheets of plastic which are thick enough not to rip when you are pouring the concrete and walking across the surface.

This plastic sheeting will keep moisture that seeps under the house from permeating the concrete and standing in pools in the basement. If you do not use the plastic, you can bet that your basement will be wet at times. If you live in a cold climate, 6-6-10-10 wire mesh placed in the concrete slab will keep it from cracking. Roll out the wire before placing the concrete. Now you are ready to begin pouring concrete.

When professionals pour a floor, they bring in truckloads of concrete and pour large areas in a remarkably short time. If you are pouring your own, you can save hundreds of dollars, but your work will be slow and at times tedious.

Your best idea may be to start modestly and work in small self-contained areas. If you plan to have a divider support wall, start behind the wall and in the part of the basement which will be least used. As you mix concrete, wheelbarrow it or carry it in buckets to the furthermost corner and start pouring it out there. If you are using wire mesh, pull it two to three feet into the slab. A five-feet-long x one-inch-thick oak handle with a hook attached to its end can be used to grab the wire and pull it into the slab.

When you have concrete piled higher than the level line and over a considerable expanse of the floor, begin what is called striking off or smoothing the concrete. If you have open forms, the striking off consists of laying a long board flat across the entire area to be concreted and two men, one on each side, pull the board from one end of the area to the other, using a sawing back-and-forth motion to move the excess concrete.

In a small enclosed area like a basement room, you cannot use a screeding or striking off board. You may have to use a wood or metal float, which is a rectangle of wood one inch thick and about five inches wide and seven or eight inches long (size can vary according to your preferences and needs). A handle is attached to the top of the wood float.

To use a float, or floats, because some people prefer to work with one in each hand, hold the float by the handle and push the float downward into the concrete. Use an up-and-down motion to push gravel deep into the concrete and to force out air pockets that will weaken the concrete.

Put a two-foot by three-foot rectangle of plywood or a long wide board on the concrete near where you

will work. Rest your knees on the board or plywood while you use the floats. Push down on the concrete until no gravel is visible on the surface. Keep the level line in sight as you work, and make sure that the concrete comes up to the level but not above it.

If you are working in the back part of the basement and if you have the support wall down the center of the house, you will have three walls to guide you. Each wall will have the level line, but you will still need to level the center of the room. The float will help you get the concrete smooth, but it will not affect the levelness of the room's floor.

One method of working out the level in the center of the room is to start, in the imaginary house described in these pages, on the far east wall and establish a floor only two or three feet wide before you start to smooth. Then, as you work, use a long and straight timber, such as a 2″ x 4″ ten or 12 feet long. As you smooth a swath, lay the 2″ x 4″ gently upon the surface of the concrete and lower your head to get a close-up view of the concrete beneath the 2″ x 4″. If the 2″ x 4″ does not touch the surface all the way across, you need to modify the floor to correct the problem. But make doubly sure that the 2″ x 4″ does not sink into the concrete and give a faulty reading.

As you work away from the east wall, keep repeating the basic steps described above. When there is ample space on the fresh surface, lay the 2″ x 4″ diagonally in both directions to check the levelness of the floor.

When you reach the doorway of that room, set up a board to mark the boundary of the concrete. As you did with footings, let the concrete line end at a barrier where the concrete will have a vertical end surface. This way, when you resume laying, you will have a straight-down start, and the joint crack will be very small and hardly noticeable, especially since it occurs in the doorway where it will be covered by the closed door.

Plan your work well in advance. Do not start the concrete part of the floor unless you know that you will have several hours of work time. It is hardly worth the effort to mix the concrete and then clean up the mortar box and tools for only an hour or two of concentrated work — unless you are close to ending the job and want to get it behind you.

As you work your way across the floor, always try to get to specific points as goals in your work. And there should be good reasons for the goals. For example, if the back storage room (or, in our case, the darkroom, which could also be a wine cellar) is to be only eight feet wide, try to cover the eight-foot expanse with one day's pouring. Set up a vertical board supported by stakes where the wall will be built later. Then, when the wall is in place, the sole plate of the wall will be across the crack where the concrete work ended that day, and no one will ever see it under normal conditions.

Do the same with the walls of the future office space or game room or work shop. When you come to the wide-open areas, you will have to work out the best solutions according to your time, energy, and needs. In the illustrative house plans, the west end of the basement is completely open. However, the imaginary line extending from the support wall to the west wall is a good limit or boundary for the next work area. This is a large space which will take several mixings and smoothings, and you will need to work a long day to get it all done by stopping time. Begin work as early as you possibly can (on a weekend, for instance), and keep at it for as long as is realistically possible.

You might even decide to work in shifts in order to keep the work going, particularly if there are three or four persons on the job. If you are working alone, you will simply have to try to work to the best possible stopping place.

When you are working in an open area, use stakes, just as you did for the footings, and run a cord to the stakes and tie it at the pour line. When you are finished in a small area, you can remove the stakes. If you use very thin stakes, very little settling will occur where the stakes were driven.

What thickness should you make the floor? The answer depends primarily on how the floor will be used. If you plan to park vehicles such as trucks, you will need a thicker floor, especially if the trucks will be loaded at times. An engineer at a local college informed me that a four-inch floor for a basement is adequate for virtually every reasonable use that might be made of the area.

How much concrete will you need for the basement? Check your local building codes. Usually you will be required to use five sacks of cement per each cubic yard of concrete for basement slabs. You will need to estimate your needs in terms of cubic yards. One cubic yard contains 27 cubic feet (3x3x3), and you can estimate the amount of surface that will be covered by multiplying width times length times thickness. Assume the basement area is 32 feet wide and 52 feet long and the floor will be four inches deep.

Multiply 32 times 52 and get 1,664. Multiply this figure by thickness, which is four inches or .333 of a foot. Use simply .33 for the math, and when you multiply you get 549.12. Now you must divide this number by 27, the number of cubic feet in a cubic yard of concrete. The result is 20.33 cubic yards of concrete.

You will actually need slightly more concrete than the figure shown, because there will invariably be waste. You will spill some, or permit some to stick to the sides of the mortar box or to the buckets or tools. Most experts agree that you should plan for ten to 15 percent waste, all things considered.

After the concrete is poured, you should not neglect it. The first 24 hours are the most critical, and during this period the concrete should not be allowed to dry too fast. You can keep it dampened during the hot part of the day by spraying it lightly with a hose. Some people like to cover as much of the concrete as they can without the covering material actually touching the surface of the fresh work. Others like to cover the concrete with wet burlap sacks.

Freezing can be just as devastating as excessive heat. So try not to pour when the weather is unusually or harmfully cold.

How much will it cost you to concrete your basement floor? If you do the work yourself you can buy a scoop of gravel, which is a good load for a pickup truck, for $10-15. A yard of sand costs about $12-16. The cement mix costs about $6 per bag, and it takes about five bags to make a cubic yard of concrete.

If you are paving or concreting a relatively small area, such as a floor 36 feet long and 24 feet wide and three inches deep, you can determine the amount of concrete needed by using the formula given above. Multiply 36 times 24 times .33 and then divide by 27. The result is 10.56, which is the number of yards of concrete you will need. It will cost you about $360 to concrete the entire basement.

When the basement floor is completed, you can start cutting framing members for the floor. There are two basic types of floors to consider: the framed floor and the puncheon floor, both of which will be discussed later in this book.

Chapter Ten:
Sawing Framing Timbers

Before you think about cranking up your chain saw, you should give consideration to two major concerns. First, will the local building code permit you to use timbers that you cut with your chain saw? Second, if the code will not permit your using the chain-sawed lumber until it has an inspector's stamp, can you transport the lumber to the kiln for drying and stamping?

There are, of course, many other ways of handling the matter, but start with these two concerns. Assure the building inspector that your timbers will be equal to or even superior to the lumber yard's products in every way. Offer to show proof, if needed, that your lumber is not only physically attractive but is also stronger than commercial lumber. Point out that there is less moisture in your lumber than in commercial-grade timbers. And you can prove it with very little trouble.

First, a commercial 2″ x 10″ is actually closer to 1.5″ x 9.5″. Your timbers will be a full two inches by ten inches, and if you choose, you can make them even thicker and wider. Remember that you can cut a 4″ x 10″ with exactly the same amount of work that it takes to cut a 1″ x 10″. You can cut any dimension you like, as long as the wood is large enough to permit it.

If you want proof yourself of moisture content, all you need to do is obtain a length of lumber with a grade stamp approval and then drive a nail into it. Often there will be a small puddle or pool of sap surrounding the nail after your driving is complete. You can even see moisture flying from the wood as you strike it, if the wood has been kiln-dried recently.

There are methods by which you can test your own lumber for moisture, and these methods will be described later in this chapter. But now you need to start cutting wood.

In truth, you should cut your framing timbers before you ever begin to work on basement excavation, foundation walls, and concrete pouring. The lumber can be air-drying while you are doing the masonry work.

In this chapter you will be told every step to take from the time you go to the woods to the moment the finished lumber is cut. Your first step, naturally, is to select the first tree you plan to cut.

My own method is to search the forest near the work site until I find a tree that really needs to be cut. In many cases, the tree has blown over but the root ball has remained intact, and the wood is totally undamaged. You then are using a tree that has no useful life left, and you are salvaging it to keep it from rotting.

The ideal tree is one that is straight for the length you will need for framing members. The tree also should be large enough in diameter at the top or small end to yield framing timbers ten inches wide. Ideally, the small end should be at least 12 to 16 inches in diameter, and the straight part of the trunk should be long enough to reach from the outside of your foundation wall to the girder running along the center of your house. That length is half the width of your house.

Cut the tree at the butt or stump as low as you can without endangering yourself or cutting into the ground. Do not waste the stump portion of the tree by cutting so high that you are leaving two to three feet of superb timber standing useless.

When the butt cut is made, measure to the other end for the length you need. If your house is 24 feet wide, you should have at least 12.5 feet of good, solid log. Always allow for a few extra inches to compensate for the length lost when you straighten the end cuts. If the log is extremely long, then cut it as long as possible, while still having the needed diameter at the small end of the log. It will not hurt if the framing timbers for the headers are 30, 40, or even 60 feet long.

You might wish to start with a shorter log, however, to help you gain the needed experience. It is better to ruin a short log than a monstrously long one.

When the log is cut, lop off all the limbs. Cut them as close to the trunk as possible. When you start to slab the log, the protruding knots or snags will present difficulties for you.

Now plan either to cut the log where it lies or drag it behind a tractor or pickup truck to the work site. If you have no access to a tractor or truck, or if these cannot reach the depth of the forest where the tree is, you may wish to cut it on site and carry the lumber to the truck or house site.

Your first step is to elevate the log so that it can be laid upon two or three saw blocks. These can be three-foot lengths of logs which are six or eight inches in diameter. The larger the saw block, the higher the log must be lifted, but this also means that you will have to bend over less in order to cut.

Earlier, in Chapter Five, a device was described that is invaluable in raising logs for cutting. You can refer to that section of the book, and at this point construct the modified ring dog, or you can use levers and fulcrums and raise the log high enough so that you can place the saw blocks under it.

If you are working alone, there are a couple of ways you can get the saw blocks under the log after you raise it. One way, if you are using the ring dog, is to lean the saw block against the side of the log opposite the side you are working on. As you raise the log, the log itself will ride toward you, which means that the log pulls away from the saw block, which in turn falls to the place where the log had been. When you lower the log, it will ride over the end of the saw block and rest where you need it for sawing.

The second way is to go to the end of the log and lay a short length of log, or a rock, or anything that will provide a few inches of height 18 or so inches beyond the end of the log. Then lay a flat length of wood so that one end rests atop the rock or other elevation and the other end rests against the end of the log. Now place the saw block on top of the slanted board and against the end of the log.

Then, when you lift the log, gravity will cause the saw block to roll downhill and under the end of the log. Lower the handle on the modified ring dog and the log will roll, as before, onto the saw block.

Your first steps from this point are to saw off the ends with a straight cut (which helps to make the measuring and marking easier), and cut off all knots and snags or broken limbs that have been left on the tree trunk. Turn the chain saw flat and run the bar up

and down the top surface of the log to smooth off any troublesome areas.

Then, and this will be explained several times in this book to keep you from having to refer to other chapters frequently, use the chalk line to mark the first cut line. This first cut line can be in either of two places: down the exact center of the log, if the log is large enough, or as a slab cut on either side of the log.

When you mark down the center, you will later rip the log along its entire length. Then you will mark and saw off the slab edges on all four of the half-log's sides. When this is done, you will stand the half-log on edge, and you will mark off and saw the dimensions of lumber you want. This will be explained in greater detail later.

If you saw off a slab on one side, you will then turn the log so that the flat surface faces upward, and then you will chalk and mark both slab cuts on the new sides of the log. After the slab cuts are made, you can turn the log back onto one of the flat surfaces and mark and saw your dimensions of lumber.

Now that you have been given an overview of the two processes and are in a better position to determine the method you intend to try, it is time to go through the two processes in step-by-step detail. Start with the ripping-down-the-center method.

Figure 10-1
Starting to chalk the line.

With the log on the saw blocks so that the bottom side of the log is at least five or six inches from the ground, go to each end and with a tape measure determine the exact center of the log. Do not go by the smallest annual rings in the heart of the log, because the tree may not have grown symmetrically. If the log is 15 inches in diameter, make a clear mark at the 7.5 inch point. Or drive a nail into the log at the exact center point, if you are working alone. See Figure 10-1.

Then go to the other end and measure, and then mark the exact center. Chalk the cut line by going to the nail in the other end and looping the chalk line tab over the nail head. Pull the chalk line along the length of the log and with one hand hold the free end of the chalk line across the top of the log and down to the center mark.

With your other hand, lift the chalk line and snap it sharply against the surface of the log. Any color of chalk will do, but I have found that blue stands out in greater contrast to all types of log surfaces. Look at the chalked line to see that it has marked clearly and that snags or irregularities in the surface of the log did not interfere with the straight-line marking.

Be sure to remove the nail before you start to saw.

Now you are ready to saw. Start the chain saw and go to either end of the log. Lower the bar tip until it touches the chalk line at the end of the log, and walk slowly backward while you hold the chain saw as steadily as possible as you cut a groove along the entire length of the chalk line. This groove can be from an inch to two or three inches in depth. Keep the saw as straight vertically as possible and try not to waver back and forth as you make the groove cut.

Now go back to the starting point and again lower the tip of the chain saw bar into the groove. Pull the chain and bar along the groove in a sweeping motion of three or four feet. Pull the bar toward you, then lift it slightly and return to the starting point, and again pull the bar tip toward you. Each sweep should cause the chain to cut deeper and deeper into the log. Stay in one position until you have cut all the way through the end of the log, and as you progress down the length of the log, keep repeating this process. Do not try to rush the work: to do so will possibly result in a ruined cut or possible danger to the saw operator — or both.

In Figure 10-2 you can see the process of cutting all the way through the log. When we first started to saw our own lumber we used one of the many chain-saw attachments on the market, but we quickly discarded the device as too time-consuming and generally ineffective. You can see one of the attachments in the Figure 10-2, and if you feel more secure in your work by using one, by all means do so, but you can saw equally well by using only a chalk line and a steady hand.

Figure 10-2
Ripping the log down the center.

If the log tends to pinch in on the saw bar, stop and cut one or two small wedges and drive them into the gap where the cut-through has been made. These wedges will hold the kerf open as you saw.

Continue this work along the entire log. It does not matter whether the log is six feet long or 60 feet; the process remains the same until you are within two feet of the end of the log. At this point you can lower the head of the saw slowly until it is almost parallel with the log. You will note at this point that the saw is pulling out slivers of wood which are four to six inches long.

Keep cutting steadily until the log halves fall apart. Stand at the end of the log while the final sawing is being done. If the very heavy log sections should roll over your foot or ankle, broken bones could easily result.

When you have two log halves, you can set both of them upon the saw blocks and proceed to complete the pre-lumber cutting. See Figure 10-3. Assume you want lumber that is ten inches wide. Lay the blade of a tape measure across the log half, and mark at the tip of the tape and at the ten-inch mark. Both marks should be equidistant from the center of the log. Do the same at the other end.

Figure 10-4
Ripping off edge of log half.

Figure 10-3
Log sections ready for edge trimming.

Chalk along these marks so that you have chalk marks running down the outside edges of the two halves. Then make the groove cut along the first chalk line, then along the other. When both groove cuts are made, go back and saw off the entire outer edge of the log half, using the same techniques described earlier. See Figure 10-4.

At this point you can stand the log half on edge so that you have the widest flat surface in a vertical position, and one narrow flat surface rests on the saw blocks while the second narrow flat surface is horizontal and at the top of the log half.

Now use the measuring tape to determine where to mark the width of the first lumber cut. If you want a full-size 2″ x 10″, measure over two and one-fourth inches on each end and mark the locations. Now either have someone hold one end of the chalk line or use the nail again. Mark between the two points already scored, and when the chalking is done, you are ready to saw.

Figure 10-5
Chalking line for board cut.

In Figure 10-5 you can see the nail in the end of the log and the chalk line looped over the end of the nail. Note that I have placed the log in a heavily shaded area for the best working conditions of the summer weather. In Figure 10-6 you can see the chalk lines; the log section is ready to saw into lumber.

Again, saw the first groove one, two, or three inches deep. This is your guide line. The question often arises as to why it doesn't work to saw along the chalk line and forget about the groove cut. The answer is that the air movement generated by the saw will blow away so much of the chalk that the line cannot be seen, or sawdust will cover the line, rendering it nearly or completely invisible.

Figure 10-6
The log section ready for board cut.

After making the groove cut, use exactly the same procedure as before. You absolutely must hold the saw straight up and down; it cannot waver to the left or right as you saw. If it sways to one side, the bottom edge will be so thin that it cannot be used. If it veers to the opposite side, the bottom edge will be very thick and the next cut will be ruined.

It is a good idea to go back to the end of the log and make the early cut deep enough so that you saw all the way through the log almost at once. Let up on the saw trigger and lean over to see that the cut is straight down, so that the board starts off at the proper width. If you get off to a good start, it is much easier to keep the cut going in the right direction.

As you move backward, lift the tip of the chain and double-check to make sure that you are staying within the guide groove. If the groove is filled with sawdust, run the tip of the bar lightly up and down the groove for a distance of two or three feet to clean away the sawdust. Do this frequently.

All that remains is to continue sawing until the board or timber is completed. When it is sawed free, lay it aside and mark and saw other timbers. Do this until the log half is used up.

If you have a really thick log, you can get three, four, or even more cuts from it. If the log is smaller, you may get only one or two cuts from each log half.

You will encounter a problem almost immediately when you have made enough cuts so that the log half is wobbly and unstable. You can handle this problem in two easy ways. The first way is by far the easier of the two.

Figure 10-7
Cutting three boards at a time.

When the very first cut is nearly completed, stop sawing. Do not cut the board completely free. Leave six or eight inches holding the board to the rest of the log half. In Figure 10-7 you can see that three timbers have been partially cut, with two of them held to the log by only three or four inches of wood, while the third cut is being completed. When you have a huge log that is unstable, mark and saw each board, but leave it connected by the same amount of wood. Do this for every cut you make until you can get no more useful lumber from the log half. Then, when all cuts are made nearly to the end, stand past the end of the log and quickly saw the remaining distance. You will experience no problems if you saw the timbers in this manner.

The other way is slightly more difficult, but it also works well. Find two short (foot-long) boards four or five inches wide. Then locate two six- or eight-inch boards and nail one onto each end of the longer board so that the two form a right angle. It works better to have the upright or shorter board lap the complete end of the longer board.

When you are ready to saw, nail one of the right-angled assemblies to the top of the saw block. Then move the end of the log so that it is pushed snugly against the first assembly. Now push the other assembly up tightly against the log and drive a nail or two through the longer board and into the saw block. Leave enough of the nail sticking out so that you can pull out the nails easily and reposition the assembly for the next cut.

first run a chalk line along one side of the log, cut the groove, and then saw the slab off. If you like, you can even mark off the cuts you wish to make. See Figure 10-8.

Be sure that when you are marking you move the line over on the log far enough so that the chalk line cut will leave a wide enough flat face, enabling you to cut a ten-inch timber. You can measure down along the small end of the log at a point where you have ten inches, and mark both ends of the log at those points.

When the first slab cut is made, roll the log so that the flat surface is on top. Mark off a ten-inch cut on each end of the log and chalk the lines. Make the two cuts and then roll the log half so that it stands with one of the cuts you just made turned down. See Figure 10-9. The side or face of the log half that is vertical will be ten inches wide. Now you can make all the cuts which are possible by marking and sawing timbers two inches wide. Remember to allow for the kerf by adding one-fourth of an inch to each measurement.

If you wish, you can saw the timbers into a square, or into a rectangle, and then saw the smaller timbers or dimensional lumber needed from the large timbers.

Figure 10-9
Making the third cut for a squared or milled log.

Figure 10-8
Marking off dimension lumber cuts.

When you cut framing timbers by using the second method, that of squaring the log on three sides, you

As you cut the timbers, stack them so that they remain flat. When you have covered the first row, lay some thin boards over the first boards at both ends. Then lay subsequent boards over the thin boards. Always stack the lumber so that there is air space between the boards, as well as over and under them. See Figure 10-10.

As you work, you can find many variations on the suggestions offered here. You can cut your lumber from a variety of angles and directions. For instance, you can start with half a log and cut off boards or timbers from the outside edge. Each succeeding cut produces a wider board or timber. See Figure 10-11.

Figure 10-10
Samples of rough-cut lumber.

Figure 10-12
Making the final cut on 2″ x 6″.

When the cuts are made from the half log, you will need to trim off the bottom edge, as shown in Figure 10-12. Do this by using the chalk line and tape measure to mark the cut line, and then saw along the line, as before.

You can cut virtually any type of lumber you need, from quarter-inch paneling to 40-foot 2″ by 4″ lumber.

Before you use the framing timbers, you need to get the moisture content reduced to an acceptable level. It is a common practice to dry lumber either in a kiln or in the open air until the moisture content is down to 15 to 19 per cent.

An ancient rule of thumb is that lumber should dry "a year per inch." This means that a board two inches

Figure 10-11
Using a chain saw attachment to cut lumber.

thick should air-dry for two years. Obviously, this can be impractical if you are waiting to build a log house with timbers that are eight inches thick. Most people do not want to wait for eight years or longer to begin work on their houses.

However, if you cut your logs first and let them start to dry, and then cut your timbers for framing the floor so that they can begin drying, you can work on footings and excavations and foundation walls while the sun and wind are doing their work. Keep in mind, too, that when you start stacking logs, the logs can continue to dry while you work on the rest of the building. About the worst thing that can happen is that there will be some cracking or checking in the logs, but this is to be expected. This is the nature of logs.

There are two ways that you can check for moisture content. The first way is to purchase a wood-moisture meter. Here you are facing the expenditure of many dollars. Some of the most sophisticated moisture meters sell for $1,000 or more, but you would not likely want to spend that much money. The cheaper moisture meters sell for as low as $150.

The moisture meter works in this manner: you press the probes into the wood and one of the LED lights will come on. The meter will measure moisture content from six per cent to 60 per cent. The green light on many meters means that the moisture content is at an acceptable level; the yellow light indicates that you should investigate further; the red light tells you that corrective action is needed. The meter is powered by a nine-volt battery.

The second method is to use an ordinary kitchen oven to make the tests. The formula is as follows: Moisture Content equals Weight with Water minus Oven-dry Weight divided by Oven-dry weight times 100.
Or,

$$MC= \frac{WW-ODW}{ODW} \times 100.$$

For instance, you have a wood sample cut from one of your boards and the sample weighs 515 grams. You oven-dry the sample at a temperature of 103° C., or within two degrees of that heat, until the free water has been evaporated. Assume that the water-free (or nearly free) weight of the sample is now 265 grams. Subtract 265 from 515 and the result is 250. Divide 250 by the oven-dry weight, which is 265. The product is 0.943. Multiply 0.943 by 100 and the answer is 94.3 percent.

Obviously the moisture content is too high.

Now assume that the original weight is 490 grams, and after prolonged drying the oven-dry weight is 375 grams. Subtract as before, and you get 115, which, divided by the total oven-dry weight, is 0.306. Multiply this by 100 and the answer is 30.6 percent moisture content.

Dry the wood longer and the oven-dry weight is, for instance, 360 grams. Divide the difference, 15, by 490 and you get an answer of .03. Multiply this by 100 and the result is three percent moisture content. While this is unrealistically low, it illustrates the formula.

Remember: start with the total weight of the wood, dry it in an oven set at 103° C, and after the drying period subtract the dry weight from the starting weight and then divide by the oven-dry weight. Multiply by 100, and the result is the moisture content.

It makes no difference whether the weight is expressed in grams or ounces and pounds, just as it does not matter whether the temperature is expressed in Celsius or Fahrenheit degrees. Incidentally, to convert Celsius to Fahrenheit, multiply the temperature by 9, divide by 5, and add 32 degrees. So 103 degrees Celsius would be 103 x 9, divided by 5 with 32 degrees added, or 217 degrees Fahrenheit.

To convert Fahrenheit to Celsius, subtract 32 degrees, multiply by 5, and divide by 9.

Figure 10-13
Installing chain-sawed beam.

When you frame the floor, start by installing sills, which are long and wide boards laid flat across the tops of the foundation walls. Any anchor bolts you intend to use should be installed at this point.

The anchor bolt is a length of strong metal with threads on one end and a crook on the other. The crooked end is installed into the wet concrete which fills the cement blocks, and the threaded end protrudes upward through a hole drilled in the sill. A washer and nut are then placed on the threaded bolt. When the concrete has set up completely, you can tighten the nuts.

Anchor bolts range in length from one foot to 18 inches or longer. Obviously, the longer the bolt, the more holding power it will have. You can make your own anchor bolts by buying threaded rods and adding a metal plate at the bottom, then filling in with concrete. The plate can be made of any heavy metal that you have available, as long as there is a hole near the center and the hole will accommodate the anchor bolts.

After sills or plates and anchor bolts are installed, you can install joists. These are upright boards that run from the outside framing to the girder in the center of the house. (See Chapter Eleven.) Chapter Twelve discusses subflooring.

Chapter Eleven:
Framing the Floor

Framing the floor of a tiny house or a sprawling mansion can be essentially identical. In virtually every instance, you start with sills installed atop the foundation walls, and then you build a network of supports covering the entire floor area.

The sill is a wide board (about eight inches under most structural conditions) two inches thick and laid flat, usually, across the top of the concrete blocks that form the foundation wall. A general building practice is to attach the sills to the foundation wall by means of anchor bolts. These anchor bolts are typically 12 inches long and have an angle at one end and threads for a nut on the other end.

To install the anchor bolts, you embed the angled end of the bolt into wet concrete that has been poured into the cavities of the cement block. The threaded end juts upward about two inches, just enough so that a washer and nut can be attached after the sill has been installed over the bolt ends. See Figure 11-1.

You can buy anchor bolts or you can make your own. And, as in so many cases, the home-made product has many advantages over the commercial product. The manufactured anchor bolt is sunk into about 10 inches of concrete at most, and sometimes into less. If the amount of concrete holding the anchor bolt is less than eight inches, the bottom end of the bolt does not extend lower than the bottom of the first course of cement blocks.

What this means is that if there should be great stress placed upon the house (stress such as that exerted by high winds), the top course of blocks can be broken loose and considerable structural damage can be sustained by the house. Stated another way, typically the anchor bolt is held by one cement block only.

But if you make your own anchor bolts, there is an amazing increase in the holding power of the bolts. To make the bolts, you need to obtain threaded rods of at least three to four feet. If you use three-foot threaded rods, you will need to use a washer and nut at the bottom

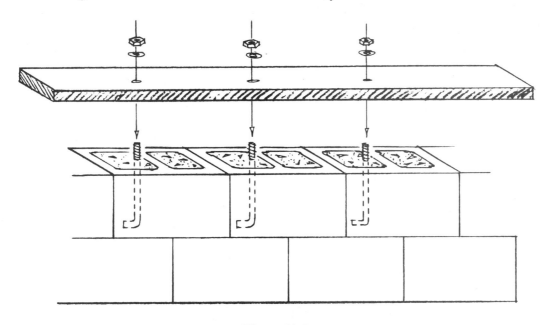

Figure 11-1
Three ordinary anchor bolts installed.

of the rod. Then slide a square or rectangle of metal, if only three or four huge washers, over the top end of the rod, and then slide the metal or washers down to the bottom of the rod. See Figure 11-2.

Insert the rod into the core or cavity of the top cement block in the foundation wall. Hold the top of the rod while you dump wet concrete into the foundation wall blocks. Leave enough of the rod protruding to extend through the sill and leave enough room for the washer and nut at the top.

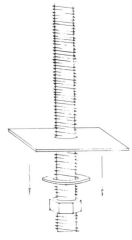

Figure 11-2
Components of homemade anchor bolt.

Now examine what you have done. The bottom of the rod is set into the concrete in one block, but the rod can-

not be pulled from the concrete of that block without also dislodging the two blocks that are bonded over the bottom block. The two blocks are held down by three blocks in the next course, four in the following, five in the next, and six blocks in the top course. This means that 21 blocks, not one, hold the anchor bolts in place. Figure 11-3 shows the relationship to the threaded rod and the blocks secured by it.

And the cost is not great. If you buy a three-foot rod for about $3, you can use it to cover an expanse of six blocks, or 96 inches or eight feet. In a foundation wall 40 feet long you will need only five of the rods. This is a total of only $15 per wall. And the protection you receive is enormous for the investment.

The next question is that of getting the sill attached to the bolts. Obviously you must drill holes in the sill, but how do you match the holes with the ends of the rods? There are two fairly simple methods. One way is to lay the sill timber over the cement blocks and drill holes to match the cores of the blocks so that each hole drilled (every eight feet) is over the exact center of the cavity or hole in the block. Then when you set the rods in concrete, you can position the rod ends to match the holes.

Another method is to set the rods in concrete and then apply blue chalk to the top of the rod ends. Set the sill timber over the foundation wall so that the bottom of the sill touches only the ends of the rods. The chalk will rub off onto the sill, and you can turn the sill over and drill the holes for a perfect match.

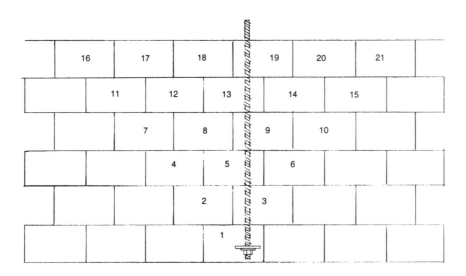

Figure 11-3
Typical installment method of homemade anchor bolt.

You will need to use pressure-treated sills. Do not risk the damage of decay by placing untreated wood in contact with cement.

When all the sills are installed, you will need to build your network of girders to support the floor framing. In our house we measured to a point exactly halfway between the two long walls, and we constructed a cement block wall down the center of the house for 30.5 feet. This left 28.5 feet open. We left the wall one course lower than the foundation walls, and then we ran a huge girder (eight inches thick and 10 inches high) from the top of the wall to the foundation wall at the end of the basement area.

By doing so, we had more than half the floor framing supported by a cement-block wall, and the open area supported by a huge girder. Under the girder we installed 8″ x 10″ oak support posts for support. See Figure 11-4.

To install the girder, if you use a log, extend the log from the interior support wall to the foundation wall. Run joists from the girder to the sills. You will need to cut out the joists in order for them to fit onto the sill and girder.

One easy way to handle the problem is to lay a course of eight-inch blocks on top of the 12-inch blocks. You will then have a difference of four inches on the inside — and you will have a ledge on which the joists can rest. Run a line level from the top of the final 12-inch block to the girder and mark the level point. Then run joists that butt into the eight-inch blocks out to the girder and, if necessary, cut into the girder in order to have the floor line level. You can cut a two-inch notch into the girder so that joists from either side will meet in the center. You can also buy plates which attach to the girder and joist and provide extra strength and stability.

Between the joists you can install wooden or metal bridging. The joists are 16 inches on-center and the bridging, if wooden, will fit between the joists and will keep the joists from wobbling or turning under the weight of the house. The metal bridging forms an **X** with one unit running from the top of one joist to the bottom of the one adjacent to it, while the other starts at the top of the adjacent joist and runs to the bottom of the first one. Every joist should be tied by bridging to the joist on each side of it.

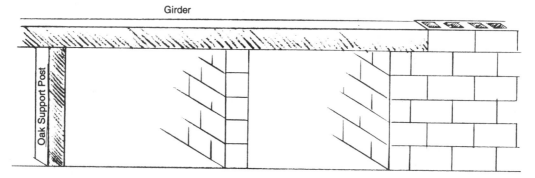

Figure 11-4
Cement block wall and girder with support posts.

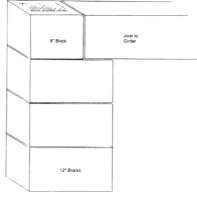

Figure 11-5
12-inch cement blocks capped with eight-inch block course and joist to girder installed.

You can make a joist spacer that will enable you to lay out and install joists with exact spacing. When all joists are installed and fastened securely to both ends, when ledger plates are nailed up and in use, and when all of the bridging is completed, you are ready to install subflooring.

We then ran 2″ x 10″ joists from the girder to the outside walls. We had used one course of eight-inch blocks rather than the 12-inch blocks we had used for the rest of the foundation wall, and the joists were exactly the same height as that of the foundation wall, plus the sill. See Figure 11-5.

To review: think of the house as a long rectangle with a wall running down the center of the house from end to end. Then, from the center wall, the joists reach out to the foundation walls. More than half of the center wall is composed of cement blocks, and the rest is made up of a heavy girder supported by oak posts. The joists were spaced 16 inches on-center.

We cut a narrow slot across the top of the girder, and the cut-out joist ends fit perfectly inside the two-inch slot. We also cut a two-inch by two-inch square out of the bottom of the joists, and we nailed a two-inch ledger plate inside the cut-out. At this point the entire floor system is supported fully.

Next we installed bridging between joists. This bridging was made up of the ends of joists that had been cut 16 inches longer than needed — for a reason. Assume that the distance is 16 feet from center girder to foundation wall. Cut the joists not 192 inches but 206 inches. The distance between joists is 14 inches, so when you are ready to install the joists you simply cut off the extra 14 inches and set the short timber aside.

You can also cut joists the regular length, and later you can cut special lengths of timbers for bridging. You can cut the timbers into 14-inch sections and use them.

To install bridging you can use one of three or more basic methods. The first is the simple 14-inch length that is placed between joists and held there while you drive nails through the outside edge of the joists and into the ends of the bridging stock. Be certain that the top of the bridging stock and the top of the joists are aligned perfectly. Never let the bridging extend past the top of the joists or you will encounter difficulties later when you start to install flooring.

A second method is to install diagonal bridging. This means that you slant-cut both ends of the bridging and nail one end to the top of one joist and the other end to the bottom of the next or adjacent joist. You can place sections of bridging side by side and have the two sections run in opposite directions. See Figure 11-6.

A third method is to nail in short sections of bridging flat and aligned with the top edges of the joists. Then at the bottom of the joists you can nail 2″ x 6″ lengths, spaced two feet apart, along the bottom edges of the joists.

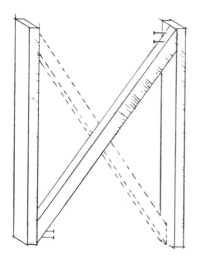

Figure 11-6
Diagram of diagonal bridging.

Remember that the entire purpose of bridging is to keep the joists from tilting or leaning and thereby weakening the strength of the framing. Your job is to stabilize the joists so that they cannot lean.

The 2″ x 6″ lengths should be spaced, if you use this method, so that they are 48 inches on center, at most. Remember that when you install gypsum board or sheet rock, if you use any, in the basement as ceiling covering, you will need 48-inch spacing. The lath structure of the bridging will provide an excellent nailing surface for the ceiling material, and the two-inch spacing between lath or timber strips will provide easy access for wiring the house later.

When you begin to install joists, take the utmost care to see that spacing is exact. Keep in mind that a joist spaced 16 inches on-center will have a distance of 14 inches from the inside of one joist to the one adjacent to it. And when you begin to work, you need to lay off your joists on both the foundation wall side and along the main girder.

There is a very easy way to lay off the joist locations, and the same device that will help you with this task will later help you even more later on with rafter spacing. I should inform you at this point that as my family and I work on various projects around our 40-acre farm, we have no one to help us. So when problems arise, we must solve them or resolve them the best we can under the existing set of circumstances. I have devised or invented a series of devices geared to help me with my work.

The joist-spacer, or the rafter holder/spacer, is only one of these common-sense devices. All you need to do is take a 2″ x 8″ board that is four feet, six inches long or slightly longer, and mark the board in the following manner. Start by laying the board flat on a work surface, and at the left end of the board measure in four inches and mark the location. Use a square to mark off a two-inch rectangle no more than three inches deep. Now measure from the exact center of the open end of the rectangle to a point exactly 16 inches away. Mark the point and move back one inch and mark off another rectangle that will reach one inch beyond the 16-inch mark.

Or you can simply measure 14 inches from the inside edge of the first rectangle. Mark off the second rectangle, then measure another 14 inches and repeat the process. See Figure 11-7.

When you have finished, you are ready to use the joist spacer. Make two of them, if you have a helper, so that each of you can use one as you work. Position the first joist by using a tape measure to get the exact location. Then lower the spacer so that the first open-ended rectangle descends over the top of the first joist. Have two other joists ready, and slide these into their position so that they will fit into the second and third open-ended rectangles.

The spacer can be located against the foundation wall or two or three feet from the wall. All that matters is that the joists are aligned according to the openings. The spacer will then hold the joists to keep them from slipping while you nail them into position. When the joists are nailed, slip the first opening over the last joist installed, and position others to be nailed. In this manner, keep moving along the length of the girder and the foundation wall until you have installed all of the joists.

A word at this point about cutting your own joists. First and always, check with the building inspector if you have any question at all about the acceptability of your materials. Then call your local building supply dealer and get prices on 16-foot joists — or whatever length you need. You will find that you will have to pay between $15 and $20 each for the joists.

At this writing, a poplar board one inch thick, two inches wide, and six feet long costs over $3. Think about it! A two-inch board six feet long costs over $3. A poplar board one inch thick, six inches wide, and six feet long costs $12!

A pine board one inch thick, four inches wide, and eight feet long costs more than $10. If you want a similar board, but one that is six inches wide, the cost is $14 for an eight-foot board.

You can cut a joist from pine, poplar, fir, or whatever kind of trees you have, for much less. In fact, you can cut a 16-foot 2″ x 8″ for about fifty cents or less! For the cost of one two-inch board six feet long you can cut *six* 16-foot joists!

Then calculate how long it takes you to cut a joist. Or how many you can cut in an hour. Assume that you can cut only four in one hour. You have saved $60 to $80.

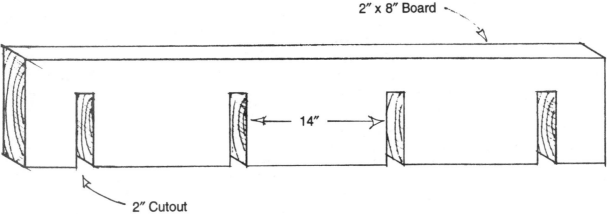

Figure 11-7
Joist spacer showing cutouts and spaces between.

Can you earn that much in an hour at your job? If not, sharpen the chain and start cutting.

Remember that when you cut the joists, rack them so that they can air-dry. You may need to weight them down with other lumber to be sure that they do not warp, check, or crack.

You may live in an area where a grade stamp is needed on all lumber used in a house. If so, check with the building inspector to see which steps you must take in order to have your wood meet the code requirements.

Remember to cut the two-inch square from the bottom of both ends of the joist before you install it. You can go ahead and install the ledger plate even before you start nailing in joists. Just measure down from the top of the girder (and later from the cement-block wall, if you built one) to get the exact location of the ledger plate.

If you cut the two-inch slot into the top of the girder, you will have part of the weight of the house (eventually!) resting on the top of the girder, and the rest of the weight of the interior of the house will be distributed among the foundation walls, the length of the joist, and the ledger plate.

It is my suggestion that you exceed code requirements in all phases of your house-building. Do not simply try to squeak past by meeting only minimum requirements. You are cheating yourself if you install inferior materials in your house. A good plan is to call the local building inspector *before* you start a new phase of your building program. Ask the inspector what the exact requirements are, and then ask about any other concerns you may have about the job you are undertaking. Get a clear understanding before you invest too many hours of work.

And now a word about nailing joists into place: unless it is necessary to do so, do not toe-nail or angle nail down through the top of the joist. The wood is highly susceptible to splitting from this direction, so you should nail through the side or face of the joist when possible. Angle-nail in three locations: top, middle, and bottom of the joist. Let the slanted nail enter the girder or other framing members at an angle, rather than nailing straight into the wood.

If you must nail down through the top of the joist, blunt the point of the nail before you drive it. As strange as it may seem, if you drive a sharp-pointed nail through a piece of wood, there is a chance that the wood will split. But if you blunt the nail, the likelihood of splitting is decreased greatly.

Why? A sharp nail actually causes a splitting action. A blunted nail punches a hole through the wood and does not split the wood as readily. To blunt a nail point, stand the nail on a solid surface, such as the head of an ax. Then use a ball-peen hammer to strike the point of the nail lightly. If you have any doubts about the effectiveness of this simple step, try nailing through a scrap of wood with regular and then with blunted nails.

Chapter Twelve:
Installing Subflooring

Installing subflooring will be one of the easiest — and most expensive — operations in the construction of your house. The work is easy because it consists essentially of laying four-foot by eight-foot panels of plywood or similar materials across the floor joists and either gluing or nailing them into place — or both.

You can cut expenses greatly, in one way at least, and add equally greatly to your labor and man-hours, by sawing your own boards — after first securing approval from the building inspector and the local code officers. To cut subflooring boards and install them, you will need logs that will yield lumber one inch thick (thicker, if you prefer) and five, six, or eight inches wide.

Approach the logs as you did when you cut floor framing units. Either slab off the sides and work from a basic square log, or saw the log down the center, cut off the side portions, stand the log on edge, and saw the lumber to its final dimensions. See Figure 12-1. When the board is cut, chalk a line along the edge, and if the edge is not straight, trim it to an exact dimension. See Figure 12-2.

Figure 12-2
Trimming fourth side of subflooring boards.

If you can cut logs that are fairly long (15 feet or so) you can save time because you don't have to stop often to set up another log. You can cut a long board without pausing, and your work is more productive.

Choose a method of cutting boards and try it for a while. If it proves to be difficult, try the other way. Either works well enough, but I prefer to square the log and then cut my boards from the squared timber.

If you want boards one inch thick, again allow one-fourth inch for kerf. So in order to get six boards from

Figure 12-1
Sawing subflooring boards on three sides.

one log, the squared log must be at least seven and one-half inches thick.

Take great care when you are cutting these boards. Once you start to install them, you will see that if the boards are not all of an equal width, you will have humps across the floor, which in turn will render the installation of finish flooring nearly impossible. There is, however, a way to handle the problem in its early stages, which requires a small amount of time and work.

First, estimate the number of boards you will need for the entire floor area. You will need more than 100 rows or courses of boards for a floor area that is 52´ by 36´. If you build a smaller cabin, the number of boards will decrease proportionately. For a house 40 feet long you will need 80 boards, assuming, as above, that all the boards run full-length across the floor area.

You will install the boards diagonally for the greatest possible stabilization of the floor joists and framing. Begin by running a chalk line from one corner diagonally to the opposite corner. You will need boards that combine for a length of almost 64 feet to reach from one corner to the other.

(Any time you are calculating the long side of a triangle — with the long wall and the short wall forming the sides of the triangle, in this case — use the Pythagorean theorem. To use the theorem, square the length of the first wall, then add that figure to the square of the second wall. Then find the square root of the combined figures.)

For instance, if the house is 56 feet long and you square that number, the result is 2,704. Now square 36, the width of the house in feet, and the result is 1,296. Add the two sums and the result is 4,000. The square root of 4,000 is 63.245.

If the house is 40 by 28, the square of 40 is 1,600 and the square of 28 is 784. The sum of the two figures is 2,384. The square root of this figure is 48.8.

After you chalk the line from corner to corner, and after your boards are cut and dried, start by laying one board from the starting corner toward the other corner. Let one side of the board align with the chalk line. You will need to angle-cut the board at the starting corner to make it conform with the corner of the building. The board will then cross several joists at an angle, depending upon the length of the board. Assume that you are building a house that is 40 feet by 28 feet, and that you will need boards combined to

give you a length of 48.8 feet, rounded off to 50 feet. To make matters simple, cut five boards 10 feet long. You will also need to angle-cut the opposite corner, to make the board conform with the corner of the house at that point.

Do not nail the boards at first; simply lay them along the line. Then by using a line level, or simply a line only, or by visual inspection, determine whether the boards are lying flat and even across the joists. If they are, then proceed and nail the boards in place. Use three nails at each end of the board and where the boards cross joists. If you use shanked nails, these are less likely to pull out or loosen.

The effect created by a nail is that as the nail, which is often only a short length of wire with a head, pushes apart the fibers of the board. The fibers naturally push back against the nail, and it is this pressure that permits the nail to hold the board in place.

If you use green wood, when the wood dries the fibers will shrink and thereby relax their pressure against the nail. The result is that the nail will pull out easily. So air-dry the lumber, unless you have access to kiln-drying facilities, until the moisture content of the wood is below 20 percent.

Earlier you were told how to calculate the moisture content in a block of wood. You can do the same with entire logs or boards that are air-dried. For boards, weigh the entire board as soon as it is cut. Then as the board dries, apply the formula described in the chapter on cutting floor framing. Remember that the old axiom is that you should allow a year per inch for drying, but you will be amazed at how rapidly sun, heat, and wind will remove moisture from a board.

If it is inconvenient to weigh an entire board, weigh only a foot-long length cut from that board or from a scrap board. Do the same with logs, which will be very difficult to weigh. But keep in mind that in the case of the logs, moisture can escape from the middle via the ends of the 12-inch section much easier than moisture can escape via the ends from the middle of a 50-foot log. So you may need to allow for a slight misreading of one percent.

As indicated earlier, if you will cut your boards, logs, and other timbers before you begin working on the foundation walls and basement, the boards and timbers can be drying while you work at masonry. By the same token, the logs can continue to air-dry after they are stacked in the walls, although some inspectors frown on this practice. If yours does, point out to him that you have all four sides of the log open to the passage of air and that the surrounding area is clear of any obstructions to the air passage. If the logs were racked, they would be so confined that air passage would be far more restricted than if the logs were stacked.

Back to the nailing of subflooring. Take comfort in the fact that the first course of boards is the longest that you will have to install. It is rewarding to realize how rapidly the rows become shorter and shorter.

It is good to appraise the situation regularly. When you think of the task of cutting 80 or more boards (each board must be the equivalent of a 50-foot board, which means actually far more than 80 boards), remember that once you have a log ready for cutting, you can cut a ten-foot board in only a matter of three or four minutes. In an hour, if you work steadily, you can cut 15 to 20 good boards. This does not take into account the time needed to locate the log, cut down the tree, and drag the log to the work site. Use your smaller trees for the boards; save the large trees for logs and for rafters and joists.

If you wish to save on time and energy by buying plywood for subflooring, you can cover an immense amount of space within a very short time. Each 4´ x 8´ panel covers 32 square feet, and the work is easily accomplished.

Start by calculating how many panels are needed to cover the first course of the floor area. If the house is 40 feet long, you will need five panels. Some builders prefer to start with half a panel, then move to full panels until they reach the end, and then finish up with half a panel. The second course will be made up of full panels. The third course will revert to the half-panel at the start and end of the course.

The reason for this approach is that two adjacent panels will never end on the same joist. The principle is the same as bonding in masonry work.

When installing plywood, leave one-half of each joist open so that the next panel can butt into the previous one. Drive a nail every six inches into every joist. This may sound like a waste of nails, but if you are skimpy with nails the floor will squeak within a few weeks, and there is little, other than taking up the flooring, that can be done to correct the problem. Many building officials require a builders' adhesive, as well as nails and screws. If you want floors that never squeak, use adhesive and screws. It is also very

helpful if you apply building paper between the subflooring and finish flooring.

When the subflooring panels are in place, you can use the surface as a temporary work area. Do not install permanent finish flooring until all the rough work is done; otherwise you will scratch and mar the finish flooring badly.

The exception comes when you decide to use a flooring that is thick enough to be both subflooring and flooring. This is a very reasonable option, particularly if you cut your own floor boards.

If you install boards diagonally, the flooring will then be installed at right angles to the joists. By doing it this way, you have the added strength of boards holding from two directions rather than only one.

However, if you choose to use ultra-thick flooring, the timbers will be installed at right angles to the joists and there will be no diagonal holding. But the extra thickness and strength of the flooring will more than compensate for the lack of diagonal holding strength.

The recommendation made here is that you use the extra-thick flooring for several reasons. First, the appearance of a floor made of six-inch or eight-inch boards of knotty pine is highly impressive and beautiful, particularly when the boards are sanded and given a high-gloss polyurethane covering. The strength of the boards is enormous, and the massive impression conveyed by the boards is overwhelming.

How much will it cost you to cut and install such a floor? If you plan to build a house 40 feet by 28 feet, you will have a total of 1,120 feet of floor space for the first floor. Each board that is 12 feet long and six inches wide will provide six square feet of floor covering. So you will need two full 12-inch boards and one four-foot board to reach from front to back of the floor area. You will need 80 courses of this pattern to reach all the way across the entire floor area.

If you prefer to run the boards longways, it will take four ten-foot boards to run the full distance, and it will take 56 courses of boards to cover the entire floor area. This equals 224 boards for the entire floor.

This sounds like an enormous amount of cutting, but remember that if you have your logs at hand and all you need to do is cut them, you can easily cut 10 boards per hour, so you are talking about approximately 22 hours of work. And with practice you can cut much faster and thus shorten the cutting time. You will find that you can cut a ten-foot board six inches wide in three minutes or so, if your saw chain is sharp.

In terms of expense, it will cost you about 25¢ per board or, in other words, four for a dollar. So the entire cost of the flooring will be about $56, perhaps considerably less. Remember that this is only an estimate. If your chain is dull, your saw (and you!) must work longer in order to cut each board, and the longer the saw runs, the more gas and oil and chains you will use. This augments the argument for keeping the chains sharp.

If you cut boards 2.5 inches thick, you will save the cost of subflooring, so in terms of savings you can deduct whatever you would have paid for subflooring plywood. Figure 12-3 shows a series of shorter extra-thick boards being readied for use.

Figure 12-3
Sawing and trimming 2″ x 6″ subflooring/flooring boards.

To install the boards, you will find that it is easier to drill a pilot hole, rather than try to drive a nail through the entire thickness. The size of the drill bit should be slightly smaller than the diameter of the nail used. If you can find fluted or spiraled spikes, these hold much better.

Plan to use two large nails (60d or so) at each joist crossing. Try to align the nails so that they look

patterned, not random. Use a straight edge if you need to do so. Mark the drill points and drill the hole through the board and into the joist an inch or so. As you drive the nails or spikes, be sure that you keep the nail shank vertical. If you allow it to slant, you may find that the point runs out the side of the joist.

You may wish to use a larger drill bit and countersink the nails a half-inch or so. This keeps the head of the nail out of sight, and you can fill in the hole above the nail head with wood putty or a mixture of sawdust and wood glue mixed so that it looks almost exactly like the wood surface.

One plan that I like very much is to cut a very small square of wood and with a pocket knife whittle it into a round shape. Then cut off quarter-inch lengths (or whatever the depth of the hole may be) and glue these in place. The overall effect is that of wood pegs holding the flooring down. This takes a lot of time, but it costs nothing in terms of money, and it adds greatly to the effect of the flooring.

Figure 12-4
Cutting 25-foot subflooring/flooring timber.

Do not install the pegs until the house work is essentially completed. You will mar the appearance by dragging huge timbers across them. You will also mar the surface of the boards, so you will need to sand them before applying the finish.

As before, cut the boards and stack them for drying. If you can cut a slightly longer board and then cut off a block of three or four inches, you can oven-dry the block to determine moisture content and get a notion of how long to air-dry the entire stack of boards.

But you must keep in mind that you are undertaking a huge task. You can handle it without problems, but do not expect to cut the boards within a few hours, and do not expect the boards to dry in a day or two. I recommend that you put one board aside (particularly one that did not turn out well) and periodically cut off a block and oven-dry it to test for moisture.

Keep in mind when you are sawing flooring that you do not need to cut such large trees, if you have smaller trees that need to be thinned. On our farm we had pine forests growing so thick that we desperately needed to thin the trees rather than have all of them stunted by too little room and nourishment. So when we needed a timber for some building purpose, we often cut a small, straight tree that would yield only one or two boards.

If you have pines or other useful lumber trees that are five or six inches in diameter, you can lay the log length over the saw blocks and chalk and cut a slab off one side, then reverse sides and cut off another slab. Leave the center as thick as you want the timbers to be.

All you need to do, then, is cut square edges on the remaining two sides and you will have a nice timber that is easy to haul, easy to hoist to the saw blocks, and easy to cut. If the log is large enough that you will have excessive waste, measure and mark off the size of timber you want and then mark smaller cuts, such as one-inch boards, on the outside part of the log. Saw these smaller cuts and get the one-inch boards and use the center of the log for the heavier timbers. The only waste will be a thin slab on the outside edges.

When flooring is completed, you can cut and install girders. The following chapter offers suggestion for this phase of work.

Chapter Thirteen:
Constructing the Log Walls

Once the logs are cut and dried, at least partially, you are ready to begin building the walls. At this point you should have the foundation walls, floor framing, and subflooring completed. The basement, if you plan to include one, should already be finished. If you have questions about these elements of your $15,000 house, consult earlier chapters for details on building the foundation walls, completing floor framing, and constructing basements.

When you start to stack logs for the walls, you must plan to handle several key steps in the building process: moving the huge logs to the house site and positioning them before elevating them to the work area, raising the logs to the subflooring, and maneuvering the logs across the subflooring to their desired location and then raising them to the needed height.

To move the logs to the house site, I recommend one of three basic methods, unless you are fortunate enough to have access to a tractor or other heavy equipment. One very useful piece of equipment is a pickup truck. If you have a truck, you can drag the logs into position. But as you do so, try not to drag the logs through mud or dirt any more than is necessary.

The best method we found was to jack up one end of the log high enough so that we could back the bed of the truck under the raised end of the log. When this was done, we fastened the log with chains so that it could not slip from the truck bed. By using the truck, we found that the only part of the log to be badly soiled was the very end, and often this part of the log could be cut off before the log was installed.

In order to elevate the end of the huge logs, you can start by prying up one end by using a pry bar and fulcrum. If the fulcrum is a foot or so in diameter, the end of the log will be lifted until it is two feet high. Place a chock block under the raised log end and shove the block as far toward the other end of the log as possible. See Figure 13-1.

Figure 13-1
Using a chock block to raise the end of the log.

Figure 13-2
Backing the truck bed under the log end.

At this point you can slip the end of the pry bar under the log and rest the far end of the pry bar in the bed of the truck. Try to keep the log near the end of the pry bar so that you will have more leverage to help you lift the end of the log high enough to clear the truck bed. While you push upward on the long end of the pry bar and hold the log end at the desired height, someone can back the truck under the lifted log end. See Figure 13-2.

Lower the pry bar and remove it from the scene. Go to the far end of the log and drive a stake against the end of the log and into the ground. Then back up the truck until the front end of the log is safely inside the truck bed.

Fasten a chain around the log and then connect the free end of the chain to a stable part of the truck so that the log will not slide as you begin to drag it. If you have a boat or trailer hitch, wrap the chain around the hitch. If not, reach under the truck bed and hook the chain to part of the frame. If there are holes or ports for sidebars on the sides of the truck bed, hook the chain into one of these ports.

When one end of the log is in the bed of the truck, the other end, because of leverage and balance, is much lighter. You can even lift the end of the log and guide it into position inside the truck bed.

You can now drag the log for a considerable distance. Check regularly to see that the log is riding safely. If the end slides out of the truck bed, you have the task of loading it again.

You have noticed that throughout this book there are special sections geared to the needs of the person who must, for whatever reasons, work unassisted. If you must hire someone to help you, you will lose much of your savings by paying salary to helpers.

If you must load the end of the log into the truck bed while working alone, here is how you can accomplish this goal. First, you need to get the first chock block under the log while you lift and hold the log end aloft. The simple way is to cut the chock block, which need not be more than two feet long, and lean the chock block against the log. Position it so that the block will not roll off when you lift the log end.

Now connect the chain of the log-lifter (a variation of the old ring-dog equipment) that you made earlier (see Chapter Five for additional details on the construction of the Ring Dog Log Lifter) and pull down on the leverage handle. As the log end is lifted, the chock block will slide down the side of the log and then fall so that one end is under the raised log. Then lower the log so that the end rests upon the chock block now under the log.

Sometimes you need to raise the log higher than the height you will achieve through regular chock blocks. You can use two blocks of wood (preferably three feet high) or cement blocks — whatever can be stacked with stability to a height of three feet — on either side of the log. One block should be no more than two feet from the log end, and the other should be at least five or six feet from the log end. This second block should be positioned right beside where you will be standing with the pry bar.

Push the pry bar under the elevated log end and to the top of the block on the side of the log opposite you. Now lift the pry bar and raise the log end until you can rest the end of the pry bar (the end you are holding) atop the nearby chock block. You now have the end of the log high enough to enable you to back the truck bed under it.

A second method is to use a small hydraulic jack under the lifted end of the log and elevate the log end to the desired or needed height.

If you have a small garden tractor with a small garden disc harrow at your disposal, you can elevate the end of the log so that you can back the harrow under the log end. Be sure the disc harrow is in the up position. Now lash the log to the harrow by using chains or ropes. You will find that even a small garden tractor will drag a very heavy log — if one end of the log is raised.

The third, and by far the least satisfactory, method of moving the logs is with a power pull or come-along. These rigs require numerous set-ups, and with each new set-up you can move the log only a few feet. If you have a considerable distance to move the logs, you must find other methods of doing so.

When you drag the log to the house site, you will need to jockey it into position by maneuvering it until the log is lying parallel to the foundation wall and at least eight feet from the foundation wall. Before you take the log loose from the pickup truck or tractor, put small chock blocks under it so you will not need to repeat the process of lifting the log a second time.

Your equipment for raising the logs to the subflooring includes a hammer, some 20-penny nails (only three or four of them), two foot-long lengths of wood with a sloped surface, and a small log ripped down the middle. The log should be 12 feet long, approximately, and eight inches in diameter.

Rip the log by chalking a line down the center from end to end and then sawing it by cutting the two-inch groove and then ripping the entire log. Position the two halves of the log so that one end of each log is resting upon the floor framing and subflooring and the other end is eight feet from the foundation wall. The log halves should be far enough apart so that one half of each log will be about two to three feet from the ends of the log to be lifted.

The foot-long lengths of wood should be four or five inches wide and about six inches thick, and the front side of the section should be cut vertically. The top side should slope down to a point. See Figure 13-3 for more details.

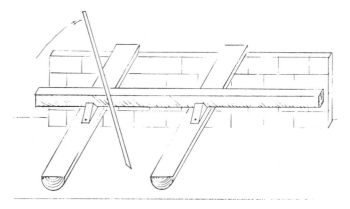

Figure 13-3
Using the chocks to hold log on split log halves.

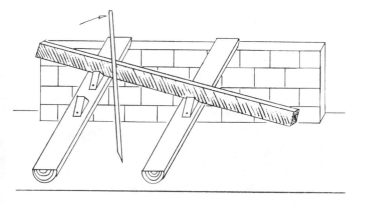

Figure 13-4
Chocks holding log in place as one end is raised.

You will also need your pry bar. Start by inserting one end of the pry bar under the log (as you stand with the log between you and the foundation wall) at least two feet. Lift the pry bar and the log will start to slide up the log halves leaning against the foundation wall and floor framing.

As soon as one end of the log is three or four feet, or even less, up the slanted log half, use your body to hold the log in position while you place the foot-long section of wood so that the straight end is against the log. Drive a nail or two through the sloping surface of the section of wood and into the log half. You have now scotched the log end so that it will remain in place while you lift and scotch the other end. See Figure 13-4.

Keep repeating this process as you work the log all the way to the top of the foundation wall and floor framing. When the first log is high enough, push it so that its weight causes the ground or lower end of the log halves to rise as the halves of logs flatten across the subflooring.

It is a good idea to start stacking logs on the wall opposite the log halves. You want to keep the log-loading side as low as possible for as long as possible.

When the first log is on the subflooring, you can maneuver it across the floor surface by using broom sticks or small, long dowels. You can also cut short lengths of limbs that are straight and round.

Use a crow bar or pry bar (often called a construction bar) to lift one end of the log three or four inches — just high enough to insert the roller (the broomstick, dowel, or limb section) under the end of the log. Do the same at the other end and in the center.

Now you can push, pull, or drag the huge log across the floor and into position. If you have cut logs that are not all the same widths, use the broadest ones at the bottom of the wall and gradually taper widths so that the narrowest ones are at the top. When the log is near the outside edge of the subflooring, you can tap it into exact position by using a sledge hammer or maul. The object is to align the outside edge of the log exactly with the outside edge of the floor framing and subflooring.

One end of the log should extend one foot past the edge of the subflooring. You will be using a log-stacking method known as the butt-and-pass system, and for better and more rustic looks you will want every other log end to extend a foot past the corner. You can saw the logs off so that all ends are flush with the foundation wall, but there is no real reason to do so.

The next step is to fasten the log to the subflooring and to the floor framing. To do this you will need a four-pound hammer, an electric drill, one quarter-inch bit and one five-eighths inch bit, a long bolt or rod five-eighths inch in diameter, a power supply, and a good supply of fluted spikes. If you are too far from power lines to have electricity, you can use a hand drill or auger. Hand-drilling is slow, but it gets the job done.

A fluted spike is typically one foot long and has a shank that is spiraled so that when you drive the spike, the spike itself turns and screws itself into the wood. To give you some notion of how well fluted spikes hold, we once spiked two logs together and then realized that we were not ready for the top log and had to remove it. We used long pry bars, a roadscraper blade, and every other leverage available to us and we could not budge the spikes. Finally we slipped a hacksaw blade between the logs and sawed all but one of the spikes. Then we lifted the end of the top log and laid a small section of log between the two logs and pried down on the top one.

Finally the two logs separated, but not because we pulled the shank of the spike from the wood. The head of the spike was actually pulled through the top log. This small incident was more than enough to convince us that logs which are properly spiked together are not likely to separate in a high wind or from buckling.

Here is the simple and easy way to spike logs together or to the floor framing. You cannot simply drive the spikes through the log and into the floor framing because there would be only two inches of spike holding to the floor framing — not nearly enough to hold together logs that weigh hundreds of pounds.

Even if the spikes were long enough, the shanks are so thin that the spikes bend very easily under the impact of a four-pound hammer. So you will need to drill a quarter-inch hole through the log as a pilot hole, as shown in Figure 13-5, and then after you drill a five-eighths inch hole to permit counter-sinking of the spikes, use a bolt or punch or other device to sink the spike deeper. See Figure 13-6.

An efficient method of spiking the log is to measure off spike locations, which should be every two feet along the entire length of the log. This may sound like a lot of spikes, but when you weigh the holding power of the extra spikes against the very minimal cost of

spikes, it is false economy to be stingy with the spikes and your labor.

Figure 13-5
Drilling the pilot holes for fluted spikes.

Figure 13-6
Using punch to countersink fluted spikes.

Mark the drill locations in the center of the log, starting one foot from the end and then every two feet for the remainder of the log. Drill all of the quarter-inch holes first, and then return to drill the five-eighths-inch holes. If you have two drills in operation, you can drill the pilot hole, and then the counter-sinking hole and then drive in the first spike, if you prefer to complete the basic steps of the operation as you go.

The quarter-inch hole is not quite large enough for the spike to slip into it easily. You will need to drive the spike with considerable force. Take care to strike directly down on the spike head. A slanted blow will cause the spike to bend instantly. If a spike does bend, stop hammering at that point and screw out the spike, if it is not in too far, or bend the spike back and forth until you break it off even with the top surface of the log.

The ideal way to drive the spikes is with a series of modest blows rather than heavy blows designed to drive the spike in all at once. If you use anything less than a four-pound hammer, your work will be too slow; anything heavier will bend too many spikes.

Drive the spike until the head is flush with the top surface of the log. Then use the five-eighths-inch bolt to help you to countersink the spike.

Place the end of the bolt evenly on the head of the spike and with the four-pound hammer hit the head of the bolt until the spike is driven in another five inches — the depth of the counter-sunk hole. It is a good idea to hold the bolt with a pair of long-handled pliers. A blow from a four-pound hammer can damage your fingers severely.

After the first few blows, the end of the bolt will be into the hole far enough that you do not need to hold the bolt, and you can use both hands on the hammer. When the spike is fully sunk, you may need pliers to work the bolt back out of the hole.

When the first log is in place (ideally, all logs reach all the way across their spanning distance, so the first log should reach from the corner of the floor to the edge of the rough door opening, if there is to be a door on that side of the house. If there is no door, the log should reach along the entire length or width of the house) you are ready to maneuver another log onto the subflooring and into position.

The plans suggested for the house under construction (see Chapter Three for details about floor plans and overall log cabin construction) include three doors: a front door, a back door, and a basement door. The number can be modified according to your own needs or desires.

For ease in floor-planning, the doors should be almost in the center of the front and back walls, and rough door openings should be 42 inches from outside to outside. The timbers used to frame the rough openings (unless you cut your own) will be 2″ x 8″s, which are in actuality only one and one-half inches thick, so you will have three inches devoted to rough-opening framing timbers and 39 inches left for the door and the hinges.

Mark off the door locations before you traverse the length of the house with the first course of logs. Let the marks for the rough door opening represent the outside limits of the opening, and let the first log end at the first mark for the rough door opening. See Figure 13-7. Drive large nails (up to 60d in size) through the door-frame timbers and into the ends of the logs, or into the timber used as a rough door opening.

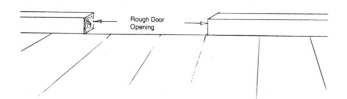

Figure 13-7
Log ends at rough door opening.

Start next at the mark on the other side of the rough door opening and locate a log that will reach from the mark for the rough opening to the corner of the house. Leave one foot to extend past the corner. Install this log as you did the first one. You are now ready to install the first log course for the other long wall of the floor plan.

Work the logs into place as you did before, but you will need to remove, temporarily, the log halves used to slide the logs into position. When the logs are installed you can replace the log halves for use with other courses of logs.

For the second long-wall logs, again mark off the rough door opening and let the logs end at the marks. Take care not to splice logs anywhere in the house. It is far easier to use short logs, but a spliced log not will have the looks, the strength, or the bonding power of an uncut log.

When the first course of the second wall is completed, you can install the end logs. Again, let these logs reach all the way across the ends, unless the wall is to be broken by a chimney or door. The end logs need to be cut precisely so that they will fit neatly between the logs for the long walls. The first course of the end-wall logs will not extend past the corner.

You should keep in mind the old construction adage: Measure two or three times, and cut only once. A ruined log is a heartbreak in terms of the time and energy expended in cutting the log and wrestling it onto the subflooring. An easy way to get the lengths of the end logs exactly right is to select logs that are a few inches or even a foot too long and then lay the end logs across the top surface of the front and back logs.

With the logs in position, use the chain saw to cut one-third of the way through the log exactly at the point where the inside edge of the long wall log strikes the top log. When the cut is one-third of the way through, put the saw bar under the top log and undercut it the rest of the way. The end of the top log will then drop gently into place at exactly the proper length needed. Do the same at the other end.

Now spike the log to the floor framing and add another spike horizontally at each corner for extra corner strength. Use the quarter-inch drill bit, stand on the ground at the corner, and drill a hole through the side of the long side log and into the end of the end log. Drill the countersinking hole as you did before, and then drive in a spike that reaches through the side of the long log and penetrates into the end of the butting log by at least five inches.

For the second course of logs, start with the end logs and cut them long enough that the ends protrude one foot past the floor-framing area. Do this on both ends and then install the spikes every two feet along the entire length of the logs. Where the second log crosses the first long log, drive a spike to tie the corners together. The spike should extend through the top log and enter five inches into the lower log. This will be done from this point on, wherever logs cross.

Your first course of end logs butted into the long wall logs, and now the long wall logs will butt into the end logs. This pattern will continue all the way to the top of the wall, with logs on each wall alternately butting into or passing over the other logs. At every

butt joint, drive a spike from the outside of the log and into the end of the butting log.

At the rough door opening, it does not matter if the logs are not exactly even, as long as the shortest logs are aligned with the rough opening mark. Later you can use a level, chalk line, and chain saw to even the ends of the logs.

When you reach the lower level of the windows, start to lay off your rough window openings just as you did the door openings. It is necessary for you to know the exact size of the windows you plan to use so that you can allow precisely for the opening.

You can also make your own windows, if you prefer. See Chapter 27 for details on installing factory windows and making your own. Keep in mind that if you are going to build the log house for $15,000, you will need to take advantage of every short cut and bargain possible. It will cost you $300 or more per window if you buy high-quality windows, so if you have 18 windows in the house, you should plan to add about $5,000 to your building costs if you buy them.

You can build your own windows and save considerable money. While a homemade window does not have the finished quality that you get in a factory window, the homemade window has a rustic and homey look that manufactured windows seldom have, and you can make them for a tiny fraction of the cost of buying them.

If you choose to make your own, your windows will likely be much stronger, and you can make one for about $5, as opposed to $300 or more for the factory articles. This is a savings of about $4,500 (or perhaps much more) on windows alone.

The point here is that if you plan to make your own windows, you can have more flexibility in rough openings. You can build your own windows in almost any dimensions you wish to have.

As your walls begin to rise, you need to make a story pole. This is simply a 2″ x 4″ or 1″ x 2″ timber that is marked off at intervals of one foot or ten inches — whatever the height of your logs may be. It is a good idea to mark off the story pole both in terms of log height and in inches and feet. See Figure 13-8.

For instance, if the pole is marked as the number of logs at a certain point in the wall, with a mark every ten inches, you can go to any corner or wall in the house and be certain that all the logs are the proper height. On the back or side of the pole you can mark in terms of feet and inches.

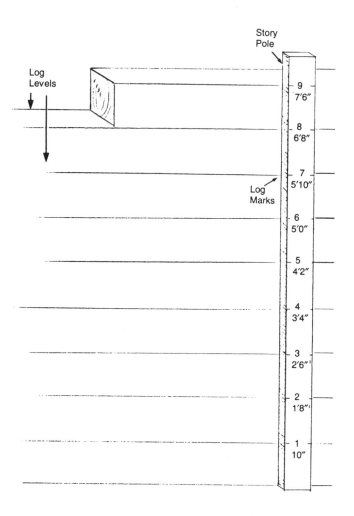

Figure 13-8
Using a story pole to keep walls at uniform height.

You can, for example, have marks of ten inches, one foot and eight inches, two feet and six inches, etc. The marks would be much simplified, such as 10″, 1′8″, 2′6″, 3′4″, etc. Each time you install another course of logs, use the story pole to check to see if you are keeping all walls at the same height. If one wall is an inch or two lower than it should be, use a one-inch or two-inch block of wood under the next log to bring it up to its required height.

You can also use the story pole for determining exact heights of windows, rough door openings, and even for such elements as heights of cabinets.

When you are ready to frame the rough window openings, you will use basically the same approach as

that used for rough door openings. The major difference is that the window opening has four sides and the door opening has only three.

When you are installing logs around rough openings, keep a constant check on the plumbness of the framing. Use a level each time you add another course of logs. Keep the framing completely plumb, and if you find a deviation of only a sixteenth of an inch, stop and correct it at that point.

Fasten the rough opening timbers to the logs by driving two 60d nails through the timbers of the framing and into the ends of the logs that butt into the framing.

Check on the distance to the top of the framing at regular intervals, and use the story pole to help you plan so that the final log around the framing — the log that actually crosses the window or door rough openings — is aligned with the top of the rough opening. Otherwise, you will need to cut out so the log will fit properly. If you have plenty of help in maneuvering the logs, this is not such a great problem, but if you are working alone or with only a mate, the problem is magnified.

When you start stacking logs onto the higher levels of the wall, the job becomes tougher and tougher. First, you will need to lean the log halves against the rising wall itself, and you may need longer log halves.

When the log is at the top of the wall and is properly chalked, you will need to go inside and pull down on the ends of the log halves so that the see-saw effect will enable you to lower the inside ends of the logs. The logs being lifted to the inside of the house will slide gently down the inside part of the logs.

When you need to lift logs to the top of the wall, you may need to build stacks of blocks of wood or cement blocks. Raise the log, for instance, to the level of one cement block, and right beside the log build a stack of two blocks. Use leverage, pry bars, and fulcrums to lift the log high enough to place it on the higher stack.

Then add blocks to the shorter stack to make it higher, and again lift the log to the higher stack. Keep going with this effort until the log is at the top of the wall.

Another way is to use a second pair of log halves inside the floor area. Lean the logs against the wall and work the next log up the incline as you did on the first logs. When you reach the top, use a pry bar or other leverage to urge the log gently to the top of the wall.

We nailed 2″ x 8″ timbers flat against the outside edge of the wall so that the timbers stuck up three or four feet above the top of the highest log. Then when we added a log, if the log tumbled too rapidly, instead of falling to the ground outside it merely bumped against the timbers. We could then jockey the log into final position and spike it into place.

Figure 13-9
Rough window opening and bracing.

As you work, keep adding braces for the walls, window openings, and door openings. Logs, despite their weight and the spikes used, are very wobbly at this stage. Go to the rough door or window opening and extend one end of a brace through the inside of the framing timbers. See Figure 13-9.

In the center of the floor nail a short length of 2″ x 6″ or larger timber to the subflooring, and then nail the end of the bracing timber to the 2″ x 8″. Then use a level to see that the wall is vertical and, when the position is true, nail the brace to the inside of the

rough framing timbers. Do this at every door and window opening to be sure that the walls are not leaning.

As the wall grows in height, frame in rough window and door openings. See Figure 13-10. If you wish, you can allow corners to extend beyond their normal length. You can cut all of the excessive length off later. See Figure 13-11.

Figure 13-10
Completed rough framing of windows and doors.

Figure 13-11
Extended corners before straight-line trimming.

When you reach the desired height of the log walls, and if your story pole indicates that the walls are all the same height and the desired height, you are ready to begin work on the interior walls and the installation of girders.

Chapter Fourteen offers suggestions on constructing hollow core partition wall framing and on log walls for interior framing. The chapter also details how to cut and install girders.

Chapter Fourteen:
Cutting and Installing Girders

With the logs walls stacked, you can start to cut and install girders. But first you must be certain that all walls are thoroughly braced. Brace the walls, if you haven't done so, by running timbers (you can use slabs off log sides, if the slabs are sturdy and strong) from the inside of the window openings to the floor. The braces should reach at least ten feet from the wall toward the center of the floor.

One easy way to install temporary bracing is to nail a block of wood at a right angle to the wall being braced and then connect the brace to the block. For instance, move out from the wall 10 feet or so and nail the block (which should be no smaller than a 4″ x 4″ or 6″ x 6″) in front of one side of the window. The block itself will point toward the window. See Fig. 14-1.

Figure 14-1
Attaching brace to block on floor.

Lay the support or brace timber with one end beside the block and the other end protruding through the window. Lift the window end of the timber and hold it against the side of the window opening and nail the brace firmly to the window timbers. Then go to the subflooring area and nail the other end to the block. Leave this and all braces in place until you have completed the installation of girders.

The log walls, you will learn quickly, are highly unstable when they are being stacked. Even when the wall is no higher than three or four courses, you can push against the wall and it will give one or two inches. As you rise higher with the log courses, the "give" in the wall becomes more pronounced.

You will also find that the corners are very sturdy. The swaying tendency occurs at breaks in the wall where doors are to be installed. But as you brace, run support timbers from all four walls to the blocks in the center of the subfloor area. Do not let the fact that you cannot shake the wall easily mislead you into thinking that the wall is sturdy. If you were to install roof trusses or rafters without installing girders, the log walls would be pushed outward and the entire assembly could collapse.

When the walls are properly braced, you can begin to cut the girders. Before you crank the saw, do some mental picturing of the installed girders. Realize, for example, that the girders are among the very few logs in the house which will have all four sides visible. Wall logs, whether interior or exterior, will have the top and bottom sides of each log hidden from view. But the girders will be exposed from all directions. So it is important that you choose logs that are straight and true, as free of all defects as possible.

When you measure, mark, and saw, take extra care to see that you are laying off the best possible logs. Start your sawing with the main girder, which runs along the entire length of the house from end to end.

If you are building a huge log house, such as the one that was described earlier, you will need a very long girder, up to 52 feet long. As you are selecting the log, use a chalk line to assure yourself that the log is straight. Do not trust your eyes. Sometimes a tiny deviation appears trivial, but when you use a chalk line or straight edge, you can see that the log curves a total of six or eight inches.

Once you are satisfied with the straightness of the log, check the diameter at the small end. It might be a good idea for you to nail strips of wood together to form an 8″ x 10″ rectangle. Hold this rectangle against the end of the log to be sure that the log is large enough to yield the timber you need. If you prefer, you can cut a two-inch thickness off an already milled log (be sure you are not shortening a log too much for later use!) and hold the thin rectangle against the end of the log.

Because this is such a crucial log, you might want to tack one of the rectangles against each end of the log. Then use a level to determine that the rectangles are aligned and that the top side is horizontal. You can also use a square to lay off the log size, if you prefer. See Fig. 14-2.

Figure 14-2
Cutlines outlined on log end.

When you are absolutely positive that the log is ready to mark, chalk the slab cut lines as you did for other cuts. This time, as you make the slab cuts, make

the groove cut as before, but when you start to cut off the entire slab, do not position the saw so that the head is resting upon the log top. Instead, hold the head above the log and run the tip of the bar up and down inside the groove cut until you have cut through the entire slab area.

As you move along the log, keep holding the head off the log and running the tip of the bar inside the groove. The reason for this is simple: if you use the spike to help you cut, the work is much easier. You are simply digging in the spike and then raising the head, with the spike acting as a fulcrum. In this manner you can cut much faster, but the problem is that the added pressure causes the bar and chain to cut somewhat erratically and the result is a very noticeable gouging or marking on the log at every point where you used the fulcrum effect.

You might, however, opt to do as we did and make the saw marks on purpose. In the traditional log house there are adz marks, so we decided to use the chainsaw to make the marks of the new tradition in building log houses.

Holding the saw engine or head higher is much harder work, and it takes longer, but the final cut is far more attractive. Remember that this girder can be seen from every point in the kitchen/living room/-dining room part of the house, and you want it to be flawless, if possible.

Make all four cuts in this way, and the finished product should be one of which you will be proud. Now comes the truly difficult task: that of getting the timber inside the house and then up to the top of the log walls.

You realize at this point that green timber will weigh about 40-53 pounds per square foot, and you are going to be moving about 2,000 to 3,000 pounds, depending upon the kind of wood you are using.

If you have a small tractor (better than a large one because it is more maneuverable) or even a garden tractor of the 15-horsepower variety, you can easily move the log to the house. But do not drag the log. By doing so you will embed dirt and mud into the pores of the wood, and these stains are very difficult to remove. Instead, let one end of the log ride on the tractor hitch or on one of the attachments, and only one small part of the log will be dragged through the dirt.

If you cannot do what is suggested above, pry up the end of the log nearest the house and roll a three-foot length of round log too small to be of use anywhere else underneath one end. Then place another length halfway down the log, and a third about 15 feet from the far end. Back the tractor or pickup truck to the end of the log and use a chain or cable to fasten the log to the truck or tractor. As you start to pull, the log will move easily on top of the rollers. The only problem is that you will need to keep watching the rollers.

As the end of the log moves off the last roller, take the roller to the front of the log and place it in position. Keep doing this as long as necessary, until the log reaches the house site and one end is pointed toward the doorway on the lower side.

Figure 14-3
Using cement blocks and ply pole.

Wait as long as possible before unhitching the tractor or truck and moving it out of the way. You will find that you can shove the log on rollers with your hands or with the help of a pry pole to complete the move. To use a pry pole, go to the back end of the log and run the end of the pole under the log and then pry upward. You will move the log a foot or so each time you pry upward.

When the end of the log is against the foundation wall under the doorway, you will need to use a different strategy that involves both lifting and prying. First, find enough square blocks of wood (preferably two or three feet long — leftovers from wall logs) and a pry bar strong enough to lift the end of the log. With the end of the log off the ground, stack the squared blocks in the old pig-pen fashion so that the first two will be crossed and bonded by the second two, and so forth. Keep lifting the log and stacking the blocks until the end of the log is slightly higher than the doorway. If you happen to have a supply of cement blocks handy, you can use these instead of wood, as shown in Figure 14-3.

Now use the pry pole again. Pry as before and shove the log, little by little, into the doorway. If you can no longer move the log by prying, find a length of rope four or five feet long and tie a slip knot around the log. Knot the other end around the pry bar at a point about six inches higher than the top of the log.

Figure 14-4
A crowbar will easily move a huge log.

Now extend the bottom end of the pry bar forward until the rope is tight. Then push against the upper end of the pry pole and use the leverage to move the log forward. If this fails, use the come-along device known as a power pull. Attach one end to the furthermost wall and the other end to the end of the log. You can move the log easily with this mechanical advantage.

The first two methods are faster and less trouble, but the third method will work when little else will. As soon as the end of the log is four or five feet inside the doorway, you can use smaller rollers, such as sections of broom handles or small round limbs, to move the log across the subflooring. You will find that you can also use a crowbar at the back end of the log, and by slipping the point of the pry bar under the log and lifting, you can steadily move the log forward. See Fig. 14-4.

A crowbar, as the tool is commonly called, is a marvel of utility and engineering. With this simple and inexpensive tool you can lift and move enormous weights with very little effort. I suggest that you have one at the work site at all times.

As the log moves inward, angle the front end so that it is pointed toward the farthest corner. When the girder is finally inside the house, it will form a diagonal line from the northeast to southwest corners.

Now comes the hardest part of the entire process. You must elevate the log so that the ends can be placed over the logs at each end of the house.

There is no easy way to do this, short of renting a lifting device or hiring someone to lift the log for you. And be warned that the job is very dangerous. You or others could be crushed if the log should fall upon you, so exhibit the greatest possible caution.

Here's how we installed our main girder. By this time, we had accumulated a considerable amount of squared logs ranging in length from a foot or less to five feet. We hauled all of these log sections that we could find into the house, and placed half of them at one end of the log and the others at the other end. Then we simply started prying up one end of the log and cross-stacking log sections under the raised end of the log. The cross-stacked log sections must be several feet away from the end wall in order for you to have working room.

We raised the girder first by prying, and within a short time we had the log as high as it could go. We could not use the pry bars after the girder reached a certain height, so we substituted a small hydraulic jack. We kept stacking cement blocks higher and higher. We made a double stack about three feet apart

and laid a section of an 8″ x 10″ log across the two stacks, and then we set the hydraulic jack atop the 8″ x 10″.

As we could do so, we kept adding 2″ x 6″ lengths on top of the 8″ x 10″ as the girder was raised higher and higher. When necessary we raised the stack of cement blocks by one block on each side. We also knotted a rope around each end of the log, ran the rope through cracks between logs, and tied another knot. We knew that the rope could not hold the log precisely in place, but we figured that if the stack of log sections toppled, the rope would keep the log from falling on one of us.

When the log was high enough, it was time for us to run freshly cut 2″ x 4″s laid side by side from the stack of log sections to the top of the highest log in the wall. We nailed each 2″ x 4″ both to the log section and to the top log in the wall. We did not want to risk having 2″ x 4″s start to slide while we were moving the log.

The same process will work for you. The end of the main girder is no more than a foot to 18 inches from the log wall at this point, and probably less. The end of the girder is also four or five inches higher than the wall. If you can pry the end of the girder upward high enough to slip the ends of the 2″ x 4″s under it, you can then use a crowbar to pry the end of the girder inch by inch until the end rests upon the log wall.

You must do this on each end of the house, of course, and you need to keep in mind that the entire job is much harder and time-consuming than the above description might suggest. At the same time, the job is also much easier than you might fear. It is simply a case of taking one step at a time, and of making no moves until you are certain that you can do so in safety.

You can also raise a heavy log by stacking cement blocks or other squared materials and then using a pry bar. When we were building our garage, we needed to raise a 36-foot green log into place, and we had only the three of us: a 62-year-old man, a 52-year-old woman, and an 18-year-old young man. The girder weighed well over 350 pounds and, in addition to the weight, it was extremely awkward to raise.

So we hauled a number of cement blocks to the scene, and at one corner we stood a long timber on end two feet from the corner of the building and parallel with the corner. Then we nailed one cross-piece at the bottom (a foot off the ground) and another near the top. The purpose of these pieces was to produce a ladder-like effect so that the elevated log could rest on the ladder "rungs." See Fig. 14-5.

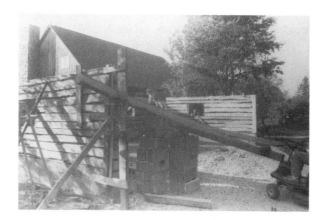

Figure 14-5
A series of "rungs" support the weight of the log.

We used a crowbar to raise the end of the log a few inches, and as soon as we had enough room we used a fulcrum and a pry bar to help with the lifting. I used a cement block with a two-foot length of 6″ x 6″ wood on top of the cement block. With one lift I could raise the log end almost two feet, and my wife and son would add another rung to the "ladder" and also build a pier of cement blocks, in case the rungs broke. See Fig. 14-6.

The entire job went smoothly, and at no time did we have to lift more than a few pounds of dead weight. When we finished at one corner, we moved our blocks and gear to the other corner and repeated the process. You can do essentially what we did, and if you work carefully and, above all, safely, you can handle the work without undue risk. The garage logs were considerably smaller than the logs used in the house, but nonetheless the garage logs weighed several hundred pounds, and the principles we used in raising these logs will work for larger logs as well.

When you have completed the steps described, all that remains is to center the girder exactly. Do this by measuring from one corner to the other at the end of the house and by marking the exact center on the inside edge of the top log. Do this on either end. Then you will know when the girder is centered perfectly. Keep prying or tapping the girder with a heavy hammer until it is in place.

Figure 14-6
Blocks and rungs provide double support.

Figure 14-7
Homemade countersinker to protect fingers and hands.

Now it is necessary to anchor the girder securely. Do this by drilling a quarter-inch hole through the entire girder from top to bottom and then driving a fluted spike into the pilot hole. You can countersink four inches, if you prefer, for a more secure hold. We used a long metal punch for a while, and then we used the broken handle of an old ratchet we had found somewhere. The handle already had a hole drilled in it, so we added a long bolt and washer so that we could hold the countersinker by the handle and not risk smashed fingers. See Fig. 14-7.

When both ends are anchored, you are ready to install the girders that run from the front and back walls to the center or main girder. But first you must install the support posts for the main girder.

Try to arrange your schedule so that you can complete the installation of support posts before you must stop for the day. Do not leave the 52-foot girder, or even a much shorter one, spanning the entire length of the house with nothing under it for support. Within an amazingly short time, such long and heavy timbers can sag considerably because of their weight. Even if you can't install the permanent support posts, at least cut pine poles and install them every 12 feet along the entire length of the girder. You will not be able to leave these temporary support poles in place, because you will need to take them down later, one at a time, in order to install the permanent support posts and finished floors. But for the present, have the girder supported at all times.

The final support posts should be the same width and breadth as the main girder itself. You should also make every effort to cut the support posts as smooth and straight as possible. These are among the other timbers which are visible on all four sides.

You will need at least four of the support posts, and it is a good idea to install the pine poles before you begin to cut the support posts. By doing so, the main girder will be supported at all times.

When you cut the support posts, try for a perfect fit. If the post is too short, it will be unsightly, and essentially worth very little. If it is too long, you cannot install it without great effort, and even if you succeed, you will cause the main girder to warp upward. The ideal fit is one that is slightly snug, so that you will need to use a heavy hammer to tap the posts into their position. See Fig. 14-8.

When the first post is cut, position it so that the top end fits under the main girder. The bottom end will probably be to one side or the other. As you tap the post into position, use a level so that you can place the post in perfect position.

Figure 14-8
Keep the support post fit snug.

Install the posts by drilling pilot holes through the top of the main girder and then a larger hole for countersinking, so that you can drive at least one fluted spike down into the top of the support post. On each side of the post, drill a pilot hole into the center of the post about four inches from the top. Angle the hole upward so you can drive a shorter spike through the top end of the post and into the bottom of the main girder.

But do not install the spikes at this point. Remember that you will need to take down the post in order to install flooring later on, and you do not want to wrestle with the spikes and risk damaging the post or girder. Instead, use 60d nails, one on each side of the post. Drive the nails into the pilot holes, but leave the head sticking out so that you can extract the nails when you need to take down the post.

Do the same at the bottom. One 60d nail on each side of the post will hold it securely, and you can remove these nails easily when you need to do so.

The next step, which is much easier in many respects, is to install the girders from the front and back of the house to the main girder.

Cut the side girders just as you did the main girder, maintaining keen attention to the fact that these cuts — all four sides of each girder — will be visible. Measure for correct length first. Start at the center of the main girder and measure to the outside edge of the top wall logs on the front and back of the house.

If you are building a large house, with a width of 32 feet, for instance, you will need a girder that is 16 feet long. One end must be square-cut, while the other end will be slanted to allow for the slope of the roof.

The slope cut can be handled in two basic ways. First, you can install the girders, and when you have determined the roof slope you can mark and cut the girder ends accordingly. The other method is to make the cuts before you install the girders. But you must know the roof slope before you make the slope cuts.

It is much easier to make the slope cuts while the girder timbers are on the ground. But in order to know the slope of the roof you need to have a fairly basic roofing plan in mind. Assume that the peak of the roof will be 12 feet higher than the log walls. This is your rise. Now consider that the distance from the center of the house to the outside edge of the log wall is 16 feet.

You are now ready to apply the Pythagorean Theorem. Square the rise (12´ x 12´) and you have 144 feet. Next, square the run (the distance from the center of the house to the outside edges) and you get 256 feet (16´ x 16´). Add 256´ and 144´. The result is 400´. Now take the square root of 400´, and you arrive at 20´, which will be the length of the third side of your triangle. Add at least a foot to this length (which is the length of your rafters) for overhang and you know that your rafters are to be 21 feet. You may want to add even more to get a larger overhang, but you need not decide that at this point.

You can now determine the slope of the roof. If you do not remember your high-school geometry, just use a basic drawing and a quick square or similar implement. Or you can use the line drawing you create.

Start with a clean sheet of regular typing paper or a page from a legal pad. If you have some cardboard that is sturdy, this is even better. Position the page so that it lies lengthwise in front of you, and make a straight line eight inches long near the bottom edge of the paper. Each inch will represent two feet, so the eight-inch line represents 16 feet, the length of your girders.

At the end of the 16-foot line, at the right side of the page or piece of cardboard, draw a vertical line at a perfect right angle to the first line. If your roof peak is to be 12 feet, and if each inch equals two feet, make the line six inches long.

Now lay the straight edge so that you can make a line from the top end of the vertical line to the left end of the horizontal line. Just to double-check, measure the diagonal line. It should be exactly ten inches, which will represent 20 feet.

You now have a triangle that represents one-half of your roof slope. By using high-school geometry equipment you can see that the angle at the bottom left of the triangle is essentially 37.5 degrees, which is your roof slope.

If you want to make it even easier, make the drawing on cardboard and cut it out. Then hold the drawing cut-out against the end of the girder. Mark along the diagonal line and you have marked the roof slope and girder cut. You can now cut the slope of the girder before you install it.

Plan to install the girders four feet apart for best results in terms of strength as well as appearance. However, if your own house plan is such that the total distance along the main girder is not divisible by four, make any necessary adjustments. It does not matter at all if the girders are four feet and five inches, for example. Just keep them spaced evenly.

It is also a good idea to stagger the girders rather than have them meet in pairs at the main girder. The reason for this is simple: if the girders meet in pairs, you will need to cut into the main girder all the way across it and five inches deep, thereby weakening the girder considerably.

A workable plan is to install the first ancillary girder on the left side of the house at a point four feet from the end log wall. On the right side of the house, install the girder at two feet. The next girder on the right will be at six feet, then one at ten feet, etc. On the left side, the girders will be at four feet, eight feet, 12 feet, and so on.

When you make the cut-out for girder installation, place the girder in exact position, and mark around the end so that you will have a perfect size. Then shove the end of the girder out of the way and make the cuts.

Use a scaffold or some type of temporary flooring as you make the cuts. Do not attempt to stand on the girder and make the cuts, and do not try to work from a ladder. The chance of a serious accident is far too great to risk.

When you start to cut, make the first cuts at right angles to the girder. Hold the chain saw so that the tip of the bar is at the corner of the cut lines. Hold the saw steady as you cut along the line. Do not push the tip of the bar tightly against the wood. To do so is to invite kick-back. Instead, maintain the slightest pressure, just enough to make the cut but not enough to cause kick-back.

Do the same on the other line. You will need to make the final cut with the grain of the girder. Hold the head of the saw about waist-high, and let the tip of the bar cut slowly and evenly along the line. As the cut becomes deeper and deeper, you will need to raise the head of the saw even higher, until finally you are cutting at an almost vertical position. You may need to complete the cut by using a wood chisel and hammer. You may find that you can make the complete cut with a chisel, but it is faster to use the chain saw.

When the cut is complete, you will need to cut the bottom of the ancillary girder. Set the whole girder end inside the cut and mark where the surface of the main girder strikes the ancillary girder. It should be at about the five-inch mark. Then mark where the ancillary girder or side girder meets the main girder, and mark along the bottom half of the ancillary girder.

Now remove the side girder and mark off the cut you need to make. When the cut is complete, set the girder back into place and check the fit. The top of the main girder should be perfectly even with the top of the side or ancillary girders. When the fit is suitable, install the girder by using fluted spikes driven through the top of the side girder and down into the main girder. Be sure the spikes are not so long that the points will protrude from the bottom of the main girder.

Then drive a spike (after first drilling pilot holes, in all cases) through the side of the main girder and into the end of the side or ancillary girder. Go to the other end of the girder and drill pilot holes down through the slope cut and into the top side of the top wall log. Use two spikes spaced at the one-third and two-thirds points along the slope at this end of the girder.

When all the girders are installed, your walls are now tied together securely. The end walls are anchored to the foundation wall at the bottom, and at the top they are held in place by a timber that is eight inches wide and ten inches high. There is an enormous amount of holding power in such a timber, and you have no worries that the walls will collapse outward. Or inward, for that matter.

The long front and back walls are anchored at their bottoms to the foundation wall, and at the top they are tied securely into the main girder by means of the side or ancillary girders. You have every four feet, a huge timber tied to another huge timber, and there is no danger of collapse in this direction, either.

Because all of the girder tops are flush, the finished flooring will blend well with the girders. You can use thick flooring that will serve both as flooring and subflooring.

When you must let girder ends meet on top of a post, slant the drill slightly so that the spike will run through the girder and into the support post at a slight angle. This slant will assure you that you have the spike imbedded in good wood, and also that the angle of the spike will increase holding power.

You are now ready to construct the roof framing. It is good to get the roof on as quickly as possible, not only to protect the wood from the weather but also to protect you so that bad weather need not curtail your work during that time period. Chapter Fifteen discusses the basic plan for installing ridge timbers and rafters.

Chapter Fifteen:
Roof Framing

Once the girder system has been completed, you are ready to begin framing the roof. But do not attempt any framing work until you are completely certain that all of the girders are secured at both ends. This system holds your walls in position against the outward pressure created by the addition of the roof, so do not neglect any part of this crucial stage in your building.

One of the cardinal rules of carpentry is that you never leave any framing member hanging from nails. This means that you should never hang a girder or framing timber only by nails; there should be some type of support under these timbers. And a spike in a sense is only a huge nail.

So if you have to bridge a gap, you must use a ledger plate or see to it that both ends of the timber are supported by some device in addition to nails or spikes. When you span a gap by using a girder, hang the ends of the girder over other girders. You can also cut into the top girders slightly so that a "tongue" of the ancillary girder fits into the space which you've cut out in the top girder. The main girder, for example, can sit atop the cap or top log in the walls. See Figure 15-1.

When all of the girders are properly secured and supported, you can begin framing the roof. You will need to make frequent use of a level, line level, square, and other framing implements.

There are several key stages in the framing of the roof. These are, in logical order: checking the level of the log walls, installing plates, erecting ridge-beam holders, raising the ridge beam, installing rafters, framing knee walls (if any), and installing collar bracing.

Other special steps, optional, include: making and using a ridge beam raiser, making and using a rafter spacer and holder, and framing dormers, if any. Depending upon your roof style and the amount of help you have handy, you may not have any need for any of these special devices or steps in building, but they are included for those who are in need of them.

When you begin, your first steps ought to be running a line level from end wall to end wall from three points: corner, middle, and the other corner. Do the same with the side walls by checking from at least three points. Then make a diagonal check from corner to corner in both directions. If you encounter any

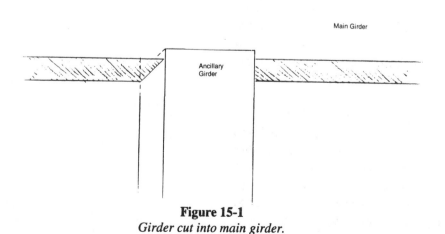

Figure 15-1
Girder cut into main girder.

discrepancies, this is the time to correct them. When you start to install rafters and learn that one wall is four inches too high on the corner, you are in trouble and the problem must be corrected.

You can correct any problems in leveling by using plates. These are simply wide boards or timbers, usually 2″ x 8″ or 2″ x 10″ (the width of the top surface of the wall logs is the determining factor), which are nailed to the top of the highest log in the wall. The purpose is to provide a level surface for the seating of rafters. Obviously, the tops of rafters must form a level line from one end of the roof to the other. Otherwise the roof would be wavy and totally unsatisfactory.

When you use the line level, if you locate a corner that is too low (and you should work from the highest corner, if you do not have a level wall system), you must shore up any low points, because you cannot reverse the process and lower high points without an immense amount of corrective work. You can cut and install shims or thin strips of wood to be installed under the plate.

Assume that the northeast corner and southeast corners are too low. When you install the plates, keep raising the corners by use of shims or thin wood strips under the plates, and use your carpenter's level regularly to get a perfect reading. When the reading is correct for that corner, drive several nails into the plate to hold it steady while you check the other wall-line areas for accuracy.

Correct the reading of the other corner, and when the level shows that the corners are correct and all other walls are at the desired level, complete installation of the plates by driving 20d nails in pairs every two feet along the entire length of the plate. When you have completed this work, the plate timbers should cover the entire top edges of all four walls.

Assuming the most optimistic of viewpoints, your logs remained level throughout wall construction and you will not need to use plates and shims to level the walls. As you raise walls, you can run the line level across to the other wall often, and make sure that you are staying level at all points. If you see that a wall is running too low, you can always cut the next log a little thicker to make the necessary compensation.

For example, if the west wall is two inches higher than the east wall, on the next course you can cut the east wall log two inches thicker (that is, higher or taller), and when you install it, the walls will be level. Or, if you do not have access to wider or larger logs,

you can always cut the west wall logs an inch or so thinner or shorter to make the necessary adjustment.

If you are working alone, you might want to stop your framing work long enough to make a small but very helpful device that I call a ridge-beam holder. This ridge-beam holder consists of several lengths of 2″ x 6″ boards assembled so that they will hold a ridge-beam in place while you start installing rafters. You will need a holder on each end of the house.

To make the ridge-beam holder, first decide how high you want the peak of the house to be. Calculate the distance from the top of the plate or top log in the wall to the height you want for the roof peak. Assume that you want the peak to be six feet higher than the top wall of the structure. The ridge-beam holder described below will be based on this desired height.

Before you make the ridge-beam holder, you may wish to go ahead and make the rafter holder and spacer, so that it will be ready for use when the ridge beam is in place.

This rafter spacer has cut-outs for either the joists or rafters. When using it as a rafter spacer, you simply set the spacer so that the cut-outs fit over the top edges of the rafters. If the rafters fit into the cut-outs, the spacing is correct. To make the spacer, use a length of 2″ x 6″ about three feet long. If the rafters are to be spaced to 16 inches on center, mark a location near one end of the timber. Draw a line across the board from edge to edge. Use a square so that you can get a perfectly square mark. Then measure out one inch on each side of the line and mark the locations by drawing a line parallel with the first line. Measure down three inches and mark across the three lines.

Figure 15-2
Second cut-out for finished rafter spacer.

Cut out the section by sawing down the outside lines until you reach the other line. Use a chisel to cut out the little rectangle. You now have a cut-out that will fit perfectly over a two-inch-wide rafter.

Measure exactly 16 inches from the center of the cut-out, and repeat the process. You now have two cut-outs, which is all you need. To use the spacer, locate the proper position and install the first rafter, which can be located so that it is over and parallel to the outside edge of the wall. For the next rafter, simply lower one end of the rafter spacer so that the first cut-out slips over the top edge. Then move the next rafter into position so that it, too, is inside the other cut-out.

This entire process takes only two or three seconds, and is no trouble at all. There is no danger that you will misread or mismark rafter locations. For even more convenience, make two of the spacers and use one at the top of the wall and the other at the ridge beam. Or nail in all rafters at the ridge-beam and then move to the wall or eaves area and nail all of the rafter ends at that point.

You can make a rafter holder which will allow you to keep both hands free while you are trying to get nails started in the rafters which are to be nailed to the ridge-beam. This device is also very simple and cheap to make, and can be created within ten minutes.

Normally, when you nail up rafters you must stand on a ladder or scaffold and with one hand and arm hold the rafter in place. Then you must manage to drive the first nails into the rafter and then into the ridge-beam. This can be tricky, particularly if you have to hold a heavy rafter.

To make the rafter holder, start with either a very wide board 16 inches long or a 2″ x 4″ and some scrap lumber. If you have a very wide board, cut it as shown in Figure 15-3. At the top end of the board, nail a short length (six inches long) across the end of the board on what will become the back side.

Now nail a six-inch length of board to the outside edge of the 2″ x 4″ and let it hang down the back side of the holder, as shown in Figure 15-4. You can now hang the holder over the ridge beam so that the short 2″ x 4″ bottom rests on the top edge of the ridge-beam. The wide board with the cut-out faces the rafters which are to be installed. When you lift a rafter into position, you can set the end inside the cut-out, and the rafter will remain in position while you nail it.

If the rafter should tend to slip or slide, you can simply drill a 3/16″ hole through the outside edge of

the cut-out area of the wide board, and when the rafter is in place, slip a nail into the hole and tap it lightly so that the point barely sinks into the side of the rafter. The nail will hold the rafter, and it can easily be pulled out when the job is done.

Figure 15-3
Early assembly stages of rafter holder.

Figure 15-4
Completing rafter holder.

If you don't have a wide board handy, use a 16-inch length of 2″ x 4″, and nail another eight-inch length of 2″ x 4″ to the bottom of it. Now cut a five-inch length of 2″ x 2″ and drill a hole two inches from the bottom of that length. This hole should be large enough to hold a nail, as before. Slip a nail into the hole and tap the nail so that this length of 2″ x 2″ can be fastened temporarily to the end of the cross-piece 2″ x 4″.

When the rafter is in place and securely nailed, pull out the nail and move the rafter holder to the next location. Nail up the next rafter as before.

This may seem like a lot of trouble, but if you are working alone, or if you are handling very long and heavy rafters, you will soon realize the advantage of having a device that will hold the rafter while you nail it. Remember that you may be using rafters 20 feet long or longer, and these timbers can be very heavy.

One other slight consideration must be made. When you angle-cut the end of the rafter so that it will fit snugly against the ridge beam side, your angle-cut will be longer than the width of the rafter. Therefore your cut-out must be deep enough to allow 10.5 inches of rafter end. So you must nail the 2″ x 4″ cross-piece 10.5 inches below the bottom of the top 2″ x 4″ cross-piece.

But before you plan to nail up rafters, you must first make some crucial decisions concerning the construction of the roof framing and, ultimately, the roof itself. Once you have firmly decided how high above the girders the roof peak will be, you can make a ridge-beam holder and raiser.

These two simple devices are described here for the benefit of those who will be working alone much of the time. You may find yourself without assistance at a time when you desperately need to get started on the roof, and you may find the help you need here.

Make the ridge-beam holder first. You will actually need two of them at first, one for each end of the ridge beam. This holder is a device that will permit you to raise the ridge beam and install it without having to make use of several other people or risk injury.

Start with a 2″ x 8″ timber that is as long as the distance from the top of the girders to the bottom of the ridge beam. If your roof peak is to be seven feet above the girders, you will then need a timber that is seven feet long, minus the thickness of a base plate (two inches) and the height of the actual ridge beam timber (presumably eight inches). So the timber you need will be six feet, two inches long. Cut it and set it aside.

Next you will need a section of 2″ x 8″ approximately one to two feet long. This plate will be nailed to the top side of the girder or final log in the wall, or to the top plate used to level the walls, if any was used. See Figure 15-5.

Cut two side pieces for the holder. These should be at least six inches long. They will be nailed to the top end of the holder, and should form a V with a square

bottom. You can spread the opening formed by nailing these pieces in place so that you can slip the ridge beam inside the holder easily.

Figure 15-5
Bracing ridge beam holder.

The ridge-beam holder will be nailed in place in the following manner. Nail a base to the assembly and then nail the base to the top of the top log or cap. Use a level to ensure that the holder is installed precisely. Once you have the holder perfectly vertical, use braces to hold it securely when the ridge beam is added. Figure 15-6 shows the ridge-beam holder in place atop the wall.

Figure 15-6
Finishing bracing and installation of ridge beam into holder.

When you are ready to make the ridge-beam lifter, you will create another device almost exactly like the holder. The only difference is that there is no plate. You can also use 2″ x 4″s rather than larger timbers.

To use the lifter, lift the ridge beam, one end at a time, until it rests upon the top of the walls. Stand the beam on edge and, working from below, raise the lifter until it slips over the ridge beam two or three feet from the end.

Lift steadily until you have elevated the ridge beam's end slightly higher than the ridge-beam holder. Gently work the elevated beam end over until you can lower it into the V of the holder. As soon as it is in place, climb up and drill a hole through the center of the ridge beam (or you can do this easily while the beam is on the ground), and run a 60d nail through the hole. You can also use a spike. This is to keep the end of the ridge beam from sliding free when you start to lift the other end.

Go to the other end and repeat the process. When the ridge beam is in place, you can nail through the sides of the ridge-beam holder to keep the ridge beam securely in place.

Keep in mind that you do not actually need to have a ridge beam at all. Many a roof has been installed without a ridge beam or timber or pole of any sort. However, your work is easier if you use the ridge beam, and it will be easier still if you use a two-inch dimension rather than a four-inch timber. The ridge beam does not truly support weight, other than rafter ends, and the rafters can be nailed to each other, if necessary.

You can also use a ridge beam composed of several shorter timbers. You use four ten-foot sections if you prefer. But you will need more of the ridge beam holders: one at each end of a section.

Now step back a few paces and review the process. When you are ready to install the holder, measure across the plate to locate the exact center of the end walls. Mark the spot clearly on the inside edge of the plate. After rigging up a scaffold or by using a ladder, use a rope or manpower to hoist the assembly to the top of the wall. This is rather heavy work, and can result in back strain if you are not careful. Take advantage of a helper's strength, if it is available.

When the assembly is sitting on the plate, center the bottom edge of the board over the center mark. Align the inside edges of the wall plate and the plate from the holder. Then sink several nails in each side of the

holder plate, which must be nailed securely to the wall plate.

At this point you need to hold a level against the side of the assembly to make sure that you have a true vertical reading. You can move the timber back and forth two or three inches to get a perfect reading. Have a bracing timber (a 2″ x 4″ five or six feet long) ready. You can nail one end of the brace to the top log five feet or so from the assembly, and have the other end ready to nail to the assembly. Once the assembly is in the exact position, hold it steadily in place and nail the free end to the assembly timber. Next add a second brace, this one coming from the other side of the assembly, for double stability.

Do the same at the other end. When both ridge-beam holders are in place, you are ready to raise the ridge beam. If you are concerned about your strength, you may wish to add a few final touches to the holder. Starting near the bottom of the holder, you can nail cross-pieces every two feet at first, and then at every foot. Let the lowest cross-piece extend from the edge of the holder to a foot beyond. The next cross-piece should be only ten inches. Keep shortening the cross-pieces until at the top you have only three inches extending.

If you have not cut the ridge beam, you must do so now. It is far, far better to cut it early so that it can be air-drying while you do other work. You will be amazed at how much lighter a timber is once it has air-dried than when it is green and filled with sap.

When you cut the ridge beam, you will need to double-check it for accuracy. You cannot afford to install a beam that is not true, at least on the top side.

You will find that many timbers, once they start to cure, will curve slightly (or, at times, alarmingly). The curve or very broad rainbow effect is called the crown, the crown itself being the edge of the timber that curves upward. This is the edge that should be installed facing upward.

Before installing the beam, lay it flat and resting upon a series of support blocks. Stretch a chalk line from the corner of one end to the corresponding corner of the other end. Snap the line and see how far from being true the timber is. You may need to use the chain saw to trim off the curved surface of the timber.

You will find that hoisting even one end of such a timber is a struggle. Only part of the problem is its sheer weight. Another difficulty is that the timber will be flexible or limber and will sag as you try to lift it.

A third impediment is that the timber will try to twist on you as you struggle with it. To help with the problem, you may find it helpful to position several cement blocks or blocks of wood in side-by-side stacks so that when you lift one end, you can rest that end on the blocks while you catch your breath. Keep raising the block levels as you lift. Rest the end of the timber on one stack of blocks while you add to the height of the other stack, and then when you are ready, lift the end another eight inches and let it rest on the alternate stack of blocks.

As soon as the first end of the timber is resting atop the log wall, go to the other end and raise that end to the top of the wall. When this is done, stand the timber so that the straight edge is facing upward.

Raise the ridge-beam lifter so that the Y-shaped top fits around the beam itself. Lift until the bottom of the beam rests upon the first cross-piece.

Get a new hold on the lifter and raise again to the next level. Keep readjusting your grip and lifting one gradation at a time, until the end of the beam can be set gently into the Y at the top of the holder.

Let the beam rest while you check the other end to make sure that the beam will reach the other holder. If it will not, pull it gently an inch or so at a time until you have the needed length.

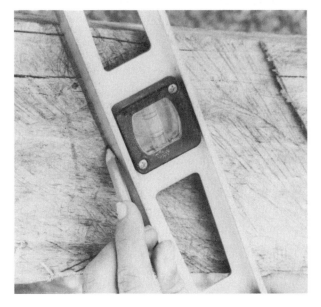

Figure 15-7
Using level to help mark vertical ridge beam cut.

With the ridge beam in place, begin immediately to install the rafters in pairs. Start at either end and, with

rafters pre-cut and air-dried enough to lighten them significantly, raise the first rafter and, if you have already cut the angle for the rafter fit, nail it to the ridge beam just outside the ridge-beam holder and aligned with the outside edge of the log wall and wall plate.

If you need to cut the angle slope for the rafters, you can select the angle in one relatively easy way. Set the angle in place so that about three inches extend over the top of the ridge beam, and the other end extends over the wall for at least a foot to form the eaves. With the rafter in position, hold a level against the ridge beam and let the level extend across the end of the rafter so that the outside edge of the level is positioned at the very corner of the rafter. Mark along the outside edge of the level to indicate the rafter cut. See Figure 15-7.

Nail the end in place loosely, and go to the other end of the rafter and mark where it just clears the wall plate on the outside of the wall. Take the rafter down and saw off the angle at the top where the mark is. Then take the portion you've cut off to the other end of the rafter, and lay the triangle so that the long edge of the triangle is aligned with the bottom edge of the rafter, and the end of the triangle coincides with the mark for the outside of the wall plate.

Mark around the triangle. This mark indicates where you need to saw out for the bird's-mouth rafter cut.

Before you climb up to the work point to install the rafters, lay four rafters so that each one's end reaches over the ridge beam, and the other end hangs over the wall plate a few inches. When you are in position to do so, lay the first rafter into the cut-out and seat it. Then nail it in place.

If you have measured correctly, the top of the rafter at the slant cut should be perfectly aligned with the top of the ridge beam. With the rafters seated, you may at your leisure complete most of the nailing. Drive one nail through the slant cut and into the ridge beam. Add at least two per side, angled into the ridge beam. When all four rafters are completely nailed, remove the holder and hang it onto the other side of the ridge beam. You can then put up four more rafters and nail these in place.

When the four rafters are nailed to the ridge beam, go to the outside wall and nail the rafter tails in place. Then install four rafters on the other side of the ridge beam.

In this fashion you can move down the ridge beam, four rafters at a time on each side, until all the rafters in the entire roof framing have been installed. See Figure 15-8.

Figure 15-8
Completing rafter installation.

At first glance the rafter holder may appear to be more trouble than it is worth, but after you have to climb up and down from the ridge-beam work area each time you need a rafter, you will soon realize that making the climb every fourth time is far superior to making it after each rafter.

When you cut your first rafter for slant and bird's-mouth cut, as well as for the tail cut (where the rafter hangs over the wall plate), you can save a great deal of time and work by using one rafter (that you know to fit perfectly) as a pattern by which you cut all the other rafters. If your pattern is correct, you can cut a dozen or so rafters at a time, and then install all of them at one work session before cutting others.

Be sure to install rafters in sections or pairs. If you should decide to install all the rafters on one side of the ridge beam before changing to the other side, the pressure of the rafters will shove the ridge beam out of alignment, and your entire roof line will be affected.

When the rafters are installed, add the collar bracing. These braces are timbers which are nailed from one rafter to the rafter just opposite it. Usually these brace pieces are installed two feet or so below the bottom of the ridge beam. To install them,

measure down the rafter on one side to a point 30 inches from the ridge beam. Do the same to the rafter on the other side, and then measure the distance between the two marks.

Cut timbers to length and hold one up to the rafters. Place the bottom of the brace on the marks on each rafter. While holding the rafter in place, mark on the end of the brace along the top of the rafters. Cut the rafter brace at these points and then nail up the brace. Use four 16d nails in each end. It is wise to install a collar brace on at least every other pair of rafters. My personal preference is to install a brace on every pair of rafters.

Do not neglect this step. It is vitally important.

You are ready now to install roof sheathing (often called "sheeting") and building paper, after which you will install the final roofing and the house will be safe from rain. Chapter 16 deals with sheathing the house.

Chapter Sixteen:
Sheathing and Roofing the House

Sheathing a roof is in many ways similar to nailing down plywood subflooring. The materials are essentially the same, and the methods of installation are identical in many respects.

The materials you will need include the sheathing panels or sheathing boards, an electric saw, if one is available (or a hand saw or chain saw if a circular saw cannot be used), nails, square, chalk line, building paper, and a few small items such as pencil and measuring tape.

Your first major step is to decide whether you wish to use a plywood sheathing or sheathing boards. The former is much faster and easier, but far more expensive. The latter is cheaper, but will require more time, energy, and effort, particularly if you plan to cut the boards. This is a good time to pause and ask yourself if the money you save will compensate for the trees you must cut in order to saw the boards.

Here is one of the problems: if you plan to use one-inch boards for sheathing, your kerf when you saw the boards will be one-quarter-inch minimum. This means that one out of every four boards will be reduced to sawdust. Still, you can saw perhaps six, seven, or even eight fairly wide boards from one good tree, and if you have the trees to spare, and particularly if you have trees that desperately need to be thinned, you may want to give added consideration to cutting your own.

But if time is crucial, plywood sheathing is the best answer to your sheathing needs.

The decision you make should be in terms of the size of the house you are building. If you choose to build a cabin or house that is, for instance, 32 feet long and 24 feet wide, you will have about 800 feet of roofing. To be perfectly safe, because you will need to include eaves or overhang, plan to sheath 1,000 square feet. You will need 32 panels of sheathing for such a roof.

To help you make a decision, you can price roofing sheathing and multiply by 32. If you can find sheathing for $7 per panel, the sheathing materials alone will cost you $224, which is not a great deal of money.

On the other hand, you chose to build a log house because you wanted to save money, and here is a chance to save $224, less the cost of gas and oil for sawing the boards. Ultimately, the choice is yours.

You may wish to try your hand at sawing sheathing boards by devoting an hour or two to cutting the equivalent of two panels of sheathing. Remember that each panel equals 32 square feet, or eight six-inch boards eight feet long. Two panels, then, would equal eight boards 16 feet long.

Why not utilize some lengths of tree trunks that are not useful for cutting wall logs or rafters and try your hand at cutting sheathing boards? If you have a 16-foot log large enough to yield boards six inches wide, square the log on three sides and then mark off a one-inch board.

If your chain is sharp and your saw is powerful, you should be able to cut off one slab from the log in five minutes or so, or no more than half an hour for the three sides, and this time includes refueling and sharpening of the chain.

Lay off the chalk lines for the one-inch board and start to saw, just as you have done on all other sawing chores. You should be able to saw the 16-foot board in ten minutes. By continuing at this rate, within an hour you should be able to saw six of the boards, for a total length of 48 board feet. This is equal to considerably more than one panel of sheathing.

Now ask the pertinent question. In your job, can you earn enough in one hour to buy 48 square feet of sheathing materials? If you cannot, you may want to consider cutting more boards and sheathing the entire roof with them.

Another thing to keep in mind is that here is a chance to use all the smaller logs or log sections that have thus far been pushed aside. Virtually any length within reason (four feet and up) and any width of board from four inches on up can be used as long as you take care to use the same width for the entire course of boards along the roof line.

If you wish, you can embark upon a sawing effort and see how rapidly the boards accumulate. If you realize that yours is one of the hopeless cases, you can always stop and save the boards for some better use later.

When you plan to sheathe with boards, start at the end of the roof at the peak and stretch a chalk line all the way from the uppermost reach of the roof to the opposite corner of the roof at the eaves. You can also use the Pythagorean Theorem to calculate the length.

The length of the roof at the eaves is one leg of the roof triangle being calculated. The house is 32 feet long, so this distance, plus the overhang, is 34 feet. Square this number and get 1,156.

The length of the line from the eaves to the peak is going to be roughly 14 feet, including the eaves. Square this number and get 196. Add this to 1,156 and get 1,352. Take the square root of this and the result is 36.8, or the length diagonally across one side of the roof. This is the longest length you will have when you start to sheathe.

Why not select a log portion that is 12.5 feet long or so and square it on three sides and then cut three boards from it? You now have the longest stretch of roof distance covered, once you nail up the boards. Each course that follows will be shorter and shorter, until you need boards that are only three or four feet long.

One of the beauties of sheathing is that, if you are afraid of heights, you can do nearly all of the work from inside. You will need to build some temporary flooring or set up scaffolds or ladders, but this is not time-consuming or strenuous work.

To sheath from the inside, climb a ladder at the end of the house and drive a nail into the top of the ridge beam at the very end. Hook the end of the chalk line over the nail head. Then work your way down to the eaves and carry the chalk line with you. At the eaves, hold the chalk line tightly against the end of the final rafter on the opposite end of the house and with the other hand snap the line to leave a diagonal chalk mark the entire distance. See Figure 16-1.

When you are ready to nail down boards, position the boards so that the top edge of each board barely touches the chalk line. Hold the boards steadily in place and drive two or three nails into the board at every point where the board crosses a rafter. You will need to angle-cut the end of each board that touches

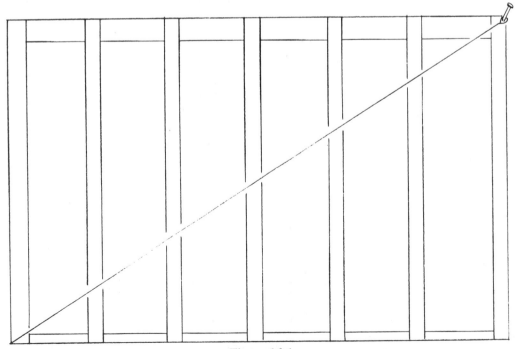

Figure 16-1
Chalking a diagonal line for sheating board starting point.

the eaves or overhang, and the end of every other board should be squared or nearly so, at least. See Figure 16-2.

When the first course is completed, decide whether to work upward or downward. If you opt to work your way up the roof, set your next course of boards against the top edge of the first course and install as before. You will now need to angle-cut the end of the top board where it reaches the ridge beam.

As you work your way upward, you will notice that the length of each course becomes encouragingly shorter. When you reach the very top of the roof section, you simply move your ladder to the other side of the ridge beam and climb up and nail from the other slope of the roof.

When you work your way down the other half of this slope, you can again work from a ladder from the inside of the house. When you are low enough that there is not room for you to stand on the ladder and nail, move the ladder outside and you can install the last few boards from the outside.

Remember that all sheathing boards should be nailed on a diagonal pattern. Diagonal sheathing has been proven stronger than right-angle nailing.

If you elect to use plywood sheathing, you can also install nearly all of the sheathing from the inside. More about that later.

When you install plywood sheathing, start at the eaves and chalk a line from the top of the very end of the final rafter on one end of the house to the same point in the final rafter at the other end of the house. You can stand on a ladder to do this. Snap the line in order to see whether your rafter ends are true.

There should not be chalk at any significant point up along any of the rafters. The line should strike each rafter end at exactly or almost exactly the same place. If some rafter ends are too long, you can cut them off.

Start sheathing by hoisting the first panel of plywood to the end of the roof. Lay the panel lengthwise along the rafters so that the eight-foot length of the panel is parallel with the wall logs on that side of the house, as shown in Figure 16-3.

Check for fit along the eaves and along the slope side of the roof. Make any small adjustments that are essential. Then begin to nail the panel to the rafters. Use 10d ring-shacked nails and drive one every six inches along each rafter.

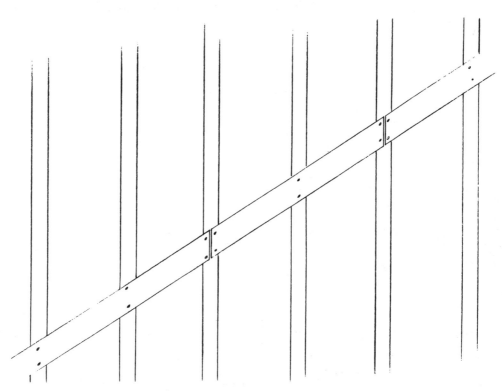

Figure 16-2
Installing sheating boards diagonally.

The pattern often used is as follows. Continue across the entire roof line. At the far end, if the roof is 34 feet long, you will need to cut a panel for the final section. Start the next course just above the partial panel and let the full-length panel lap the partial one completely.

You can buy sheathing clips that fit onto the edges of the plywood panels. These clips are slipped in place before the two pieces are joined and the nailing is completed. If you choose to use the clips, they are very inexpensive and can be purchased from nearly any building supply dealer.

As you work your way up the slope, you can nail small blocks of 2″ x 4″ to act as footing. These blocks, which will be removed later, offer stability in the event you lose footing or balance.

If you wish to install sheathing from the inside, you can complete the first course by working outside, and then move the work base inside. As before, you can do all the nailing from a ladder or temporary floor or scaffold.

Lift the panels upward between rafters. Once the panel has cleared the rafters, turn it so that it is in the proper position and then let it slide downward to make contact with the previous course. Check the end for correct fit. If you prefer, you can lay the panels upon the eave end of the rafters and push them upward to their correct positions.

Figure 16-3
Locating first plywood panel.

Then nail as before. When you reach the top, you can move the ladder, as you did earlier, to the other side of the ridge beam, and climb a rung or two higher to complete the nailing. In this manner you can install sheathing right up to the ridge beam.

When you start the other slope, use exactly the same pattern of work. Start from outside and then move inside. As you reach the top of the slope, you will see that you will no longer have room to maneuver the panels through the sheathing. All you need to do is set out the extra needed panels and let them lie on top of the installed panels until you need them.

When you come to the final course, you can cut the panels into four-foot sections and continue nailing as before, or you can leave the panels whole and climb out onto the installed paneling. When you come to the very last panel or portion of a panel, you have no choice but to work outside, unless you want to go to a slightly more extreme length of action.

When we built our house, we took the extreme method — for two major reasons. Our roof slope was almost a 45-degree angle, and the footing was very uncertain. Not only that, if any of us had lost our footing, we could have rolled off the end of the roof and then fallen 18 feet to a paved patio below.

The second reason is that my left leg was in a hip-high cast and I was somewhat less than agile. That fact, coupled with the possible — and probable — damage that would be done to an already badly broken leg, discouraged me from going out onto the roof unless there was no way to avoid doing so.

So how, then, can the final sheathing panels be nailed in place without having to go onto the roof at any point? Here's how we did it.

Assume that all of the roof is sheathed except for one small corner at the peak. Measure the length of the space and cut a small rectangle of sheathing to fit into the space. After it is cut, try it for size, and if it fits, set the piece into the location and make certain that it is situated well at every point.

Now mark with a pencil along both sides of all rafters that are covered by the section of sheathing. Remove the sheathing and locate short lengths of 2″ x 4″s or rafter-sized short lengths of stock. Stand the rafter-sized length of stock on edge and then position the sheathing section so that the rafter material is aligned on either side of the pencil marks.

Drive nails through the top of the sheathing and down into the top edge of the 2″ x 4″ or rafter sections. Use plenty of nails to hold the pieces together.

Then, when the assembly is completed, push the section back up through the rafters, turn it appropriately, and lower the sheathing into position.

The short sections of wood that you nailed to the sheathing should now drop in alongside the rafters already in place. The short sections should, in fact, fit snugly against the genuine rafters.

Now all you need to do is drive nails through the side of the short wood sections and into the rafters. The final section of sheathing will hold perfectly. There is no weakness in this type of construction. The scrap wood is nailed to the sheathing and then to the rafters. At no point is there a problem. You have just proven that a house can be sheathed without the sheather having to go onto the roof section at any time.

You may now install the felt paper over the sheathing. The purpose of this paper is to provide a moisture barrier between shingles and rafters and to help prevent leaks and decay. This, too — or nearly all of it — can be installed from the inside, but at this point the topic is the installation of the felt paper in the traditional manner.

Climb upon the sheathing and move to the very edge of the eaves where you will align the felt paper with the end of the sheathing panels. Allow a couple of inches to hang over. Then use a stapler to fasten the felt to the sheathing. You can, if you prefer, use large-headed roofing nails.

When the paper is in place, cut another strip and align the bottom edge of the paper with the clearly marked line on the felt itself. This line indicates the proper amount of overlap to keep out wind and moisture. When you reach the top, lap any surplus paper over the peak and ridge beam and fasten it on the other side. Then do the other slope in the same manner.

Can this be done from the inside? Yes! When you install the first course of sheathing, stop and install the first course of felt or building paper. Lean out over the first course of sheathing and nail or staple the bottom edges of the felt paper. When the first course of paper is done, start the second course, which will reach too high at this point. So fold the paper back over the previous course and lay blocks of wood on it to keep it from blowing away.

Then, when the next course of sheathing is completed, reach down and pull the felt paper up and spread it as before. Nail it or staple it into place. Con-

tinue this progression all the way to the top of the peak. As suggested earlier, leave a small escape route for now, and this can be eradicated, from the inside, later.

You can also install the final roofing from inside, or, as before, most of it. The next few paragraphs will explain how to install roofing in the basic manner.

Starting out, you will probably choose 36-inch shingle strips for the basic roof. You can buy fire-retardant wood shingles, but these are often hard to locate or they may be too expensive for your budget.

To install shingles in the traditional manner, measure from one end of the roof line to the other, with your measurement being taken at the eaves. Locate and mark the exact center. At this point the felt paper has already been installed.

The reason for starting in the center rather than at one end is that shingle strip lengths vary slightly, and if there is to be a discrepancy, it should appear at the end of the shingle line, rather than in the mid-portions.

Begin, after marking the mid-point, by chalking a line that will mark the topmost part of the shingle strip. In a typical pattern, each shingle, 12 inches in height, will have seven inches covered and five inches exposed. Remember that the more you have exposed, the greater the possibility of a leak. Be sure to let two or three inches hang over the eave, so make your chalk line accordingly.

Start by installing the first strips of shingles upside down across the eaves. By "upside-down" I mean that the slits that are normally turned to face downward will face upward for only this one course, which will be doubled.

When you start at the center and work your way to either end, keep the shingle strips aligned with the chalked line. After the first upside-down course is laid, return and lay the second course directly on top of the first one. In this manner, the cut-out sections in the lower course will be covered, and the next course will be laid in the traditional manner.

Use plain barbed roofing nails. You will need about 2.5 pounds per square (100 square feet) of asphalt roofing. To determine how many squares of shingles you will need, determine the number of square feet in the roof and divide by 100.

When the first course is installed, return to the middle point and install the next course. Note that on the strip of shingles there is a lighter-colored portion of the shingle that contains the cut-out, which divides the shingle strip into one-foot lengths. There is a darker-colored section on the upper half. When the shingle strip is in place and the course is complete, install the next course so that the cut-out section is lapped an inch or so by the next shingle.

Keep chalking lines as guides. If you are not careful, you will begin to drop or rise in the course, and soon your shingle line will not look or perform to your satisfaction. When the first slope is taken to the peak, shingle the other slope. At the peak you can install a cap that will cover any exposed shingle ends. Your best bet is to buy the cap and install it according to the manufacturer's directions.

When you reach vents, lay shingles right up to the bottom edge of the vent. Cut out a shingle to fit around the vent stack, and then install a vent flange that fits over the vent stack and is cemented to the roof. Then shingle courses are laid over the upper portion of the flange.

Around chimney areas, install aluminum or copper flashing that is nailed to the roof sheathing and waterproofed with a sealer. Shingles are then laid up to the base of the chimney. The same is done for dormers and any other irregularities in the roof line.

Here is a helpful hint for getting the sheathing to the rafters for installation. Position a wide board in an upright position, so that it leans from the ground to the edge of the rafters. Set a panel of plywood, or the OSB material often used in place of plywood, so that it leans against the wide board, as shown in Figure 16-4.

Figure 16-4
Starting panel up to rafters.

Then slip your fingers under the bottom edge of the panel and lift, and at the same time slide the panel up the board. See Figure 16-5. Slightly lift the panel, one corner at a time, and slide the entire panel over the end

of the rafters. Then slide the panel all the way upon the rafters.

Figure 16-5
Slide panel up to rafters.

Finally, position the panel so that it is aligned perfectly with the rafters, See Figure 16-6. You are now ready to nail the panel in place.

Figure 16-6
Locating panel for nailing.

Chapter Seventeen:
Framing the Third Level

If you plan to have only a one-story house, you can skip over this chapter because nothing in it will relate well to your plans. However, if you think you might decide to add a third floor, then peruse this chapter and let your thinking expand.

First, why add a third floor, particularly if your family is small and your needs are not great? One reason is economy in the actual construction. Remember that one roof will cover two or more stories as cheaply as it will cover one. So if you want to invest a little more money, you can add greatly to your floor space and not have to spend very much more money.

A second reason relates to resale value. While you may not have any intention of ever selling the house, you cannot see into the future so well that you can totally rule out the possibility. And if the time should come that you do need to sell the house, the added space will likely make the house more attractive to a buyer, and will probably result in a higher selling price.

But if you are undecided, you can always find the happy compromise and settle for half of a second story. Consult the floor plans in an earlier chapter and you will see that the third level in the house described in this book contains a sitting room that overlooks the family room and fireplace area as well as the kitchen. Such a sitting area has the double attraction of being high enough that it catches the heat from below in winter, and remains at a cozy and comfortable temperature.

While the room is left open in the plans, you can always close it in if you wish. By doing so, you could create another bedroom or closed-in den or office area.

A small hallway or alcove leads to two bedrooms in the east part of the house. These two bedrooms are delightfully suited for a second (or third) den, or office, or sitting room, if they are not needed as sleeping quarters.

If you plan to have a third level, you will need to frame the roof differently and include what is sometimes known as a knee-wall. What is involved here is making the peak of the house high enough so that there will be plenty of

head room in the extra rooms and an abundance of dead air space that serves as an attic. Figure 17-1 shows knee-wall construction.

Figure 17-1
*Knee-wall allows maximum room
width and heigth for bedroom.*

So you will need to frame the roof at least 14 feet higher than the top of the ground-floor walls. By doing so you will have a steep roof that can be considered dangerous to shingle, but keep in mind that you can do nearly all of the shingle work from inside the house.

Start the framing by installing girders, as suggested earlier, in the western half of the house, and install joists in the eastern half. The western half can remain open, with the cathedral-ceiling format, and the eastern half will be closed in and will have rooms above it. This is a heavy job, and if you have help available, by all means use it.

Frame the floor just as you would if it were the ground level. Run the joists, spaced 16 inches on-center, from a central girder. Use bridging and supports, just as you did before. When this is completed, install subflooring by nailing down plywood to cover the entire area which will have rooms above it.

Remember that you have a second option. You can cut or buy the double-thick flooring that will serve as both layers of the floor, and save the time and money involved in putting down traditional plywood sub-flooring.

Now raise the ridge beam and frame the roof as suggested earlier. Remember that the peak will be much higher now, and the roof slope much more severe. Figure 17-2 shows the installation of a very high ridge beam in sections. Notice that the first and last pairs of rafters are installed first, and the middle rafters are added later. Notice, too, that the ridge beam is braced securely at all times. The open area near the left is there so that the dormers can be added without having to remove the rafters.

Figure 17-2
*Ridge-beam and rafter installation
with open area left for dormers.*

Building codes generally will not permit you to run the floor of a room out to the corner where the roof slant meets the floor of that level. The space is so small and congested that it is worth very little, so many people choose to frame a knee-wall to get around the problem.

Some building codes specify that the knee-wall must be at least four feet high. Many building inspectors, on the other hand, do not know what a knee-wall is, and will not object strenuously to the use of the space.

Plan, at any rate, to include a knee-wall. Your rafters are already installed, and your job is to frame the walls and the knee-wall. Start with the full-length walls. In this case, you will need to lay out a traditional hollow-core wall, including a sole plate, top plate, studs, and top cap.

Decide how large the rooms are to be. If the entire house is 32 feet wide, you will lose eight feet because of the knee wall, leaving you a width of 24 feet. You can

frame a wall down the exact center of the area and have rooms that are 12 feet wide, less the thickness of the four-inch wall.

If, however, the house is only 28 feet wide, you will still lose eight feet, leaving you with rooms ten feet wide. If the house is only 24 feet wide and you lose eight feet, your rooms could be no wider than seven feet, which is unrealistic.

For the smaller houses, then, the best option is to have one large room, or to convert the sitting area into a second large room. If the area is to be only 14 feet, you need not worry about the basic hollow-core walls. Frame the knee-walls and the front walls only.

Start work by laying off the dimensions of the rooms and by chalking a line upon the subflooring where the partition walls will be located. If it will help you to visualize the rooms better, go ahead and frame the knee-walls.

Start with the sitting area. Begin work where the kitchen-dinette-area wall rises to the third level. Go to the final rafter at the dinette wall. Use a tape measure to determine exactly where the distance between the sub-flooring and the bottom edge of the rafter is four feet. Mark the location on the subflooring and also on the bottom of the rafter. Do the same at the end of the house, and also at the final rafter on that end.

Now use a chalk line to mark along the subflooring for the entire length of that side of the house on that level. Use a nail to hold one end of the chalk line if you are working alone, and pull the line tight and snap it sharply to get a clear line.

The next step is to fasten one end of the chalk line to the bottom edge of the rafter at the dinette wall, and then to pull the chalk line to the final rafter at the east end of the house. Again, hold the line securely, pull it tight, and snap the line. You now have a chalk line on the floor and on the rafters.

Cut and install a sole plate--a length of 2″ x 4″ on which the wall frame will rest — so that the inside edge of the sole plate is aligned with the chalk.

Now measure the rough length from the top of the sole plate to a point midway across the width of the rafter. Cut a 2″ x 4″ that length and stand it so that the edge toward the center of the house is aligned with the inside edge of the sole plate. Use a level to get the stud into a vertical position, and hold the stud against the side of the rafter. Mark along the underside of the rafter and onto the side of the stud.

Saw along the line, which will be diagonal, and stand the stud in position again. The inside edge should be aligned with the inside edge of the sole plate, and the point of the stud should match the mark on the underside of the rafter.

Move along the entire wall and install studs atop the sole plate. When you have finished, that wall is framed.

Do the same on the other side of the house. When both knee-walls are in place, lay off the other walls and frame them.

Decide where the walls will go, then chalk a line along the predetermined boundary. If you are to have only one large room, chalk the line across the entire upper-level area except for the sitting room. Cut and install a sole plate along the entire length of the chalked line, which will reach from the beginning of one knee-wall to the opposite knee-wall.

The bottom side of the rafter will serve as the top plate for the wall, up to the point where the ceiling will be installed. So measure to locate the point on each side of the house where the rafter bottom is exactly eight feet high. Mark the location and measure, mark, and cut a top plate that will fit between the rafters snugly.

If the room is extra wide, you will need to piece the top plate as you install studding. Start by installing all of the studs that will be shorter than eight feet. Do this on both sides of the area you are framing. If you have a top plate long enough to reach the rest of the way across the area, install this now. You will have to angle-cut each end of the top plate and install it flat. This means that unless you double the rafters, you will have only half of the top plate in contact with the rafters.

If the house is 32 feet wide, the top plate must be 24 feet long; if the house is 28 feet wide, the plate must be 20 feet long; if the house is 24 feet wide, the plate must be 16 feet long. If you do not have long timbers or if you cannot handle the weight of the unwieldy lumber, cut an eight-foot stud and install it eight or ten feet from the knee-wall. Brace it so that it will not sway. Double the stud and run a top plate from the rafter to the doubled stud. Then fill in the spaces in between.

You should lay off the stud spacing before you start to install studs in order to make sure that you don't ruin your pattern.

When you complete the section you have laid off, lay off another section just like it, and in this way make your way across the entire area. This process of sectioning off a few feet — 10 feet at a time, for example — and

completing each will keep you from having to work with long timbers.

As you set up the studs at the end of the sections across the upper level, let the top plate reach only halfway across the top of the last stud. You will now have space for the end of the next section of top plate to fit over the stud.

In the wall framing, you will need to leave rough openings for doors to upstairs rooms and to closets. If you plan to use any sort of heating system upstairs, allow for duct space and for equipment that needs to be housed in a closet or other similar area. If you are going to have water and bathrooms upstairs, these should be provided for as you frame.

This chapter assumes that the upstairs will have only one or two rooms and a closet for each room. You should add any other necessary or desirable aspects of the living area that you require.

You can utilize space effectively and have the rooms and closets you want without undue difficulty. As always, these simple suggestions can be modified to meet your own needs.

The rooms shown in the basic house plans are long and narrow out of necessity. No room could be spared from the width of the room to be used for closet space. On the other hand, the length of the rooms was more than adequate, and it seemed logical to use the ends of the rooms for the needed storage space.

To frame such an alcove, you will need a corner post on both sides of the alcove framing. The post consists of two 2″ x 4″ studs nailed together, with a third stud laid over the first two and nailed in place. Note that there is space on one side of the flat 2″ x 4″. This space is to allow for wall covering to be installed over the stud-ding. Note too that there is a series of spacers nailed between the two even studs to provide greater width.

As you install the corner posts, let the edges of the two even studs align with the outside of the sole plate. One edge of the third stud will also align with the outside edge of the sole plate.

When you frame the rough door opening, measure the width of the door you plan to use or make. Remember that in this book there is a chapter on making your own doors for only a fraction of the cost of a store-bought door. You can make a superb door, in fact, for about $7. You can even make a highly attractive and serviceable door for less than one dollar. If you make your own doors, you can modify the width and height of the doors to fit virtually any rough opening. If you buy doors, however, you need to tailor the rough opening for the dimensions of the door.

Generally speaking, you can leave a height of 80 inches for the rough opening. The width is more variable, but a 40-inch rough opening is common for outside doors and a 36-inch opening is often used for indoor doors.

At the rough-door opening, double the studs on each side. You can use a single stud and a trimmer, which allows for installation of the header. Let the sole plate extend all the way across all the door openings. It will be cut out later, but leave it for the present. The last full stud will be installed 1.5" from the end of the wall frame. The final 1.5" of space will be devoted to the trimmer stud.

Nail in the final studs just as you installed all the others. Then cut the trimmer to a length of 80 inches rather than the usual eight feet or 93 inches. Nail the trimmer to the common stud on either side of the rough opening. Then make the header and install it.

Figure 17-3
Starting to frame the dormer.

You can make a header easily by using two short lengths of 2″ x 4″ or 2″ x 6″ stock and some thin spacer material. This spacer material could be thin plywood or strips of thin wood.

Lay one of the header pieces flat on a work surface and lay the spacers in position. These spacers need to be thick enough to make the two header timbers plus the spacer thick enough to equal the width of the wall frame. If you are using a true four-inch 2″ x 4″, then the header needs to be four inches thick. If you are using purchased studs, the header should be only three inches thick.

Nail all three sections of the header together, after first aligning them so that all their outside edges are even. Then stand the completed header on edge atop the trimmer-stud ends. You can then toe-nail the header to the studs, or you can nail through the back edge of the studs and into the ends of the header.

When you are framing closets, you employ exactly the same methods and techniques which are used in wall framing. Frame doorways and walls by studding them in the ordinary manner. You can use corner posts constructed like the ones which were described earlier in this chapter.

Figure 17-4
Completed dormer framing.

When walls are framed and you are ready to finish the roof framing, proceed as described earlier in this chapter. If you want to add dormers, you can follow the basic outline as depicted in Figure 17-3. Once the basic frame is completed, frame the dormer roof just as you did the regular roof, except that you can use 2″ x 4″ or 2″ x 6″ ridge beam and rafters. Figure 17-4 shows the completion of the basic framing for the eastern end of the house.

When you are framing the roof of a house this size (and with a height like this!) you need to be ultra-careful. If you must go out on the roof area, be sure to install walkers. Figure 17-5 shows walkers nailed to sheathing to provide footing for workers. Be doubly sure to nail both ends of the walkers.

Figure 17-5
Nearly completed sheathing with abundant walkers.

As you continue to work toward the top, keep adding the walkers. If you lose your footing, you will slide all the way off the roof if there is not something you can grab. See Figure 17-5 for details.

When the entire roof is completed, you can see that the addition of the dormers complemented the overall house greatly. Later you will need to decide whether to add a partial deck, a full deck, or no deck.

The next chapter deals with partition walls (as opposed to load-bearing walls) for the various rooms in the house.

Chapter Eighteen:
Building Partition Walls

No matter how large you like your rooms, there are times when a partition wall is necessary. Such walls, unlike load-bearing walls, do not support any of the house weight other than the weight of its own lumber and wall covering. Their only purpose is to divide bathrooms, bedrooms, and other private areas from the rest of the house.

There are two types of partition walls that are practical to build and at the same time inexpensive. One of these types of walls is the log partition wall. The other is the hollow-core wall.

Of the two, the log partition wall is probably more in keeping with the log decor of the house. The hollow-core wall is made up of sole plate, top plate,

studs, and wall covering, while the log wall is composed of nothing but logs.

This chapter will discuss both types of walls, with the hollow-core wall receiving first treatment because this is the kind of wall that most people build. It may not be the type they prefer, but it is simple and easy to construct.

The first element of the wall is the sole plate, which is composed of a series of 2″ x 4″s that lie along the top of the subflooring and outline the exact boundary of the wall. The sole plate is unbroken when it is laid out: even door openings are not included. The sole plate, then, is the bottom unit of the wall.

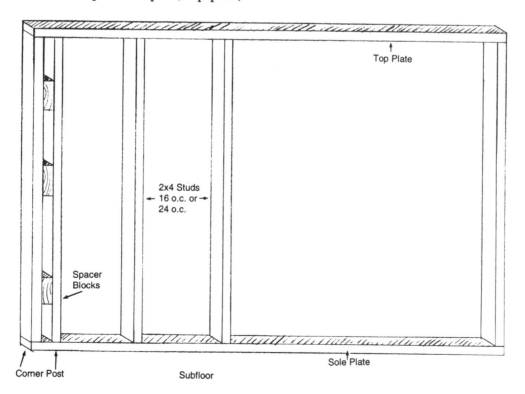

Figure 18-1
Starting a wall frame.

The top unit of the wall is the top plate, which connects the wall to the ceiling. This unit is installed exactly above the sole plate but about eight feet higher. The third component of the wall is the series of studs that reach between the sole plate and top plate. See Figure 18-1.

To build such a studded or hollow-core wall, start by laying off the room by chalking lines wherever you want a wall to be built. The first chalk line comes out at a right angle to the outside wall on one side of the house, and the second line forms a right angle to the other wall of that end of the house so that you are left with a square or rectangle.

Cut and lay out the sole plate for the first wall. Stand the sole plate on edge, and on the bottom edge (the edge away from the studs when they are added) lay off stud locations. Start by marking off the studs at the very end of the wall. Usually, two studs are used for maximum strength and stability. You can also use a 4″ x 4″ if you prefer. This end of the wall will attach later to the exterior wall.

From the end of the plate, measure over to a point exactly 16 inches from the end of the plate. This is the point for your next stud. Continue marking off stud locations so that the distance from the center of the edge of one stud to the center of the edge of the next stud is exactly 16 inches.

Lay out the top plate about eight feet away from the sole plate, and mark the stud locations on it just as you did for the sole plate. Then cut and place studs between the two plates and move the plates close enough together that the studs touch both the plates.

Nail up through the bottom of the sole plate and down through the top of the top plate, and into the ends of the studs. It is a good idea to nail only the first and last studs before you measure diagonally across the wall frame to see if you have a square construction. This diagonal measurement must be equal. If there is a problem, correct it at this point. If the measurement is a good one, you are ready to complete the wall frame, and raise and install it. See Figure 18-2.

Stand a foot or so from the top plate and lift the top of the entire assembly. There is considerable weight, but if the wall is short, you can lift it alone or with the help of one other person.

Have lengths of bracing wood (such as 2″ x 4″s) handy, and as soon as the wall frame is erect, nail a

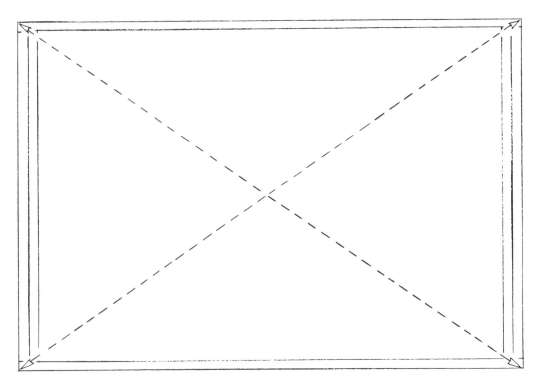

Figure 18-2
Diagonal measurement for squareness.

brace to one of the studs and then hold the frame in position while you nail the other end of the brace to the subflooring.

As soon as the temporary bracing is complete, use a heavy hammer to tap the sole plate into perfect position along the chalk line. When the plate is aligned correctly, drive 16d nails down through the sole plate (between studs) and into the subflooring.

Adjust bracing as needed to position the wall in a plumb or vertical position. Hold a level along a stud to be sure you have a level reading, and then renail the brace again. With the wall frame in place, nail through the end stud and into the log wall. At this point the wall frame is ready for covering. Check with your local building officials. At this point, they may require an inspection prior to covering the wall frame.

When you frame the wall that intersects with the one you've just erected, lay out the sole plate and top plate as you did before, and double the studs at the end. You can construct a corner post by nailing two studs together with small spacers of plywood or similar thin material, and then you can nail a third stud across the edges of the first two studs. You have now created a corner post to which you can attach the adjoining wall.

In each partition wall where there is to be an interruption, such as a rough door opening, you must frame a header as well as the rough opening. A header is an assembly made up of two timbers and spacers between them, and the assembly reaches across the top of window or door openings.

Above and below the rough openings you will need to install cripple or short studs, and trimmer studs are installed alongside the sides of the openings for windows, etc. The point here is that nothing should be supported only by hanging from nails, and the trimmers permit the header to rest on the top end of the stud. Figure 18-3 shows cripple and trimmer studs.

If you want to use log partition walls, you can handle the job easily and very inexpensively. You need to decide first how thick you want the wall to be. Almost any thickness works well, so you can use logs from four to six inches wide to form the wall.

Here is a simple method of building a log partition wall. Start by cutting the logs needed. Measure the height from the floor to the ceiling, and then determine how many logs will be needed to make the wall the proper height. If the ceiling is to be eight feet, you have 96 inches to fill. If you choose to use six-inch

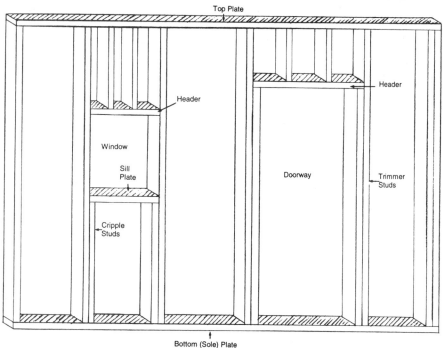

Figure 18-3
Wall frame showing cripple and trimmer studs.

logs, you will need 16 of these to fill the space. If you opt for four-inch logs, you will need 24 logs.

You can, of course, use a variety of heights as long as the thickness' are the same. The final appearance is actually more creative looking if you have logs of four-inch height balanced every few courses by a log of five or six inches in height.

When you have sawed your logs, lay the first one along the chalked line that serves as the room's boundary. If possible, locate the log directly above a floor joist. You must now fasten the log to both the floor and to the exterior wall; otherwise the wall will rock in a very unstable manner.

There are two easy ways to stabilize the log. First, as soon as the log is laid in a stationary position, drill a quarter-inch hole into the end of the log nearer the exterior wall. Drop back about one foot for the hole. Then drive a fluted spike through the hole and into the subflooring.

Move to the other end of the log and drill a hole about four inches from the end itself. Drive a fluted spike into this hole as well. Space a series of other holes about two feet apart along the length of the log and spike the log to the sub-flooring at these locations.

At the end near the exterior wall, start a hole about six inches from the exterior wall and drill down one inch or slightly less. Then remove the drill bit and drill again angling the bit so that the tip is pointing in a seven-o'clock direction. Continue to drill until the bit passes through the end of the log and enters the exterior wall.

When the hole is completed, drill a slightly larger hole so that you can countersink the spike. Then drive the spike into the hole and into the exterior wall. Countersink as you did wall logs. The log along the floor is now stabilized along the floor length, and also fastened firmly to the exterior wall. See Figure 18-4.

For the next log, follow exactly the same procedure. This time you will drive spikes through the second log and into the first log. Spike the log to the exterior wall as well.

If you want to use fewer logs, you can use spacers between the logs. These spacers can be one inch shorter than the thickness of the log. If the log is five inches thick, the spacers should be four inches long and at least two inches wide.

Position the spacers so that you have one every two feet. Nail the spacers to the log below by using 10d nails or even smaller ones. The next log will rest upon these spacers, and the spacers will help to stabilize the next log.

If you use spacers one inch thick, and if you are using four-inch logs, you will save the equivalent of one log every fourth log. The problem, if there is one, is that you will need to fill in between the logs with chinking of some sort. So you are faced with the question of whether you prefer to use more logs or more chinking.

No matter which approach you take, you will need to chink the cracks between the logs in order to guarantee privacy for those inside the room being partitioned. For chinking you can use mortar or a vinyl chinking substance which spreads like putty when moist but which dries into the consistency of hard rubber.

When the log wall reaches the ceiling, you can fasten the final logs by drilling through the exterior wall and driving a spike into the end of the top log. You can also employ a slanted hole through which to drive a spike. You may need to slant the spike upward rather than down in order to drive it in spike easily and effectively, although either way works.

You will find that the log wall remains slightly unstable at this point. The second wall that butts into the one just completed will stabilize the two walls perfectly.

To build the second wall, first decide where the rough door opening will appear. If you are partitioning a corner bedroom, you may wish to have the wall which is at right angles to the front or rear exterior

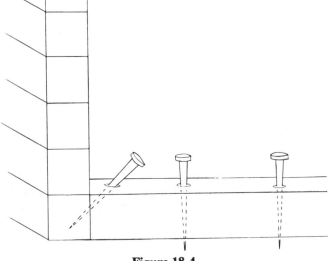

Figure 18-4
Stablizing bottom partition log.

wall remain uninterrupted. The wall which is at right angles to the end wall can have the rough door opening in it. The best place for the door is at the corner, rather than in the middle of the wall.

When the first wall is completed, chalk the line for the second wall. Determine how wide you want the door to be and mark off the rough door opening. For interior doors a rough opening can be 34 to 36 inches. The door framing will account for two to four inches, leaving room for a door about 32 inches wide.

If you are buying doors, you will need to adapt your rough opening to the size of the door, or you can modify the size of the door slightly. If you plan to make your own doors, you can fit the door to any rough opening size you have.

Start with a rough opening that is 36 inches wide. Mark the spot where the first log must stop. Cut the log and place it in position so that you can spike the log to both the floor and to the end wall.

Next, cut a rough framing timber for the door. The term "rough" should not be taken too literally. Make the framing piece as smooth and accurate as you can. The framing member should be as wide as the wall logs are and as high as you wish the door to be. A workable height is 82 inches. Thickness should be two inches.

Now cut another framing member that is 38 inches long and the same width as the wall logs. Let the end of the shorter member lap the top of the longer framing member, and you will have an opening of 36 inches.

To install the framing members, stand the 82-inch member on the subflooring and hold it as erect as possible. Nail the bottom of the member to the end of the first wall log. Use a level to get the best possible reading, and then run a brace from the side of the member to the side of the wall log. It is always a good idea to nail one end of the brace to the wall log and leave the other end of the brace free. Then, while holding a level against the upright framing member, nail the framing piece to the brace once you have a perfectly vertical reading.

Start three nails one inch from the end of the short framing member. Drive the nails until the points just appear on the bottom side of the framing piece.

Hold the cross piece in place and drive the first nail into the top of the upright framing member. Check to be sure that the two pieces fit together perfectly. When you are satisfied, drive the other nails all the way into the board.

The other end of the framing member is loose at this point. Cut another 82-inch framing piece and install it against the logs on the other side of the rough opening. When this is done, lay the loose end of the short framing member across the top of the second framing timber and nail the two pieces together.

Your rough door opening is essentially complete. For the rest of the logs in the wall you need to measure the distance from the outside edge of the framing timber to the exterior wall, and then cut logs to fit the space. Try to space your logs or to choose heights that will work out perfectly to fit over the rough door opening. You don't want to have to shape a log to make the fit a good one, but if you cannot work it out otherwise, you may have to do so.

As you work your way up the rough framing timbers, you can drive nails through the framing timber and into the end of the wall logs. Use 60d nails or fluted spikes.

Now you are fastening each log to the log beneath it, to the door framing, and to the exterior wall. As soon as you rise to the top of the wall frame, you will be fastening logs to the first wall, in addition to the other stabilizing points.

If you are unable to work out your log height properly, cut out the end of the log that crosses the door frame. For instance, if the last log before the top of the door frame lacks two inches of reaching the top of the frame, go ahead and install the log. When you start to install the next log, however, you will need to measure over from the end 38 inches (the total length of the top framing member) and up from the bottom two inches. Mark off and cut out the 2″ x 28″ inch section of log. Now the log will fit perfectly over the door frame.

Carry the log plan all the way to the top of the wall area. At the corner you can use the butt-and-pass method that you used for exterior walls, or you can let the ends meet flush against each other.

The partition wall is now completed. Later you can install the door and door trim, and the room, other than floor covering and ceiling covering, is essentially complete.

Chapter Nineteen:
Rough Wiring

This chapter could easily be the shortest in history: Call an electrician.

This is not frivolous advice. You are at this point dealing with one of the most important aspects of house building, and it is one of the most crucial, most exacting, and most dangerous in the long run.

If your roof leaks, you can find a way to patch it. If any of a thousand other parts of the house are less than perfect, you can find ways of dealing with the problem. But if you grab a hot wire you may be seriously injured or killed.

This does not mean that you cannot do some or even a major part of the rough wiring. However, unless you have some previous experience or background in the matter, you are advised to seek and use experienced assistance.

The first suggestion here is that you might try to work out a trade-off. If you know an electrician who is also interested in chain-saw work, you might offer to trade your knowledge for his: an hour-for-hour arrangement.

The second suggestion is that you look for cheap (but not shabby) help outside the profession. A great place to search is on the maintenance staff of a public or private school, a college campus, or similar locations. On the campus of the college where I taught English and literature for three decades, one of the requirements for anyone who wanted to advance in the maintenance department was that he be licensed in plumbing and electrical work and experienced in carpentry.

The logic is sound. If the maintenance staff can handle all of the major and minor problems of the physical plant on the campus, there will seldom if ever be a reason for calling in the professionals. The college is thus assured of having not only inexpensive but, instant service when problems arise.

But what does this have to do with wiring your house? The answer is simple: many of these maintenance men, like the rest of us from time to time, want to supplement their incomes in order to have Christmas shopping money

or funds for a vacation or car upgrading or major renovations of their houses.

So locate a college or university or public or private school and learn whether the maintenance staff members are indeed licensed as electricians. If so, ask how much one of them would charge you to serve as the head electrician, while you work as his helper.

(Later on, you can arrange the same type of deal with a mason, plumber, or other craftsman. If you can't trade off services, you can pay one person and you can serve as his laborer.)

In the meantime, here are several other suggestions that you might consider for your house. First, last, and always, check with the building inspector or the building code to learn exactly what must or must not be done in the wiring of your house. Some codes require a receptacle (socket) every ten feet of wall space. Others insist upon ground-fault receptacles in all "wet" parts of the house. These wet parts include any portion of the house where there is a constant use of water: sinks, bathrooms, darkrooms, etc.

A ground-fault receptacle is worth its weight in gold. The purpose of these devices is to shut off electricity in an instant: a tiny fraction of a second. So if you are washing dishes or mixing a cake and there is an electrical malfunction or accident, you will not be electrocuted.

There are many who whine about the high cost of the ground-fault receptacle, but the cost is inconsequential when you think of the benefits which are entailed when you install them. Take heart concerning the cost: you do not need one of these expensive receptacles at each and every receptacle point within ten feet of the sink. The electrician will tell you that one ground fault receptacle on each circuit is sufficient to activate the power cut-off.

As you ponder the wiring of your house, give a great deal of thought to exactly what you want. Do you, for instance, want to have a light in the center of the den ceiling? Or in the center of the bedroom ceiling? More and more people are getting away from these light fixtures and are more interested in having the wall switch activate a bedside lamp or a lamp beside the couch.

Do you want ceiling fans? Do you want flood lights for the front and back yards? There are literally hundreds of possibilities, and you have the opportunity to make the choices.

In my particular case, it was having the receptacles mounted on the baseboard or near the floor that gave me pause. I have given the matter a great deal of thought, and I can find no rhyme or reason for putting these electrical outlets in the hardest-to-reach places in the entire room. In virtually any house you enter, if you should need to plug or unplug a lamp, odds are great that you would have to move the couch, crawl under a coffee table, or wedge your way behind and around heavy items of furniture.

Why? Why not install the receptacles at the same height as that of the light switches? Why not make it easy for the people who live in the house to unplug the television set in the event of a heavy electrical storm? I have never fathomed the reason for our custom of locating these outlets in the unhandiest points inside the house.

So think of your own irritations and frustrations, if any, and plan the wiring of your house to meet not only your needs but also your wishes and desires. Do keep in mind, however, that if you should later decide to sell the house, your preferences might stand in the way of selling the house quickly and for the right price.

Now to the problems of wiring a log house. Ask electricians and they will tell you, in all probability, that you have only two reasonable choices in the wiring. You can install the wiring while you are stacking logs. You can cut a groove along the center of the log, from end to end, and you can then lay the wire inside the groove to keep the wire from being crushed or broken. Or you can drill holes in the logs and pass the wires through the holes.

There is, of course, another possibility, one that is very handy and practical and in no way expensive or troublesome. You simply use conduits or pipes. You can work from the basement or from the crawl space and drill holes through the flooring just against the wall, and then you can run the conduit up six or eight inches or a foot above the floor level.

And here at last is a reasonable excuse for locating the electrical receptacles close to the floor! Otherwise you would need to run the conduit as high as the switches, and the results would be unsightly and more expensive.

So for log houses there can be a justification for low-to-the-floor receptacles.

When you install switches, you will need to run the conduit higher — to the level of the normal or ordinary light switch. And to the minds of many people, this sort of conduit is unattractive. But you can cut one-inch boards and box in the conduit and the wood will either turn through aging to the color of the logs, or you can apply a stain, particularly if you also stained the logs.

You will use the conduit or pipes for all walls that are made of logs. For hollow-core walls, those that are studded in the more traditional manner, you can run the wiring through the walls by drilling holes in the studs.

But however you do the work or hire it done, you can still make a wiring diagram that will govern the entire electrical work in the house. You must, of course, install a wall switch next to every door. You must use special wiring for the electric range, hot-water heater, dryer, some heating systems, and well pumps in many instances. These are the 240 wires, as opposed to the 120 circuits, which are far more common. (These were called, only a few years ago, 220 and 110 circuits.)

If you will be working with an experienced electrician, you can do a great deal of the work even when he is not around. But be sure to check with the local authorities. In some parts of North Carolina, for instance, an unlicensed electrician cannot contract to wire a house for another person. However, that same unlicensed person may wire his own house without encountering problems. And in many parts of the state anyone, without any previous knowledge or experience, can wire his own house.

This arrangement is not limited to North Carolina, and the entire guidelines will speak volumes to you, if you happen to live in a similar area. Just remember that you must be the person of record as far as the wiring is concerned.

Before the electrician appears on the scene to work, show him the wiring diagram to see if it meets regulations. If so, then you can drill the holes, fasten the electrical boxes or receptacles to the walls, install the switch boxes, and even pull the wires to the proper locations.

A word of caution: when you are working around any form of electricity, make certain that the power is off before you touch any wires. Theoretically, if the switch to a lamp or other connection is off, no power can reach past the switch. All the same, I have enough of my own insecurities and I use the old lamp test. If I plan to re-wire or correct a problem in a receptacle, I take a lamp with me — one that is working and which has a good bulb in it.

Keep that in mind. If you plug in the lamp and the light does not come on, you assume that the power is off. But if the bulb is bad, the power could very well be on.

Try the lamp in a hot receptacle, and if the light comes on, you know the wires are hot. Then try the same lamp in the box to be repaired. If the bulb does not come on, you can feel reasonably certain that the power to that receptacle is off.

But my insecurity tells me that it is just barely possible that the bulb burned out between sockets, so I always return to the first receptacle and try again. If the bulb comes on, then indeed the receptacle which was tested second is powerless.

Some people use a radio, which works just as well, but I suggest that you remove the batteries to be certain that the radio is not playing off battery current rather than household current.

When you are ready to work, you might wish to start wiring in the basement. At least, you can start installing the metal boxes for the conduit and wires. Be advised that electrical boxes come in metal or plastic form. Use the metal for your work here.

The metal boxes for the conduit should be installed four feet from the basement floor. To install the boxes, use a battery-operated drill with a masonry bit to drill holes. You can use a pencil to mark the locations of the holes. Take an empty box and measure up from the floor to a height of 48 inches. Mark the spot. Then place the bottom of the box at the mark. While holding the box in place, stick the point of the pencil through the holes in the back of the box and mark the locations for the holes for the screws that will hold the box on the wall.

When you buy the metal electrical boxes, you should also buy a supply of screws and plastic anchors. If you have ever tried to use a screw in a masonry hole, you know that the screw will hold for only a very brief time. But if you drill the hole, then tap one of the plastic anchors into the hole, and then run the screw into the anchor, you will have a permanent fastening. Check with your supplier to get the right sizes of drill bits, anchors, and screws.

Unless you can accurately "eyeball" the position of the box, use a small level to prevent yourself from installing the box in a crooked manner.

When you pull the wires to the box, you will first run the wire through a length of metal pipe or conduit. Pull out enough of the wire so that you can pull it down into

the box and allow it to hang out six or eight inches or more. When you later install the actual receptacle, you will not be able to work well if you must pull and try to stretch the wire.

There is a nut that slides over the end of the conduit. After the nut is in place, you can flare the opening of the pipe so that the nut will not slide off. After the wire is in place, the nut is then tightened onto the top of the metal box. When the connection is completed, you can drill small holes on each side of the conduit and slip one of the curved support brackets over the pipe. One screw on each side will hold the pipe in place. You may wish to use two of the supports if the stretch of pipe is longer than four feet. In that event, use a support bracket every four feet. At this point, except for the actual connection of wires to the receptacle, the work is done for this box and conduit.

You may find that you need to buy, borrow, or rent the flaring tool for the pipes. And you may need to obtain the equipment for bending the conduit. The conduit seats in the top of the box, and in order for the connections to match, the pipe must be bent out slightly so that for the final six inches the pipe does not stay in contact with the masonry wall.

When you have installed the receptacle boxes (but not made any of the wire connections at this point) you can also begin to install the switch boxes. These, too, are mounted onto the masonry walls just as the receptacle boxes are. The switch boxes come in the small metal format similar to that of the receptacles, and the mounting basics are the same. Pull the wires through the conduit and into the switch box. Seat the lock nut atop the switch box and clamp the conduit to the wall.

Switch boxes are usually located at a comfortable height, with the bottom of the switch box four feet from the floor. When you are installing switch or receptacle boxes on a studded wall, you do the work before the wall coverings are installed. The boxes are installed on the sides of studs, and the height is the same as that used in the basement.

Instead of drilling holes and using anchors, you can use nails to mount the boxes on the studs. Note that on the sides of the boxes there are two openings through which you can slide nails. Insert the nails and use a hammer to drive the nails into the wood of the stud. You cannot mount the boxes with the outside edge flush with the edge of the stud. You must allow for the thickness of the wall covering. For instance, if you plan to use gypsum board (Don't! The effect of sheet rock in combination with the rich and soft yet sturdy effect of the logs is unsatisfactory, to say the least. Use boards for wall covering. You can buy or cut your own tongue-and-groove wall covering or find your own materials that will blend well with the logs.) for interior walls, the boxes should extend past the outside edge of the stud as much as the thickness of the sheet rock. If you plan to use one-inch boards, let the box extend accordingly.

Again, pull the wires to the switch boxes and leave enough of the wire hanging through for you to wire in the switch itself. Do not make any connections at this point, and do not install switch box covers.

When you are ready for the actual wiring, there will be three major elements to the job. First, you will need a meter or service box for the outside of the house. This box is installed on the masonry wall, if there is room, or as a last resort, against the wood inside a storage room which is accessible from the outside. This box contains, when fully activated, a meter to register the amount of power used during a time period, a ground that leads into the soil under the box, and a lead-in to the electrical box mounted inside the house. This inside box holds all of the fuses or circuit breakers, and all of the circuits end here.

What is a circuit? In its simplest sense, it is a complete round trip in which you start at a certain point, travel for a period of time and distance, and return to the starting point. In baseball a circuit blow is a home run in which the batter is able to touch all bases without interruptions as he proceeds from home plate back to home plate. If you are a hiker, many trails are said to be loop trails. This means that you return to the starting point via the trail.

And that is a circuit. In electricity, power starts at the service panel on the outside wall or, in a stricter sense, at the electrical box inside the house. You flip a switch and the current flows through the wires from the switch to the light bulb and to all of the receptacles on the circuit. There is no point at which the potential power supply is interrupted.

Remember that in all electrical activity within the wiring of your house, there must be a complete circuit if the work is done properly and if the wiring functions properly. When you are drawing your electrical layout, use a copy of one level of the house plans. Mark all doors and windows clearly, and then determine where all ceiling fixtures will be located. Do this for all chandeliers or pull-chain fixtures mounted in the ceiling, and indicate on the drawing whether the fixture is pull-chain or chandelier.

Now locate or mark all switches, which are placed near doors in most circumstances. If a light or fixture is governed by only one switch, this is called a single-pole switch. If there are two doors in the room and the switch nearby each door operates the lights in that room, the switch is called a three-way switch. When you are preparing to buy, count the number of two-pole and three-way switches you will need. Buy one or two extra (with the understanding that they can be returned if they are not used) so that you will not need to immediately drive back to the store in the event one of the switches is defective or is damaged.

Next, locate the receptacles or outlets. There should be one on each wall, and if the wall is very long, there should be more than one. We have as many as four outlets on one wall in our house.

Mark the location of wall-mounted lights or lamps, such as those used in a bathroom near the mirror or medicine cabinet.

When you are wiring a circuit, you must run wire from the fuse box or breaker box to all of the switches or outlets on that circuit, and all switches and outlets must be wired into the circuit. In all wiring, the red- and black-covered wires are said to be hot. The white-covered wire is neutral. The white wire is on the return side of the switch or outlet. When you are connecting wires, be sure to connect red to red and black to black. Always connect wires of the same color, unless there is a clear reason for doing it otherwise.

At this point, run wires to all active points and be sure to leave enough so that connecting them will not be difficult. To repeat what was said at the outset of this chapter, if you do not know what you are doing, call in outside help. All work must be done to the satisfaction of the local building inspector, and you will need his approval before permanent power can be turned on.

Chapter Twenty:
Wall Covering

One of the most important — and pleasant — aspects of log-house construction is that of covering the walls. One reason that the task is so pleasurable is that you have several delightful materials or methods from which to choose.

You can, of course, install gypsum board or sheetrock. And there is always paneling of various sorts. A third option is half-log or slab wall covering. Finally, for our purposes here, there is tongue-and-groove wall board or tongue-and-spline wall board covering. Each of these will be discussed in this chapter.

Sheetrock or gypsum board has long been a favorite with home builders, and for several good reasons. The panels are fairly inexpensive and are easily transported. You need only a hammer and some sheetrock nails to install the panels, and each one covers 32 square feet. If your rooms are 12´ x 12´, you can hang three panels on each wall and you are essentially finished with the rough work.

If you need to cut sheetrock, you can do so with a knife. You can also use a razor knife, a fine-toothed saw, and even a special circular-saw blade. To install sheetrock, all you need to do is measure to see that the panel will fit easily into its position and then stand it in place and drive a sheetrock nail every foot or so around the entire border and then every foot or so along every stud that is covered by the panel.

There is one other major consideration. Your first panel on any wall must be hung true in a vertical or plumb sense. If the corner of the room is not square and/or if the floor is not level, your sheetrock panel will not hang levelly, and all other panels will be off plumb.

Worse, if the panels are uneven, there will be a slight gap at either the top or bottom, and with each successive panel the gap becomes wider and wider until the wall is a grotesque effort rather than a neat affair. You can get started with a plumb panel if you will stand the panel in the corner and push it against the wall and hold it there while you hold a level to the vertical edge of the panel. If the level shows a true reading, you can proceed with the nailing.

If the level shows that the corner is not true, you must make adjustments in the shape of the panel itself. For example, if the top corner fits well but the bottom corner is two inches off, lay the panel on a work surface and chalk a line from the bottom corner to a point two inches back from the top corner. Use a razor knife to cut the line you marked and the panel will now fit. So will all subsequent panels on the wall.

Once the sheetrock is nailed up, you must fill nail-hole areas, and apply compound or joint filler along the seams. When you drive a nail into sheetrock, you should drive the nail slightly deeper than the surface of the panel, and later you can use a putty knife to spread compound or putty over the indentation and nail head. Smooth the compound and feather it around the edges.

At all seams you will apply a layer of compound, and then press a length of tape into the compound and cover it with yet another thin layer of compound or putty. You must then smooth and feather the joints and later sand all areas you compounded, before the sheetrock is ready to paint.

So, you can see that the sheetrocking of a room is not quite as simple as it appears at first glance. Your initial work goes very fast, but the taping and compounding and sanding take a much longer time. Your cost also increases in terms of the compound you must buy, the tape, razor knife, putty knife, nails, and other materials. You later have to add the cost of sandpaper and paint, brushes, rollers, drop cloths, and related materials.

One other viewpoint that may be important: logs, wood, and sheetrock do not mix really well aesthetically. With log walls, a wood appearance is generally more satisfactory, although this must ultimately be a matter of personal taste and preference.

You can also install simulated wood paneling or any of the other paneling surfaces and designs which can be very attractive. These panels come in a variety of sizes, but the most universal is the four-by-eight-feet format. You install the paneling in much the same way that you nail up sheetrock.

Start with a true corner, modify the panel if necessary, and nail the panel in place. Use special paneling nails, some of which are colored to match the hue of the paneling, with nails every foot or so around the edge and up and down every stud that is covered by the panel.

The next panel fits neatly against the first, and with better paneling the edges are manufactured to give an invisible joint, or one that is nearly invisible. You then apply molding around the top and bottom of the wall and you have a very neat and finished appearance.

The problems here are that paneling is usually either very thin or very expensive. If you use thin paneling, the wall can be easily damaged and will "give" if any pressure is applied against it. With the better grades of paneling these problems generally disappear, but the increase in price often offsets the advantages of the paneling over the thinner varieties.

Do not be discouraged by these minor problems, if you really want and feel like paying for sheetrock or paneling. Other than the minor difficulties mentioned, they serve very well. If you elect to use these wall coverings, you need to handle problems of installing the panels around light switches and receptacles, and the following paragraphs will help.

When installing paneling around a light switch or receptacle, the first step is to remove the switch plate or receptacle cover so that you will have all the work room possible. Then measure carefully from the floor to the bottom of the light switch or box and again from the ceiling to the top of the box. Write down all of these measurements.

Next, measure from the edge of the last panel installed to the near side of the box and then to the far side. Then stand the next panel in front of the box or boxes and reach behind the panel to make a mark in the exact center of the box, if you can do so. If not, come as close as you can.

Lay the panel upside down on a work surface (and be sure that the surface is not in contact with anything that will damage the finish on the surface) and begin to mark off the box outline with respect to the new panel.

Mark down from the top the distance of the measurement you made earlier and mark the point. Move over an inch or two and measure and mark again, to guarantee accuracy. Then use a straight edge to draw a line connecting the two marks. Make the line five or six inches long.

Measure up from the bottom of the panel to the point where the bottom of the box occurred and mark as before, including the six-inch line. Now do the same with the near and far sides of the box. When you are through, you should have a rectangle with four clearly defined corners.

Use a drill to make a small hole at the upper left corner and at the lower right corner. Take care that the holes do not go past the outside of the outline. Drill another hole at the corner diagonally opposite the first hole. Now use a razor knife, a pocket knife, a jig saw, keyhole saw, or whatever other fine-toothed cutting edge you have. Cut along the outline and then lift the rectangular cut-out from the hole.

When you stand the panel back in place the hole you cut should fit neatly over the box. Make any minor adjustments that are necessary and then nail up the panel. You can then remount the switch box or receptacle box covers.

Use the same approach to cutting out openings for windows and doors. As always, remember that you are working from the back rather than the front of the panel and you must reverse the measurements and sketching of the outline. That is, if the panel is in place and the box is 18 inches from the right side, when you lay the panel upside down you must then measure to a point 18 inches from the left side of the panel.

A third option is available for paneling and sheetrock work. If you can find a superior bargain in both of these items, you may emerge financially victorious if you install the sheetrock first and then add the paneling over it. The result, if the cost is not too great, is that you will have a very solid wall. You must, of course, make cut-outs for interruptions in the wall for both paneling and sheetrock. However, you do not have to joint and compound the sheetrock surfaces.

A third type of material used for wall covering is that of half-logs or even thick slabs. When you squared logs, you made the slab cut, and some of the slabs were a foot to 18 inches or more wide. You may wish to peel off the bark, even up the slabs in terms of thickness and width as much as possible, and use them as wall covering.

Generally, you come out better if you use shorter sections, but in most rooms the walls will be short in any event, and the slabs can be used easily and effectively. Assume, for instance, that you have a stack of very wide slabs, many of them as long as 56 to 65 feet. You will notice that the slabs may be 24 inches wide at the butt of the log and as narrow as ten inches or so at the top end.

However, the 24-inch width may taper only to 22 inches or so during the first eight to 12 feet. If this is the case, you can use eight-foot lengths in a vertical arrangement, or 12-foot lengths in a horizontal arrangement. You can chalk the lines and saw the slab so that the width is the same at both ends.

You will likely have a difference in the thickness of the slabs, and you may wish to set up a rig to allow you to saw the slabs to a uniform thickness. To set up such a rig, I have found the following method to be both fast and efficient.

Locate a short length of board (12 inches long and six inches wide is ideal) and a block of wood eight or ten inches high and four inches wide. Stand the block on edge, narrow side up, and nail the wider board to the top surface of the block. Now turn the assembly upside down and nail the edge of the wide board to the top of your saw log.

Six to ten inches away from the nailed assembly, nail another similar assembly in place. Now locate a strip of 2″ by 4″ or 2″ by 6″ wood and keep it ready. When you are ready to use the holder rig, use a C-clamp to hold the 2″ x 6″ section tight against the side of the block assembly.

Stand the slab on edge so that the flat or cut surface is against the first assembly. Push the slab in as tightly as you can, and then loosen the C-clamp slightly and push the 2″ x 4″ or 2″ x 6″ tightly against the back side or bark side of the slab. Then tighten the C-clamp securely.

Such a simple device works wonders. It will hold the slab so tightly that it cannot move, wobble, or fall as you saw. It can be set up and taken down in a matter of seconds, and it costs virtually nothing to construct. Best of all, it offers you a chance to cut the slabs in safety.

Another fine feature of this simple home-rigged device is that there are no metal elements such as nails for the chain to hit as you work. You can hold and cut

any thickness' you wish, as long as there is room for the bar to pass between the two block assemblies.

The only slight problem you may encounter is that once the chain has cut between the two assemblies, there will be a kerf differential of one-fourth inch, which will permit some movement of the slab. But if you wish to pause for a moment and tighten the C-clamp again, the problem is eliminated.

Another method of using slabs is to take small logs that were too narrow to be useful earlier and saw off all four slab sides. Then remove the bark, if you wish, and nail up the slabs as wall covering.

Still another possibility for wall covering is to cut wide boards and install these on the interior walls. It is easy to cut boards eight to 12 feet long and six to 12 inches wide, and these look great when installed. You have two basic options: first, cut and fit the boards edge-to-edge with as tight a fit as possible. The second option is to fit the boards side-by-side loosely and then cut two-inch strips to cover the edges. By doing it this way you need not worry about having perfectly straight edges. See Figure 20-1.

Figure 20-1
Nailing up batten-and-boards wall covering.

To cut the two-inch strips, your best bet is to cut a two-by-eight-inch or similar timber and then simply slice off two-inch boards a half-inch thick or less. You can also try for a tongue-and-groove effect in the lumber you cut. It is impossible, so far as I know, to cut a true tongue-and-groove piece of lumber easily with a chain saw, but you can use one of two possible methods to deal with the problem.

The first is to locate a tongue-and-groove plane. These were at one time very plentiful and low-priced, but when there was no longer a demand for them, they disappeared. Still, you may be able to locate one at an antique shop or in tool sheds of older people who are selling their equipment. If not, at least you can use a traditional plane to smooth the edges on the boards. When you have a board with a rough side, turn the rough side away from view.

When you saw a board, stand it on edge and use a rig such as the one suggested above, and use one side of the plane to cut the groove in the edge. Turn the board over and cut the tongue. This is rather slow and tiring work, but it works well.

One hint for ease of work: Try to cut boards as wide as you can. One board 13 inches wide will yield more wall covering than three boards four inches wide. Yet the 13-inch board had to have only two edges planed, while the more narrow boards had to have six edges planed. And the work is the same, whether the board is two inches wide or a yard wide.

You can use yet another method: spline-and-groove lumber, which you can cut with a chain saw. You saw a board just as you would for any other purpose, and when the board is completed, stand it on one edge and chalk a line down the center of the edge. Then saw a groove about one inch deep along the mark.

Turn the board over and saw another groove in that edge as well. Do this with every board you saw for wall covering, and when you are ready to use the boards, saw a 2″ x 6″ board and then slice off thin strips two inches wide. Each strip should be no more than one-fourth inch thick.

When you are ready to install the boards, nail up one board in a horizontal position (you can also use vertical installation just as easily) and then slide one of the thin strips into the groove. Tap the strip with a hammer to seat it completely into the groove.

When you are ready for the next board, position it so that the groove is against the strip, and tap the other edge of the board until the groove is again seated. Be sure to use a block of wood against the edge when you tap. Hit the wood with the hammer rather than hitting the board edge itself. Prolonged or hard hitting with a hammer can damage the edge of the board.

This is not as easy as it sounds, and you may have to work at the job for an hour or so before you get the hang of how to do it. One helpful suggestion is that you turn the bar back and forth just a very little as you saw the groove and in this manner you can saw the groove a little wider than the ordinary kerf. Do not exaggerate the zig-zag movement of the bar tip or you will saw the kerf too wide and the strip will fit too loosely.

Another suggestion is to saw the groove as straight as you possibly can. Any slight deviation in the groove will make it much harder for you to fit the strip inside. The strip, or spline, should also be cut as straight as possible.

When you are ready to install spline-and-groove boards, start with a board without a groove in the bottom or corner side. When you are ready to insert the spline and then fit the second board onto the spline, you may find that you can perform this task better if you do not drive the nails all the way into the first board. Use a crowbar to pry out the free end of the board an inch or so in order to give you more freedom of maneuverability as you work.

If you find that you are having an inordinate amount of difficulty in combining the splines and grooves, you might wish to try a lap cut to create essentially the same effect but with an easier methodology. Stand the board on edge as before and cut the groove, and then lay the board flat and chalk a line from end to end of the board and exactly one-half inch from the edge. Very carefully saw off the top edge of the groove so that what is left is a lip that extends half an inch from the board.

Then saw another board in the same fashion, and turn the second board so that the lip is now facing the outside. In other words, the lip faces opposite from the first one. Slide the two boards together so that the lips overlap. The effect is that the board edges fit together easily and the overlapping lips create a windproof seal. The appearance is good, and the effect is equally good. It takes very little time to saw boards in this manner and also very little time and effort to install them. See Figure 20-2 for an end view of ship-lap boards.

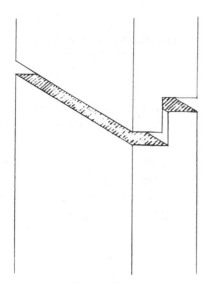

Figure 20-2
Ship-lap joint.

We even used it in our bathrooms. See Figure 20-3 for the effect created by using it.

Figure 20-3
Tongue-and-groove in bathroom.

Do not nail through the lips. The wood is thin and can be cracked easily. If you absolutely must for some reason nail in this area, blunt the tip of the nail before driving it.

This method of lapping the wood edges also works well when it is time to fit the final piece of board into corners. You will have trouble fitting tongue-and-groove or spline-and-groove into corners and still get a tight fit, but with the lapped-edge approach you can handle the tight situations very easily.

You can make your job even easier if you will cut the laps so that the top one is slightly longer than the bottom one. If the bottom one is longer, there will be a crack between boards. If the bottom one is shorter, you will still get the wind-proofing effect, but there will be less chance of a wide joint.

If you use tongue-and-groove lumber that you bought, pick out the lumber carefully and reject any boards that are obviously warped or unfit to use. We were able to secure a superb bargain on ready-to-use lumber, and we installed it in some of our rooms. We found that the knotty-pine lumber blended well with our logs, support posts, and stair-and-railing work.

Chapter Twenty One:
Rough Plumbing

Like wiring a house, plumbing one may be a trifle demanding for many would-be builders. But do not let the apparent enormity of the job discourage you. Yes, it can be difficult, and yes, it does require some special tools to get the job done.

And, yes, you can hire someone to do the work and perhaps come out better from a financial standpoint. Before making a decision, look at your own situation and options.

First, try to estimate what it will cost you if you must buy or rent tools and equipment in order to complete the job. Add to this amount the cost of materials.

Then ask a plumber to give you an estimate. If it turns out that you can get a real bargain by hiring someone, by all means do so. Ask whether it would be meaningful to you to be allowed to work on other parts of the house while the plumber is at work.

Here is one important consideration: Many times the plumber will make you a complete price on his time and labor, plus the cost of bathtub, toilet, hot water tank, holding tank for fresh water, and other elements of the job. He may give you such a discount on the tub and other fixtures that you can emerge in very sound shape financially, particularly if you can work out a trade-off such as the one suggested in the chapter on wiring.

When we were building our house, a man appeared at the door and said he wanted me to teach him to write for publication. He said that he was a builder and would happily work for no pay, and in exchange I would teach him to write and sell articles and stories.

I happily took him up on the offer, and he regularly appeared to help me. He never missed a scheduled day. And afterward I was happy to spend hours teaching him what I knew about publishing.

While you might not have this particular ability on which to capitalize, you could have other talents and skills that are in even greater demand. And, as suggested earlier, check with college and university maintenance men to see if any of them are willing to work for you during their weekends or vacations. You will be amazed at how much work someone is willing to do just so he can earn the money needed to help finance the cost of a fishing trip.

But if you decide that you must do the actual work, check to see if you can buy all materials at a contractor's price. You were advised earlier in this book that if you agree to buy a large part of your supplies from a dealer, he will very likely give you the contractors' discount.

As for the actual plumbing, the job can be as simple or as complicated as you make it. For starters, make the work a great deal easier by backing bathrooms against each other. By doing so you can make one basic set of pipes serve both baths. If you plan to have an upstairs bath, locate it over the downstairs bath. If possible, keep the kitchen close to the immediate vicinity of the baths.

Your job is essentially divided into two general areas: you must bring water into the house and direct it to all needed areas; then you must take the water and human waste out of the house and direct it to a specific area. Keep in mind that the fact that water flows downhill.

If you are installing your own well pump, carefully follow the directions on the pump itself. You must connect the water lines to the pump and sink the lines into the well until the pump and lines are submerged, if you are using a submersible pump.

Connecting a pump is very simple, but because there are many makes of pumps, your best bet is to consult the manufacturer's diagrams for wiring and connecting the pipe. Essentially, it is a matter of connecting three wires and one pipe. The easiest method is to lay out the line and attach it to the pump by using screw-tightened clamps and a screwdriver, after first heating the plastic pipe so that the material will become elastic and will fit easily over the pump connector. Use rubberized tape or its equivalent to fasten the wire snugly against the pipe all the way from the pump to the top of the well.

The length of your pipe will depend upon the depth of the well and the distance from the top of the well casing to an acceptable depth into the water.

You have essentially two types of wells: drilled and bored. A bored well is one in which water is reached before the bore hits the solid rock. Such a well is often supplied primarily by surface water that seeps into cracks and crevices and finds its way to the bottom of the well.

A drilled (or punched) well is one in which you hit rock first and then drill through the rock until you hit a huge pocket of water. Often the water is in the form of an underground stream or aquifer. Such water typically is good, virtually pure, and filled with minerals.

In all cases, locate the septic tank and drain fields downhill from all types of wells. You may also decide that a spring, if you have one which will provide the needed water, will suffice as well as the drilled or bored well. It will certainly be a great deal cheaper. You may need to build a spring house, complete with the footings and waterproofing necessary for keeping outside water from entering the spring.

Your actual plumbing starts when you run the water from the well to the house. You need to bury pipes below the frost line (at least 18" deep in the middle-Atlantic states and deeper in the more northern states). You can also buy insulating tape that will help to keep your pipes from freeze damage.

Where the water pipes enter the basement (or crawl space), you will want to run a line to the hot water tank after you have drilled a hole in the masonry wall. Install a cut-off in the line between the entry pipe and the hot-water tank. Then install a cut-off between the entry point and the holding tank for the well water. This holding tank is used so that your well pump does not have to run each and every time you open a faucet. The cut-off is necessary in the event you need to shut off water while you repair a problem with the holding tank or hot-water heater.

The cut-off from the hot-water tank is there in the event that you have a problem with the tank and have to shut off water to it, but you don't want to turn off the water to the entire house.

At this point you have pipes leading to the holding tank and to the hot-water tank. On the top of the tank you will see two pipe connections: one is labeled cold water, the other hot water. The cold water enters, the electric coils heat the water, and the hot water emerges from the other connection.

Note how far the hot water must travel before it reaches its destination. Perhaps it must travel only six to eight feet before it reaches the bathrooms. It may need to travel 15 feet to reach the kitchen sink and dishwasher, and it may need to travel 30 feet or more to reach distant parts of the house, such as a faucet on the third level. Obviously, you must pump hot water to push out the cold water in the pipes, and when the faucet is turned off, the hot water remains in the pipes and eventually cools. So you are pumping money through the pipes, and you will economize by keeping the travel distance as short as possible.

Above the cut-off to the holding tank, you will install a T-joint in the cold-water pipe, and then send cold water in two directions: toward the kitchen and bathrooms, and toward the outside faucets, if any.

To install these fittings, you can buy a special connector that is shaped like a capital T. The fitting has three openings: one at the bottom or stem of the T and one at each of the ends of the cross piece.

You will probably want to use a one-inch pipe to bring the water into the house from the well. From that point to the various destinations inside the house, you may wish to reduce the pipe to three-fourths of an inch to carry the hot and cold water. At a plumbing-supply store you can find many types of reduction fittings which will enable you to go from one size to another without difficulty.

You may wish to go to an even smaller size of pipe as the water is delivered to faucets at sinks and lavatories. As the pipes run along the masonry walls or inside hollow-core walls, you will need to use a series of braces to hold the pipes in place. By reducing the freedom of the pipes to move about, you not only reduce the chance of breakage but also cut down on vibration.

Your pipes can be either plastic or copper. You will find that people generally are divided in their preferences. When you begin to reduce pipe size, you will need to buy what is often called a single-nipple transition or reducing coupling. This device has one end the size of your pipe and the other end the size of the new pipe size. On the nipple end there is a type of socket, and on the other end there are threads, although you can also buy couplings with nipples on both ends. The so-called triple-nipple fitting is like the T device described earlier.

On couplings with double nipples, you will insert the nipples into the open ends of the pipes to be coupled, and seal the two connections. In many cases you can make the insertion and it will hold without any other assistance. If there is to be considerable pressure on the connection, you can use glue and also add a clamp where the fitting is made.

There are so many possibilities that no chapter (or book) could ever deal satisfactorily with all of them, so you need to ask your supplier for help. Tell him or her exactly what it is that you need to do, and the supplier can find exactly what you need.

When you are working with plastic, you can cut it to length by using a hacksaw or sharp knife. When using copper tubing, use a hacksaw and miter box (to prevent the pipe from slipping and crimping) or a pipe cutter.

Most people who prefer plastic do so because the material is so easy to work with. You do not need any special tools, except for possibly a torch to heat the fittings before joining them. One of the most common ways of joining copper tubing is to use the hacksaw and flaring tool. Once the pipe is cut, ream it out with a reamer which will remove all sharp edges. Insert the flare into the end of the pipe and tighten the pressure until the force of the flare opens the end of the pipe. Be sure that you have your fitting on the pipe before you flare it, because otherwise the fitting will not go over the flare.

When you are joining plastic pipes, cut the pipe where needed and sandpaper the last inch of the pipe. After cleaning the outside of the pipe and the inside of the fitting with the pipe manufacturer's recommended cleaner, use plastic glue to coat the outside of the pipe, and then slip it into the fitting. You can also add a small amount of glue to the inside of the fitting to get a better bond.

When you are using copper tubing, you can bend the tubing gently if you need to round a bend, but be careful that you do not bend too severely and crimp the tubing. Crimping will either cut off or severely restrict the passage of water, or it will create a split in the pipe. When you run water pipes to locations in a log house, you should stay under the flooring when possible. When you must go above the floor, drill holes under the sink and lavatory and at the commode. Keep the holes as close to the walls as you can, and when possible and practical run pipes inside the walls.

Inside a studded wall you will need to drill holes through the studs or cut into studs just enough to permit the pipes to fit inside the cut-outs. Do not weaken studs any more than is absolutely necessary. The code in many areas states that at no time can a cut-out or hole account for more than 40 percent of the width of the stud in a load-bearing wall, and no more than 60 percent of the stud in a non-load-bearing wall.

Be sure to include water cut-offs under all sinks and lavatories and on the supply pipes for commodes and bathtubs and showers. The purpose for the cut-offs is that if there is a plumbing problem you can cut off the water in that one area without having to cut off water for the entire house or even for the entire bathroom.

When you have carried the pipes to all the destinations and have stabilized the pipes so that they cannot move about, put caps on the ends of the pipes. These caps will prevent debris, insects, and other foreign material from entering the pipes.

Once the fresh water has been delivered, you need to concentrate on eliminating waste water. Here the key words are gravity and venting.

Depending upon where you live and the particular circumstances of your house, you have several options. One is to dispose of waste through a sewer system, if you live in the city; you can also have a septic tank; and, if you live in the real boondocks, you might even settle for an outdoor privy.

But we are concerned here with a septic tank. You can do the excavating yourself and dig the pit for the septic tank, but you will need to buy the tank itself and have it installed. Once it is in the ground, you can tap into the knockout space and install the sewage or plumbing lines running from the house.

One line typically carries all: bathroom waste, bath water, and dishwater. All of this waste is conveyed through one channel, but other lines feed into the one large line. You will run one line down straight from the commodes, and other lines downward from the bath tubs and the sinks.

In the rough plumbing stage, do not plan to connect anything to the open end of the lines. A cap will suffice for the moment.

To attach these lines to the main line, use plastic line and plastic fittings. You can usually connect these by using glue. There should be a clean-out plug at the end of the septic line inside the house.

If you are uncertain about line sizes, contact the office of the building inspector. Get all of the specifications, and when you must buy fittings, if you can't keep the sizes straight just carry a sample of the line with you and tell the supplier what type of connection you are making and ask his advice.

Rest assured that if you are doing business with a reputable company, virtually anything in stock will be acceptable. The better stores derive much of their business from people who are installing materials or upgrading or repairing their houses in one way or another, and it makes little sense for these people to stock supplies which are not acceptable to the code inspectors. Who would buy them?

When you are connecting some of the lines you may find that you need a medium-sized pipe wrench. Go ahead and spend the money. Do not attempt to slip by with workmanship that is at best only modestly acceptable. Get the supplies you need and the equipment you need to install the materials you bought.

When you install the main line and all ancillary lines, be certain to use a level regularly so that you always know that the lines are slanting in the proper direction and that there is sufficient fall to allow the lines to work correctly.

When all connections are made, stop your work at this point and resume later when you do your finish plumbing.

Chapter Twenty Two:
Chimney Construction

Building a chimney is a challenge, even for the experts in the field. Properly built, a chimney will draw remarkably, keep a good fire going, produce sufficient heat to create astonishing comfort, and offer aesthetic joys that are incomparable. If you have read the many articles that disparage chimneys and remind you over and over that they are worse than inefficient, that they actually lose more heat than they produce, disregard that information and build your chimney.

Regardless of what critics say, the chimney produces a copious amount of heat, if the construction and the fuel are both good. One winter my family heated its house by a woodstove in one room and a fireplace in the other end. We had a 4,000-square-foot house and the temperatures dropped to as low as minus 14 degrees that winter. We had a 4,000-square-foot house and the temperatures dropped to as low as minus 14 degrees that winter.

And we stayed warm!

Before you start any form of work, decide where the chimney should be located. Two obvious possibilities are inside and outside the house. The advantage of the inside chimney (that is, one with all sides of the chimney located inside the house) is that you can enjoy the benefits of the heat that escapes through the outside of the chimney.

Go outside and place your hand on a chimney when a fire is burning in the fireplace. The chimney will be toasty-warm. If this surface were inside a room, the heat would help to heat the area, even though the room is not exposed to fire.

The disadvantage is that if you should have a chimney fire and the heat from the fire cracks the bricks and other materials, the next time there is a chimney fire the flames could possibly escape into the walls or attic of the house. Read some statistics on the number of lives and amount of property lost because of chimney fires before you make a decision, and keep in mind that building techniques and materials are now better than they were when many of the older chimneys were constructed.

The advantages to the outside chimney are that if there should be a chimney fire, the odds are immensely great that the fire will not spread into the house, and if there is

chimney damage, it can be repaired much easier than can the indoor chimneys.

There is also the aesthetic advantage of the beauty of the huge, even massive chimney standing against the outside wall of the log house.

The disadvantage of the outdoor chimney is that of heat loss.

After you have made your decision, the next step is to dig and concrete the footing. The size of the footing is controlled in a large sense by the size of the chimney. Assume that you will build your chimney on the outside of the house. The width of the chimney will be seven feet, and its thickness or depth will be 40 inches.

This depth includes nine inches inside the interior wall, the thickness of a 12-inch cement block wall, plus 19 inches extending out from the house. The footing should be one foot larger than the outside dimensions of the chimney, or nine feet long and 69 inches deep.

The depth of the footing is another matter. In our county the footing must be at least nine inches deep. Ours is 38 inches deep.

Why so deep? Concrete is cheap, compared with the cost of rebuilding a chimney and repairing the damage incurred when the chimney topples or pulls away from the house as the too-thin footing permits the chimney to shift and settle.

In all probability, we went deeper than necessary. You can dig a footing 12 or 14 inches deep and feel totally confident. For starters, have the masonry products delivered to a predetermined location which is near enough to the chimney work site without actually being in the way of the work.

Before you start to build, you should be aware of several key factors in chimney construction. First, the purpose of the chimney is to carry smoke and gases to the outside of the building. While the smoke angle is obvious, the gases produced by combustion can be deadly, so you must vent these to the outside of the house.

The key to successful venting is draft, which is the action created by wind or air blowing down the chimney, then turning and traveling back up and into the outside air. This draft sucks the smoke and gases from the house area.

Inside the chimney there is a flue liner, which is made of terra cotta or fired clay. These liner sections will later be mortared into position, just as bricks and blocks are. Do not consider for even a moment the possibility of building one of the old-fashioned chimneys without flue liners. You can buy masonry blocks that have sections of flue liners built into them.

After you mix the concrete and pour the footing (see the earlier chapter on mixing mortar and concrete), lay out the chimney in your mind and then sketch it on paper. You will want, for best results, a lip inside the house that extends a foot or at least eight inches beyond the rough opening of the chimney. Let the final distance be determined by the number of cement blocks and bricks needed to fill the opening.

The purpose of this lip is to bond the chimney to the wall inside and out, so that the chimney cannot possibly fall as long as the house stands. See Figure 22-1 for a better understanding of how the lip is constructed. The viewpoint is from above the house.

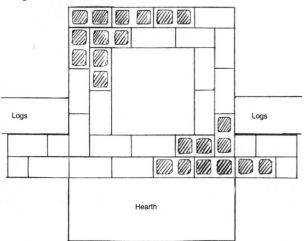

Figure 22-1
Top view of chimney, hearth, and profile.

Start with cement blocks laid around the perimeter of the outside dimensions of the chimney. If the chimney will be seven feet wide, you will need 5.25 blocks for the width. If you wish to narrow the chimney (assuming that the rough opening will permit you to do so) two inches on each side, your blocks will come out even.

A far better idea, however, is to allow two extra inches on each side for the installation of a rock surface for the chimney. You will not affix these rocks to the chimney walls until the very end of the job, however.

When you lay the first course of the outside wall, you will then lay the narrow courses, which are 40 inches, plus two extra feet for the hearth, if any, in the basement. The total depth, then, is 64 inches. This length will work out to four 16-inch blocks. When you lap blocks for the bonding pattern, you will have to cut or break a block to make the course work out perfectly.

Lay the complete outside area of the chimney, then pour two inches of mortar over the entire inside area and set cement blocks side by side and end to end to fill the area. Many building codes require that you fill the cores of the blocks with concrete. If you plan to do so, fill them as you work. You can also fill the entire area with concrete, rather than cement blocks, if you prefer.

Build the entire hearth-chimney area two full courses high, or 16 inches from floor or footing to the top of the structure. At this point you will start up with the chimney. One effective way of doing so is to start a narrow wall of one cement block laid squarely on top of the other. The blocks should lap part of the ends of logs on either side of the chimney area. The blocks are laid on the inside of the living area, and other blocks are butted against the outside of the log ends when you are high enough to do so.

Figure 22-2
Chimney blocks butted against foundation wall.

Look at Figure 22-2. You can see that the blocks are butted against the outside of the rough opening for the chimney. Such a pattern of construction eliminates any possibility of a crack forming if the chimney should settle slightly.

One of the tricky elements of a fireplace is the angle of the throat where the damper is installed. You do not want to have a gaping hole above your fire, or virtually all of the heat will escape up the chimney. At the same time, you do not want to choke the opening down so that there is no draft.

Before you take the chimney upward through part of the floor area, you will need to cut away floor joists and install a new header to permit room for the chimney to climb.

As you stand inside the house and look toward the fireplace, at the back of the fire area the bricks used in the throat must be edged forward a small amount each time until the back wall leans forward gently. The interior of the fire chamber, and this includes all walls, must be lined with fire bricks, not the traditional bricks used in other construction.

When the opening is narrowed to five or so inches (depending upon the side of the throat) you install the damper with the handle hanging down into the fire pit. Mortar the damper in place so that when you open or close it, the assembly stays solidly in place. Above the damper you should start installing sections of flue liners.

Keep moving upward with the chimney at this point. Lay the outside courses, then fill in the center around the flue liner with blocks, concrete, concrete-filled blocks, or bricks. As soon as you are a few feet above the fireplace, light a crumpled section of paper inside the fireplace and see if the draft seems correct. If not, you should correct the throat and flue at this point.

If all is well, you will need to erect scaffolding for the rest of the chimney. You can borrow, rent, or buy. If you have no further use for the scaffolding after the chimney is built, you may wish to rent, unless you can borrow the equipment. If you think you will have continuing needs, you can buy the sections and, later, when you are through with them you can sell them and regain at least part of your investment.

As the chimney continues to climb, the scaffold levels must be raised higher and higher. When you floor a section, you can use 2″ x 10″ timbers, at least three of them, covered by a 4′ x 8′ section of plywood. Be sure to nail the plywood to the timbers so that it will not slip and cause you to lose your footing.

Stabilize the scaffolding as well as you can. Note the long timber in Figure 22-3. The timber is fastened

securely to the rail of the scaffold, and the other end is anchored securely to a stake in the ground. This timber keeps the scaffolding from swinging and swaying with the movement of the workers.

Figure 22-3
Stabilizing scaffold for safety.

At the top of the chimney, you will need to cut back into the eaves so that the chimney can stay against the wall of the house and yet extend through the roof line. Notice in Figure 22-4 that there is a board anchored to the roof and a ladder is positioned against the board. The purpose of this rig, of course, is to keep the worker from slipping and falling from the roof. Note also that the chimney is starting to rise through the roof line.

You should also note that when the chimney reaches its maximum height, the flue liners extend a few inches above the final block and brick courses. See Figure 22-5

You are not finished inside yet. You can go to the front of the fireplace and nail a length of plywood two feet wide and eight feet long to the subflooring. This plywood (and you can double the thickness for greater support) is for the hearth.

Figure 22-4
Toe-board anchored to roof to keep workers from falling.

Figure 22-5
Flue liners extending past roof line.

with the fire bricks in the bottom of the fireplace. See Figure 22-6.

Figure 22-6
Finished hearth is even with firebricks in fire box.

When the chimney exterior is completed, you will want to parget (or "parge") the surface by spreading a coating of rich mortar over the cement blocks. This parget coating will permit you to affix rock or stone to the chimney, creating the most beautiful part of the entire structure. Figure 22-7 shows the application of a parget coat of mortar. The work in progress is an entire masonry wall, but the principle is exactly the same. Apply the parget on both inside and outside surfaces.

You may be surprised to learn that you affix, rather than lay, the rock or stone surface to the chimney. You may be even more surprised to learn that you start at the top and work your way down.

The reason for starting at the top is that when you drop mortar (and you will), it will not adhere to the chimney where it must be cleaned off later. The rocks or stones are in reality thin layers of a shale-like rock that are merely attached with a mortar adhesive to the parget surface of the chimney.

When you mix the mortar, use Portland cement rather than the usual mortar. Make the mixture slightly thicker than you would normally use. Hold a stone in one hand, and with the other hand use a trowel to smear a thick layer of mortar onto the back surface of the stone. Then press the stone against the surface of the chimney, and

Use bricks to form the hearth. A six-inch length of plywood extends past the hearth outline. The inside of the hearth is filled with bricks. When the final touches are put on the hearth's basic structure, the assembly is even

while you apply pressure toward the chimney, turn the stone a quarter of a turn while maintaining the pressure. Then let go of the stone, and it will cling to the chimney.

Figure 22-7
Pargeting provides a base for sticking rock.

Figure 22-8
Sticking rocks to pargeted wall of chimney.

The stones do not touch each other when they are attached. Leave rather large spaces between them, as shown in Figure 22-8. Later you can return and spread mortar between the stones. For a very impressive appearance, use a black mortar (which costs slightly more than regular mortar, but the effect is worth it) to fill in the spaces between the stones.

One practical work method for completing the top parts of the chimney is to mix both types of mortar and haul them to the top of the scaffold. When you have fastened the stones which the scaffolding will permit you to reach, apply the mortar while you are still on the scaffold and while the scaffold is at that height. See Figure 22-9.

Figure 22-9
Start sticking rocks at top and work down.

To apply the mortar, use a small trowel and cut into the mortar with the back of the blade. Then turn the blade so that the back faces the stone, and press the blade against the side of the rock. The mortar is dislodged and wedged into the spaces. More experienced masons will sling the mortar into the spaces, but if you are not skilled at this you will smear black mortar across the surface of the stones, and this stain is incredibly difficult to remove.

When the chimney is completed, it will add greatly to the visual effect of the entire structure. The overall effect of the black mortar can be seen in Figure 22-10.

Figure 22-10
Mortar's effect on chimney rocks.

And finally, the total effect of the fireplace and profile can be seen in relation to the entire room.

Chapter 23 discusses finish plumbing and wiring.

Chapter Twenty Three:
Finish Wiring and Plumbing

At this point you have completed your rough wiring and rough plumbing. The wires have been pulled from the various circuits to the box on the inside wall of your house, and the pipes have been connected from the sinks and bath tubs to the main septic line, which has in turn been connected to the septic tank.

Your job from this point is detailed but not difficult. Start by going to each outlet on every wall of every room and in the hallways and any other areas where there is wiring to outlets. You will start by recalling that at the outside meter box you have wiring coming into the house. From the inside box you have red and black wires leading to outlets and switches. These red and black wires are the hot wires, while the white wire is the neutral wire.

At each outlet you will see the plug for the various lights or appliances that will be installed, and on the sides of the outlet receptacle you will see a pair of screws on each side. One hot wire will be connected to the top screw on one side, and the other hot wire is connected to the top screw on the other side. The ground will be connected to the bottom of the receptacle.

When the wires are connected (after you have made sure that no uncovered or bare part of the wire touches the sides of the receptacle box or any other foreign surface) you can push the now-wired receptacle back into the box. At the top and bottom corners of the receptacle there are ears, and below the ears you will find a small slot. You will tighten a screw that holds the receptacle unit to the box itself. The box, you recall, is already installed by means of screws or nails to the wall or to the studding inside the wall.

Next, you will go to every other outlet or receptacle in the entire house and make similar connections. When this is done, you will need to wire the switches. This is done in essentially the same way. When the switch is removed from the box (and the box is left installed on the wall surface or studding), you will see a screw on each side of the switch. Connect one of the hot wires to the screw on the left side, and the other hot wire to the screw on the right side. As before, bend the wire tightly and snugly over the screw shank and then tighten the screw until the wire is held securely so that it cannot wiggle or move about.

When this is done, push the switch back into the box and tighten the screws to hold the switch securely in place. You are now ready to install the switch and receptacle covers, once the inspector has given his approval to all of the work.

The building inspector will need to see your work in the various stages, so be prepared to call him at the appointed times or stages. Depending upon the part of the country where you live, you may need to call the inspector when the wires are first pulled, and again later when the switch and receptacle wiring has been completed.

Keep in mind that anywhere in the house that wires are joined or spliced, you must use wire nuts to hold the wires together, and then the splices must be enclosed in a box. To use the wire nuts, strip an inch of coating from each of the two wires to be joined, and then hold the wires so that they are side by side. Slip the wire nut over the two ends and turn the wire nut in a clockwise fashion. As the wire nut turns, the wires will be twisted and held together. Remember to connect black with black, red with red, and ground with ground.

Turn your attention now to the wiring of light fixtures. Here you will have a series of tasks to handle. Many fixtures have a metal or plastic box that is attached to the ceiling to hold the fixture in place. This is so that the fixture will not be held only by the electrical wires.

You will pull the black wire away from the fixture and connect it to the black wire in the wiring system. Do the same with the red wires and ground wires, if appropriate. Then use screws to connect the entire fixture to the box at the ceiling.

If the fixture hangs down a considerable distance from the ceiling, you will probably have wires which you will thread through the links of a chain leading from the bulb to the connection itself. Connect fluorescent fixtures in the same manner. Then use the screws to connect the fixtures to the ceiling.

Follow these same principles throughout the entire house until everything is safely connected. Then turn your attention to the finish plumbing.

This is often somewhat more complicated and difficult. When you are ready to install the kitchen sink, for example, you may need to install cabinets, if you plan to use any at this stage of the house. Whatever you decide, you must have a surface on which the sink is to rest.

Generally, you have a wide expanse of wood or wood product which will house the sink. You will need to cut a hole for the sink to fit into, and you will need to drill holes for the faucet connections. Your major problem is that if you cut the hole for the sink too small, it will not fit inside, and if you cut it too large, you have ruined the plywood.

To get the right size for the hole, start by turning the sink over and looking at the bottom side of it. You will see a lip that goes completely around the sink top, and this lip will rest upon the plywood when the hole has been cut. You will also see that the lip is at least an inch wide, and usually it is much wider, so you have some play or freedom in the hole cutting. If you purchase new sinks, a template is provided that you can use to make surface cut-outs.

Lay the sink upside down over the plywood. Adjust the position of the sink until it is located straight and even. When you are satisfied that the sink is located correctly, use a pencil to trace around the entire sink. Also mark inside the holes in the sink where the water faucets will be located.

Now use the pencil to draw another line an inch or so inside the first lines. This second mark is your cut line.

Remove the sink and use a drill to bore a small hole (a half-inch hole is sufficient) along the line so that the major part of the hole is inside the line and only the outside edge of the hole touches the line.

When the hole is drilled, use a jig saw or keyhole saw to cut out the entire inner circle. Start the point of the keyhole saw into the circle so that the teeth of the saw are aligned with the line, and begin sawing. Continue all around the entire sink area. If you use a jig saw, do the same, but pause every few inches to be sure that you are not deviating from the line. When the oblong oval is almost cut through, you may need to reach under the sink area and support the oval so that it does not sag and

create too much pressure at the saw area. Be careful you don't touch the saw-blade.

Use a larger drill bit to drill the holes for the water-supply fixtures. When the cutouts are done, set the sink inside the hole and make certain that it has seated properly. You will have some small brackets with the sink that you attach around the underside of the sink. These metal or plastic brackets hold the sink tightly against the plywood.

If you plan to use a Formica or similar cover for your plywood area, you can install this before making the lines and cuts. It is much easier to cut tile and wood at the same time than it is to try to cut them separately.

You are now ready to connect the supply lines. Typically, copper or plastic feed lines are used, and the connecting procedure is very easy. Cut copper tubing to fit, allowing two or three inches in case of a mistake, and install fittings as you did earlier. Or cut the plastic lines and use the proper fittings to install the lines.

Connect the hot and cold supply lines. If your copper line is too long, you can gently bend it at a gentle angle. The deviation from a straight line will have the effect of shortening the line so that it will fit correctly. Your sink will come with printed instructions on how to install the plug and other aspects of the fixture. Follow the directions exactly and install faucets and double-check all connections.

In the bathroom you may have a cabinet with a sink built in. You can position the cabinet, make certain that the sink is seated correctly, and make the connections as you did before. Be sure that your water lines include individual cut-offs, so that you can turn off the water to the sink or commode without losing water to the entire bathroom.

When you install the commode and tank, you will use the same basic connecting principles. However, for the commode you must install an O-ring over the septic connection in the floor, and then set the commode into position and push down upon it, applying steady but not great pressure until the commode pushes the O-ring into a somewhat flattened condition, at which time the water seal from the toilet to the septic connection is made. There are screws on the sides of the toilet that will be tightened until the entire assembly is held tightly secure.

If the weather is not sufficiently warm, you may need to heat the bathroom or warm the O-ring so that the gel-like substance will be malleable enough to shape itself under pressure to the floor, the drain, and the commode.

You may need to buy a small roll or more of Teflon tape with which to wrap the threaded ends of fittings in order to prevent leaks. Water under pressure can find its way through the tiniest holes imaginable. You will need to correct all leaks at this stage of construction. When the wall coverings are installed and you find that there is a leak, you will need to take down sections of sheet rock, ceiling tile, or wall covering in order to locate and repair the leak.

It is far better to turn on the water and test for leaks long before you do the finish work inside the house. Turn the water off, then on, several times. Flush the commode and watch it refill. Check for any leaks or any other problems that may surface.

Shower stalls and bathtubs must also be connected. Shower supply lines enter about 80 inches high from inside the wall. The lines are in place but have not been connected. As you slide the shower unit into place, there is an opening for the shower head connection. Make certain that the connection is lined up with the hole, and when the shower unit is in place, lay a level on the bottom of the stall and make certain that your unit is slightly off-level enough so that water will flow toward the drain.

The drain line can usually be easily reached from under the bathroom and between joists. While you are down there, use a level again to make sure that your septic lines also have sufficient drop so that water will flow readily toward the septic tank.

Go through the house and shake receptacles and switches to be sure that none have come loose or have any play. You should not be able to move the switches at all, and the receptacles should not move more than a fraction of an inch.

As with all phases of your building, check with building-code inspectors to be certain that your wiring and all plumbing supplies are in conformity with the code. Call the building inspector if you have questions.

You are now ready for the finishing touches. One of these is to connect the ice maker, if you have one. This is one of the simplest of tasks. The newer models have a screw-in connection that connects itself by allowing you to simply tighten a fitting which in turn causes a penetration of the water line and permits a supply of fresh water to the ice maker.

Another finishing touch is that of connecting the dishwasher and washing machine. These two appliances must funnel their water discharge into pipes which flow into the main septic line. At the end of the septic line inside the

house, make certain that the clean-out plug is tight and seated properly.

Finally, turn to the outside faucets. Installing a faucet is astonishingly easy. In some instances you need merely screw on the faucet. In other cases, you may need to use Teflon tape or employ glue and a torch to get the proper seal.

If you wish to run a water supply to a vegetable garden or flower garden, tap into an existing line with a T-connection. If the line is plastic, cut the line with a sharp knife or hacksaw and then use sandpaper and a pocket-knife to clean off the shreds and tatters remaining after the cutting.

Also sandpaper the ends of each pipe back for a full inch. You can buy a fitting that has three nipples — the triple-nipple fitting mentioned earlier — and you can insert two ends into the ends of the cut line. Use glue and clamps for a secure bond.

For only a few cents, you can buy a metal clamp that fits around the pipe with the fitting inside. Position the clamp and then tighten the screw as far as you can take it without stripping the threads or breaking the clamp strap.

Install the new line over the third end of the fitting and take it as far as you wish into the garden. If you decide to add faucets along the way, cut the line as before and use the triple-nipple again. Then add a short length of pipe (about three to four feet long) and allow this to jut into the air. Install the faucet on the open end of the line. You can drive a stake into the ground and attach the line and faucet to the stake if you wish.

By doing this, you can have a series of faucets along the length of the new line. We installed more than 2,000 feet of water line to various points on our property, and rather than buy a long series of hoses to drag across the vegetables and berries, we simply set up the series of faucets. One short hose then served multiple purposes.

You are now ready to move on to other projects. When the inspector authorizes the power company to initiate service, you can check all of the circuits for proper performance. If you have problems, turn off the main power supply and correct them.

Chapter Twenty Four:
Installing Flooring

For a log house the flooring of choice is very likely to be knotty-pine tongue-and-groove lumber. If you are lucky and can stumble over or locate a good buy for the lumber, it is easy to install, is not incredibly expensive, and looks great for a long, long time. It is also easy to maintain.

If you want to save money, cut your own flooring and install it. This is harder work and the time required is longer, but you can do it and save hundreds of dollars.

Then, if you wish, you also have a choice of tiles and ceramic floors in a series of designs which are attractive and range in cost from inexpensive to very costly. You may need to shop around to find the best deals for these items.

The traditional word of caution follows: when you buy tongue-and-groove flooring, make certain that the dealer has enough of the lumber to floor all of the house that you intend to floor with it. If you can possibly afford it, buy the lumber all at one time and store it until it is needed. When you buy tiles or other man-made flooring, make the same inquiries. Ask also whether you will be able to find the same style and pattern in later months and years when the original flooring starts to fade in the most-used areas. If you cannot, you will be forced to remove the good flooring and replace it, along with the worn parts.

Start with the idea of putting down vinyl tiles or other ceramic flooring. There are two basic approaches: either the tiles have their own adhesive on the backs and all you need to do is remove a thin sheet of paper before you lay the tiles, or you need to buy your own adhesive and apply it underneath the tiles before placing them.

To install tiles, clean the subflooring carefully. Leave no grit or grease or other foreign matter on the surfaces. Buy a bag of filler (to be mixed with water to form a paste) and fill all of the cracks. Let the filler dry, and sand the areas to get a smooth surface throughout the room.

If you do not fill the cracks, the tiles will sink and crack at even the smallest fissures. Don't try to slip past this fairly minor chore, or you will regret it.

There are many ways of installing tiles, and everyone has his own favorite method. Some people like to start against a wall and work their way along the wall all the way to the opposite wall. They then move over the width of a tile and repeat the process. My personal favorite way is to start in the exact center of the room and work my way over to one wall, then work to the other wall. I have reasons for this method.

First, if you start at one wall, and if it turns out that the wall does not have square corners, by the time you get to the other wall you may have a discrepancy of two to four inches, possibly even more. There is no way to correct this problem other than taking up the tiles and starting all over.

If you choose to start in the center, measure carefully at both ends of the room and in the center to be certain that you have located the exact center. Then mark the locations along each wall and snap a chalk line along the long direction of the room.

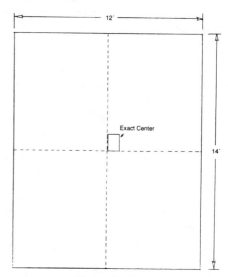

Figure 24-1
Chalking off the exact center and starting point for tiles.

Measure along the short direction and again mark the exact center of the room. Chalk a line in that direction as well. Where the two chalk lines cross marks the perfect center of the room, and this is where you begin. See Figure 24-1.

Tile one quadrant of the room at a time. Assume that the room runs east to west, long-wise. Begin, arbitrarily, at the southeast quadrant. Lay the first tile so that the edges of the tile barely touch the two lines where the chalk lines cross. Position the tile precisely and then install it permanently.

Next, lay the next tile along the south-pointing line. You can follow that line all the way to the wall if you wish, or you can follow the east-pointing line all the way to the wall. Keep on laying tiles along each line to the wall. Manufacturers sometimes suggest that you leave a tiny space between tiles, about the thickness of a dime. The space allows for expansion and contraction of the tiles when weather conditions change. Follow the manufacturer's guidelines and suggestions.

When the first quadrant is completed, lay tiles to cover the next quadrant. Do all four quadrants in succession. Then, when you reach the walls, if there is a discrepancy, you can trim the tiles to fit, and even if you do not get an exact fit, your molding will cover the flaws later. You can do a very reputable job, without any previous experience, of laying tile for your floors.

If you buy the huge sheets of linoleum, empty the entire room of everything that is movable. Leave only a fully empty floor. Then lay the roll against one wall and unroll the linoleum all the way to the other wall. Generally, you do not need any type of adhesive to hold the floor covering in place. The ends may tend to curl upward until the covering becomes more flexible and lies flat of its own initiative.

The major precaution here is to unroll the floor covering when the temperatures are in the sixties or higher. Linoleum which is very cold is also very stiff and may break or crack if you force it to unroll before it reaches room temperature. Linoleum or sheet vinyl should be stored at a temperature of 60° or higher for at least 24 hours prior to its placement upon the floor. Refer to the manufacturer's suggestions and specifications.

Now consider tongue-and-groove floor covering. The knotty-pine covering can be used in every room in the house, including hallways and bathrooms. When you buy the knotty-pine boards, do not buy anything under a five-inch width.

When you pick up the lumber, add another chore to your work list and help load the lumber yourself. In fact, insist on doing all of the loading if the dealer will permit it. Then, when you see a board with a crushed tongue or groove, set it aside as not usable in your house. Or, if you decide to take the damaged lumber (which can be used in several ways, to be described later), make the dealer an offer to buy it at a much-reduced price.

If possible, buy lumber long enough to reach from one end of your room to the other. If you have smaller rooms, such as 12´ by 12´ bedrooms, buy all 12-foot pieces if possible. If not, buy 12-foot pieces and six-foot pieces so that you will not have to do any sawing at all.

In our particular case, our living room is almost 40 feet long, and it is impossible to find lumber of that length. But if you have a room that is, for instance, 36 feet long, buy all 12-foot sections of lumber. If the room is 30 feet long, buy twelve-foot and six-foot sections of lumber. If it is an odd length, buy the dimensions that will work best for you so that you will have less waste and less cutting. Any time you cut a board, you will need to take the time to measure the space and the length of the board, and then you will need to mark and cut. Each time you cut you risk ruining a length of expensive wood.

Always remember the old carpenter's maxim: Measure twice and cut once.

When you have the lumber on hand, stack it in a room where it will stay dry and where it is less likely to be damaged. Do not stack it in a haphazard manner. The stress and strain will cause the boards to warp or break. And keep the lumber as secure as possible. Thieves or vandals would not hesitate to haul off or destroy the lumber.

When you are ready to install the flooring, buy a supply of cut nails and be sure you have a punch ready for use. Begin with the first board pushed flush against the wall and with the groove against the wall and the tongue facing outward toward the room. Be sure that the first board is straight and true and that the tongue and groove are not damaged.

There is a reason for this: You cannot nail through the tongue edge of the board.

When you start to nail, make certain that you have a good, easy fit. If the wall is crooked and the board refuses to conform to the wall line, do not force it. If you decide to use pressure to make the board fit against the wall, the board will be forced out of alignment and the next board will not fit against it. Then, if you force the second board, the third will not fit. So you will need to maintain the time-consuming and energy-consuming efforts to make each board fit.

Instead, get the best fit you can (once you have determined that the board and not the wall is crooked) and push the board up against the wall as snugly as you can without force. Start one of the cut nails about a foot from either end. Do not nail closer than a foot to the end. If you are too close, the cut nails might split the board.

To drive a cut nail, turn the nail so that the flat side is facing you and position the point in the angle formed by the tongue and the remainder of the board. Hold the nail at an angle to the flat surface of the board. If straight up is 12 o'clock, let the nail head (if you are starting at the north wall and working your way to the south wall) point at two o'clock.

Notice that the cut nails do not have a sharp point. Earlier you were told that a pointed nail is more likely to split a board than is a nail with a blunted point. The cut nail is evidence of that fact of carpentry.

Drive the nail until the head is level with an imaginary line running from the lip of the board to the end of the tongue. Do not try to seat the nail completely. By doing so you will damage the tongue and make it virtually impossible for the next groove to fit over the tongue.

Instead, hold the punch by the pointed end and lay the punch flat against the head of the nail. You will see a flat surface of the punch, and it is this surface that needs to be against the nail.

Now hit the punch, and the punch in turn will drive the nail until it is seated properly. If you need to do so, you can hold the punch by the shank near the top and direct the point of the punch against the head of the nail. Use a hammer to hit the top of the punch to seat the nail fully.

Drive a cut nail every two feet along the entire length of the board. Do not make the angle so acute that the pointed end of the nail will not dig deeply into the subflooring.

If the first board does not reach the entire length of the room, select another board and lay it so that one end is against the other end of the wall and the length of the board rests against the side of the first board. Use a straight edge to mark a line from the end of the installed board and across the new board.

Cut along the line just marked and then fit the board into the space at the end of the first board. Here is your cautionary note: Do not try for a perfect fit!

This may sound like foolish advice, but take it. If you try for a perfect fit, you may cut the board too long by a tiny fraction of an inch. Then, when you try to take off

another tiny fraction, you will perhaps make a bad cut and the result is either a bad fit or a board which is too short to use.

When you allow a tiny space between board ends (as opposed to trying for the flawless fit) the spaces are not noticeable.

Remember that you have molding to add to the flooring, and this molding will cover any poor fits up to half an inch or worse. So try for a comfortable, rather than perfect, fit.

When you start the next row or course of boards, position the long board so that it laps the juncture of the first two boards. Do not let any two boards in succession end at the same juncture.

As you nail succeeding boards, you will occasionally encounter a board that is slightly bowed. As a rule, gentle pressure will bring the board into conformity with the others. If a board is badly bowed and you cannot urge it into position, set the board aside and use it later when you can cut it into short lengths for use in filling out a course.

If you must use the warped board, there are a couple of ways you can make the fit a good one. Assume that the two ends of the board make good contact with the installed board but the center part of the board bows away by as much as two to four inches. To correct the problem, nail a 2″ x 4″ length (two feet long) to the subflooring two inches from the outer edge of the bowed board.

Now find a six-inch length of 2″ x 4″ and set it on edge between the bowed board and the 2″ x 4″ you've nailed to the subflooring. Wedge a crowbar point between the two sections of 2″ x 4″. Then pry outward, away from the installed board.

The pressure of the crowbar will cause the 2″ x 4″s to separate, and because one is nailed to the floor, there is only one way that the pressure can be directed. The loose 2″ x 4″ will force the bowed board into conformity with the installed one.

If you have a helper, he can nail the bowed board in place. If you are working alone, start the cut nails before you apply the pressure on the 2″ x 4″s. When the pressure has forced the board into place, hold the pressure on the crowbar with one hand while you drive the nails in far enough to hold the board in place with the other.

You can use this same principle if the bow is in the opposite direction and the ends need to be forced into alignment. You will need to move your pressure point from one end to the other and do the correcting work in two steps rather than one.

When you have worked your way across the entire floor, you might have room for a complete board to make the final fit at the opposite wall, but the odds are great that only a partial board can be used. You may have to rip part of the board away in order to get it into position.

If the board is only *slightly* too wide, you can trim off the tongue, and the loss of the quarter-inch width will allow the board to fit into place. If the board is still slightly too wide, you can set the groove into position and let the back side of the board tilt slightly against the wall. Then set a 2″ x 4″ on edge atop the tilted board and with a hammer drive the board into place.

Do not strike the wood with a hammer. You will badly damage it. Always place a section of wood over the board and hit the wood with a hammer, but do not hit the board itself.

The only time that you will have to strike the floor itself is when the boards become damp and bow slightly upward. Because the floor is already installed, you can't toe-nail or angle-nail. In this case, which is rare, use a small finish nail to drive through the boards and force them back into position. See Figure 24-2.

If the nails will not force the boards back into position, one final resort is to use a circular saw and run the blade along the crack. Be sure that you do not hit nails. If the bowed boards are really bad, you can see and remove the nails before you make the cut.

Notice in Figure 24-3 that the floors and the ceilings match perfectly. Notice too that the walls were allowed to darken in a natural manner. If you want your walls lighter, a 1:1 mixture of commercial bleach and water will lighten them. But be very careful when working with bleach, and do not mix products as such bleach and ammonia.

Figure 24-3
Blending of walls, ceiling, floors, and girders.

If you choose to cut your own flooring, remember that if you want to cut flooring extra-thick, you will not need the subflooring and you can save a considerable amount of money. If you have serious doubts about cutting your own thick flooring, keep in mind that you can cut a board or timber that is three inches thick with the same effort it takes to cut one a half-inch thick.

You can cut the boards with straight edges and fit them side-by-side across the joists and across the floor, or you can cut a type of ship-lap edge. To cut the lap edge, stand the first board on edge and determine which is the bottom and which is the top of the board. Chalk a line down the center of the edge and cut a groove an inch deep. When you install the board, let the lip be positioned at the bottom. When you cut the next board, this time the lip will be at the top (to fit into the allocated space) on one side and on the bottom on the other side (to provide room for the next board).

Follow this pattern all the way across the floor. If you cut a board but then find that it is too thick to use, set the

Figure 24-2
Using finish nails to remove a slight warp or bow.

board aside and use it elsewhere. If you must use the board, stand it on edge and on saw blocks and then use the chain saw to slice off a small part of the board's thickness.

You can also lay the board in place, reach under it and mark along both sides of the joists, cut a small groove on each line, and then use a chisel to chip out the wood. The best solution, however, is to install the boards, and then rent a powerful sander. Within a couple of hours you can sand the entire room, and perhaps other rooms as well. The result is a good finished floor that is smooth and very attractive.

Your flooring work is now complete, and you can move on to other facets of your work.

Closely related to flooring work is ceiling installation. The only real difference, in terms of basic work practices, is that in one area you work underfoot, and in the other you work overhead. The principles are virtually the same.

Begin with a basic suggestion: Determine what lengths of boards you can use without cutting. If the room is, for example, 18 feet long, you might wish to buy a number of ten-foot boards and eight-foot boards, usually an equal number of both. Now you can nail up a ten-foot board and then finish the course or row with an eight-foot board. On the next course you can start with an eight-foot board and finish with a ten-foot board.

By doing so, you will not need to stop to measure, cut, and perhaps re-cut. You will save time, energy, and lumber. You will have little, if any, waste. Keep in mind that tongue-and-groove lumber is expensive, and if you must cut one or two feet of waste off each board, soon you have soon discarded a considerable amount of money.

If the room is 20 feet long, buy equal numbers of 12-foot boards and eight-foot boards. Again, you save time and money.

It is a good practice to begin ceiling installation (if you are using tongue-and-groove lumber) with the board placed so that the groove is toward the wall and the tongue extends into the room area. The purpose for this is twofold: first, you must have the tongue exposed so that you can nail the board in place; second, you will be able to exert a slight force to push the groove side and seat the next board properly without damaging the board.

If you are using four-inch boards, the actual width of the board is three and one-half inches. Measure out from the wall at each end of the room and mark the spot where the outside edge of the board will rest when it is installed. Chalk a line along the entire length of the room. Then hold the board up so that the groove is against the wall,

and make certain that the outside edge aligns with the chalk line. If there is a slight discrepancy (of one-fourth inch or so) you can push the board into alignment with little difficulty. If the problem is greater than one-fourth inch, you need to check the board to make certain that it is straight.

Smaller-dimension lumber will often tend to curve or bow, but it is usually easy to install the boards, if you follow the suggestions offered in this chapter. Begin by holding a chalk line or straight edge from the edge of one end of the board, and then stretching the line to the opposite edge. If there is a space of more than half an inch or so, set the board aside for later use. You may need to use it for shorter spans where the curve will not be so troublesome.

To nail the board into place, use flat or cut nails and place the end of the nail in the V formed by the tongue cut. The flat side of the nail should be parallel with the length of the board. The nail should be located so that it will enter a joist when it passes through the board. Hold the nail at about a forty-five-degree angle and drive it in until the head is almost flush with the wood surface. Then use a punch to seat the nail the rest of the way. Do not hammer against the wood and damage the surface.

You may choose to install traditional boards rather than tongue-and-groove lumber. These boards are easier to install, but the finished look is not quite as neat and professional-looking as the tongue-and-groove look is. If you wish to cut your own boards from pine or poplar logs, you can create a professional and trim look by using a ship-lap cut. This type of board will fit together neatly, and it is easy to cut.

The only minor problem with ship-lap boards is that you will have exposed nail heads. You can use finish nails, but the heads of these nails are so small that the boards may work over the heads in time, and become loose and unsightly.

If you have a cathedral ceiling, you will start at the top of a wall and install the boards along the ceiling slant. Work your way to a point near the peak. Do not try to install boards all the way to the peak. You will need to leave room for collar braces, if these have not been installed already.

Because of the collar braces, you will have a flat or horizontal area at the very peak. The point where the angle or slant and the horizontal section meet is the only difficult spot to handle. When the final slant board is in place, you will need to trim off the back side of the first horizontal board. Trim on the groove side so that when the board is set into position the bottom side of the groove will fit exactly over the tongue, and the trimmed back side will not cause the board to buckle or fit in an awkward manner.

Follow the same procedures for the ceiling boards as you did for the wallboards. When you come to the light fixtures, use the same methods you used to work around receptacles and switches on the walls. When the ceiling is installed, you can cover it with a clear sealer in order to keep the wood from darkening with age.

Chapter Twenty Five:
Cutting Molding

At this time you are ready to take on one of the most challenging elements of chain sawing: cutting molding. However, like many of the other activities, once you get into the job you will find that it is not nearly as difficult as you had feared.

You will start the task by cutting lumber to the dimensions you will need for the molding. This means cutting 2″ x 2″ units, or 3″ x 3″, 2″ x 3″, or whatever you decide will work best for you. Start by selecting some good stock or wood from the scraps you have been accumulating for the past days or weeks. You will need floor molding and ceiling molding that is long enough to cover the entire wall. If you choose to piece the units, there is no real reason you should not do so. If you bought the stock from your lumber dealer, you'll need to piece the molding.

Start by deciding on the size of molding you want to use. Hint: Most people tend to choose molding that is too small for the job. With massive logs (or even modest-sized logs), the decor calls for wide and thick molding. Molding that is too small looks highly fragile and out of place.

My suggestion is that you cut 3″ x 3″ units as long as the room, if you have the stock on hand. Good woods for this work include pine, poplar, fir, maple, and even cedar, if the coloring will work with the other logs. A 3″ x 4″ section of wood, when cut diagonally, will result in a wide surface of approximately 4.25 inches (4.2426″).

Here's how to do it the easiest and best way. Start by picking out of the scrap pile two 6″ x 6″ (or 5″ x 5″ or 4″ x 4″) blocks. Even 2″ x 4″ blocks will work. These need to be no more than six inches long, although it does not matter if they are shorter. They can be as short as four inches, if you have nothing better. Select the straightest side of the scrap lengths and mark off and cut out a V that is as close as you can get it to a right angle. I suggest that the cut-out be at least two inches at the outside surface of the wood. You can do this on both short

lengths of wood, but one cut-out will also work effectively.

When this is done, stand the section on end and drill a hole one-quarter inch in width down through the top of the section. Put the hole in the center of the block. Now find a saw log three or four feet long and place it in a good location. Set another log of the same dimension or close to it about ten feet away. Saw two more of the short blocks with the cut-outs in them.

Drive fluted spikes down through the holes until the end of the spike is even with the bottom edge. Now set the block atop the surface of the first saw log and drive the spike into the log. You will need at least three inches of spike to penetrate the log.

At this point set the 3″ x 3″ length adjacent to the first block with the cut-out. Position the 3″ x 4″ so that it stands on one corner and the right angles extend on each side. Slip the right angle into the cut-out and then drive the other spike into the log so that the second cut-out aligns with the other side of the 3″ x 3″ unit. The entire assembly works best if the corner of the 3″ x 3″ can rest on the top of the log. See Figure 25-1.

Do the same at the other end. Now the 3″ x 3″ is held in a tight-fitting V on each side of it and at both ends. To saw the molding, start at one end and cut carefully along the top edge. Make a groove an inch or so deep. Then return to the starting point and saw all the way through the 4.25″ thickness. Pause in the sawing long enough to peer over the edge to ensure that the saw is cutting perfectly vertically through the 3″ x 3″.

Now, maintaining the same angle of the saw, cut along the entire length of the 3″ x 3″. When you are finished, you will have two pieces of molding which measure three inches on two sides and 4.25 inches on the wide side. When you install the molding, insert the V-sides so that they are flush with the wall and ceiling. You will then have a superb molding strip ready to nail into place.

As always, it may seem that this is a lot of work for one piece of molding (actually, two pieces), but remember that when you are ready to cut the next pieces, all you need do is feed the 3″ x 3″ into the cut-outs, and you are ready to saw again.

You can follow this procedure for cutting floor molding as well as for ceiling molding. In fact, you can cut virtually any type of molding you need by using the V-notches to hold the lumber for you.

You are not limited to 3″ x 3″ molding. You can cut any size you want. All you need is a squared length of molding stock and notches to hold it. Your cuts will be much better if they are cut with a ripping chain rather than a cross-cut chain.

To install the molding, simply hold it in place and drive finish nails through the wood and into the ceiling or wall or floor, depending upon where the molding is to be installed. Hold a nail in place one inch from the bottom edge of the molding and position the nail so that it is perfectly horizontal. Sink it. Then drive a series of others across the entire length of the molding, with the nails spaced every two feet.

Do the same at the top edge (again, this is for ceiling molding) and hold the nail perfectly vertical. Space as before.

If you want molding that is a different size, cut the stock into smaller or larger squares. If you don't want a triangle that is perfect, use stock that is 2″ by 4″ or 2″ by 3″. Be forewarned, however, that it is much more difficult to cut anything that isn't a square.

If you want very small molding, you are better off to cut the material with a circular saw rather than with a chain saw. If you happen to have access to a table saw, you can cut smaller widths very rapidly and neatly with the table saw.

For floor molding, you might wish to cut only a 1″ x 4″ or 1″ x 5″ board to use. If you want larger dimensions, expand to 1.5″ by 4.5″ or similar versions. Cut these just as you would cut any other boards, and install them by standing the boards on edge and nailing them to the bottom logs.

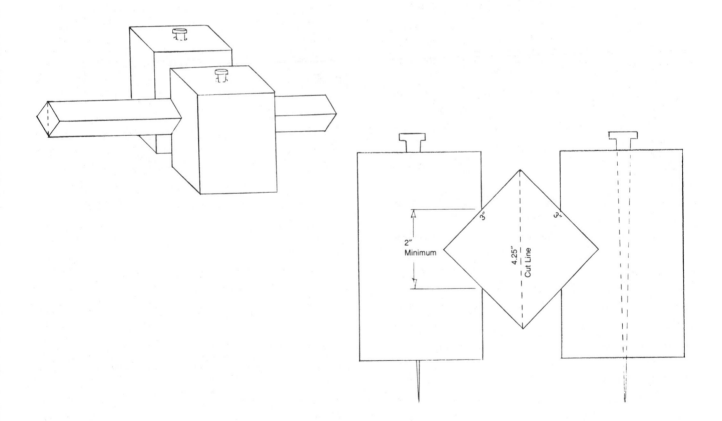

Figure 25-1
3″ x 3″ molding held by cutouts in blocks.

Now comes the hardest part of installing any trim you cut or buy: fitting corners. The only satisfactory ways to handle the problem are, first, to cut 45-degree angles at the ends of the corner trim pieces. The first molding end will be slanted back toward you, with the long end reaching into the corner. The piece that fits against it will be slanted in the opposite direction, with the long end near you and the short end fitting against the long end in the corner.

You must realize that you are shortening the usable length of the molding by two inches on each length, so if you have a 12-foot room, cut the molding slightly longer in order to have adequate length. This factor is the greatest single argument for piecing the molding. You can cut and fit the first piece, and then, using stock that is too long, cut and fit the other corner. Then, with the molding in position in the corner, lay the second length side by side with the installed piece, and mark where the second length should be cut.

One workable idea is to use a scrap length on which to make the final corner cuts, and then use that length as a pattern to mark the actual molding which you will install. If you make a crucial mistake on the test length, no harm is done.

The second method of getting an acceptable corner fit is to hold one section in place, and then push the end of the other piece forward so that it butts into the first piece. Then, while holding the pieces in place (you may have to use a nail driven only partially), mark along the end of the second piece onto the end of the first piece. Then cut the first piece.

In case you are confused, place Unit A into the corner but do not nail it in permanently. Use a couple of small finish nails to hold the unit where it will be installed.

Now raise Unit B and push it against the end of Unit A. Hold the two units in place and use a pencil to mark along the end of Unit B, but the mark must be made on Unit A. Then cut Unit A along the mark. When you are ready to install the molding, Unit B will be nailed in place first. Then Unit A, which has been cut diagonally along the mark you made, will fit neatly against Unit B.

When you are installing trim work on doors, you will want to cut some door-stop molding. This will probably be a thin strip of wood (about one-half inch in thickness) that will be pushed into the door framing to cover any crack left when the door was installed. The molding might be 1.5 inches with a square edge where the molding fits against the framing or along the framing. The other edge can be beveled to provide a neater appearance.

It is somewhat difficult to bevel-cut with a chain saw (but it can be done), so you may need to make the bevel cut with a circular saw or table saw. If you are a purist and wish to make the bevel cut with the chain saw, you need to devise a method by which you can keep the molding strip standing erect.

You can do this by cutting a groove into the saw logs. The groove should be as wide as the molding is thick, and at least an inch deep. Set the molding upright in the groove. If the groove is too loose, push some wood chips in beside the molding to hold it in an erect and steady position.

Now the problem is that the molding will tend to slide as the saw pulls on it. The solution to this problem is to make the second or back groove cut so that it doesn't reach all the way across the top of the log. Instead, leave a sort of back wall to the groove. Use a chisel, if necessary, to cut the small wall vertically true. See Figure 25-2.

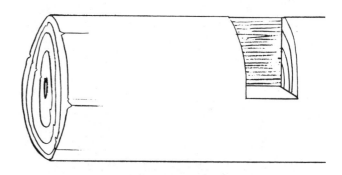

Figure 25-2
Groove in log to keep molding from sliding.

Let the molding butt against the wall, and when the action of the chain pulls on the molding, it will not slide.

Now it is time to make the cut. You must stand to the side of the erect molding and angle the chain-saw bar appropriately. If, for example, you want an average slant to the edge, hold the chain saw about waist-high and point the bar at a location that would be comparable to four o'clock. For a more severe cut, point the bar at five o'clock.

As you cut, you must watch the top edge of the molding very carefully to see that the chain isn't digging too deeply into it and damaging the molding. Let the cut start at the corner of the inside top edge of the molding. This will be the high point of the cut. The low point will be on the side of the molding opposite you. Make the cut as even and smooth as you can.

You can chalk a line on the opposite side of the molding and let it represent the bottom or low point of the cut. The problem here is that you may have difficulty in seeing the line from the angle from which you are cutting. By this time, though, your eye has become accustomed to observing the cut line, and you should have no real difficulty in cutting usable molding angles.

Use the same principles and techniques for cutting all other types of molding. Let your own imagination and creativity take over the planning processes. Be bold and experimental. After all, if you try something which doesn't work, the experiment has cost you merely a few cents in gasoline and oil, a few minutes of labor, and a scrap of wood that wouldn't have been worth much more than firewood.

As an example of what you can do, buy a few feet of half-inch or larger rope. Push the rope into joints formed by two walls or by wall and ceiling. Use small colored nails to tack the rope into place. You may be pleasantly surprised to discover how attractive a rope molding can be.

All that you really need to keep in mind, other than safety, is that wood is rich, heavy, strong, ponderous, masculine, and often massive; yet it can be as feminine as virtually any other building material. It is so flexible and universal that it can be used to create almost any atmosphere you wish.

When moldings are cut, it is time to learn to make windows with a chain saw. Chapter 26 details how to do it.

Chapter Twenty Six:
Making Rustic Windows

You can visit the supply house and price windows and come away with a renewed determination that you will find a way to make your own rustic windows and save literally thousands of dollars. It is not at all unusual to learn that a double window will cost you far in excess of $300, and single windows are incredibly expensive. These features are, in fact, among the most significant expenses when building a house.

But nearly everything that goes into a house is staggeringly expensive in these times. So every penny that you save is indeed a penny — or many dollars — saved in the long run.

There are some parts of windows that you cannot cut with a chain saw, but you can saw out the most expensive parts. Start by going to your rough window openings and measuring the width and height of the opening. Then set about making your windows.

As you built the walls of your house, you framed window openings as you stacked logs. Figure 26-1 shows the basic rough window opening in a log wall.

Do not try to make the windows fit exactly. You allowed for some play or space between window frames and rough window openings.

Start by planning and then constructing a single window. This window can be used in a kitchen, above the sink, in a bathroom, or any other place where a full-size window is not needed. Or, and this is the logic behind the plan, you can also use the window as half of a large window.

Assume that you are going to make a window that is 36 inches wide and 24 inches high. The dimensions given here are for the inside of the window; that is, the area covered by the panes and by the mullions and horizontal bar. This will be a six-pane window, with three 12-inch panes across the top and three more across the bottom.

Pause long enough to learn the names of the window parts.

Imagine a window, or look at one. The long piece going down each side of the single window is called the upper stile in the top window and the lower stile in the bottom window. The piece across the top is logically called the top rail and the piece across the bottom is the bottom rail. In the center of each single window there is a length of wood running horizontally across the window and halfway between the top rail and the bottom of that single section of window. This is called the horizontal bar.

In that same single window there are short strips of wood that run vertically and separate the panes of glass. These are called the mullions. Where there are two windows, the two overlap in the center of the window opening. These two overlapping rails are called the upper meeting rail and the lower meeting rail. See Figure 26-2.

To make a single window, start by cutting the stiles. These can be 2″ x 2″ pieces or 2″ x 3″. Do not make

Figure 26-1
Rough window opening for log wall.

them much larger than these dimensions or they will be too heavy for convenient use.

Cut the stiles just as you would cut any other dimension lumber in the house. If they are to be two feet long, make them not 24 inches but 30 inches, for the sake of the probability of human error. You can later trim off any excess you do not want or need.

Now cut the upper and lower rails. These should be the same dimensions as the stiles. Again, if they are to be 36 inches long, make them 40, to allow for error.

Now assemble the four pieces. The easiest way is to lay one of the rails on a work surface and place one of the stiles at a right angle and at the end of the rail. Then drill a hole down through the top of the rail and into the stile. The hole should be about 1/8". Use a quarter-inch drill to bore a very shallow hole for countersinking a screw later. This hole should be no more than 1/8 inch deep.

Apply a liberal amount of wood glue to both surfaces that will be joined. Sink a long screw through the top piece and into the end of the bottom piece. Do the same at the other top corner, after first cutting off the rail to the proper length, if you are sure that there are no problems.

Now measure down from the bottom edge of the rail to a point 24 inches below. Be sure to allow the full 24 inches and perhaps one-eighth inch extra.

Cut off the extra inches once you are certain that you have all measurements correct. Then attach the lower or bottom rail just as you did the top rail. You now have a rectangle with four perfectly square corners and with inside dimensions of 36 inches across and 24 inches down.

The outside dimensions depend upon the width of your stiles and rails. If you used three-inch stiles and

rails, the outside dimensions will be 42″ by 30″. Be sure that this size will easily fit into the rough window openings.

Here is a second way to assemble the window frame. At the end of each stile and rail cut out a right angle, all of the same size. If the window stile is two inches thick, make the cut-out space one inch thick. If the width of the stiles and rails is three inches, make the cutout three inches long.

Now lap the stiles and rails into a perfect rectangle and fasten the four corners by using screws, nails, brackets, or glue, or a combination of glue and one other of these.

Now add the horizontal bar. If you are using 2″ x 3″ borders, make the horizontal bar two-by-two. Install the horizontal bar just as you did the other units by drilling a hole, applying glue, and then sinking a screw through the stile and into the end of the horizontal bar.

Now you are ready to install the mullions. These strips should be 1″ by 2″ stock, and they should be installed in exactly the same way as the horizontal bar was.

Now you are ready to install the pane stops. You can easily do this easily by cutting very thin and very neat strips of wood no more than one-fourth inch thick and one-half inch wide. Spread wood glue thinly over one surface of the stop and press it into position so that the outer edge aligns with the outer edge of the mullions and horizontal bar. You will need four of these strips for each pane, so when you are cutting, you might choose to cut long strips rather than cut them one at a time.

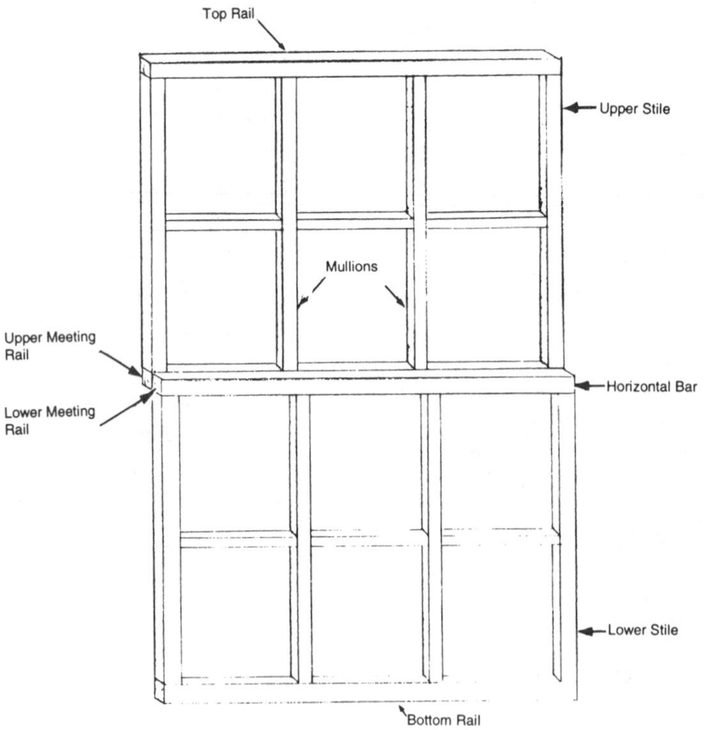

Figure 26-2
Basic parts of a window.

(labels in figure: Top Rail, Upper Stile, Mullions, Horizontal Bar, Upper Meeting Rail, Lower Meeting Rail, Lower Stile, Bottom Rail)

When all four strips are glued in place, you can install the panes. If you have panes, you can use a glass cutter and cut them to size, or, if you prefer, when you are constructing the window you can expand the size of the window, or make the stiles and rails more narrow, so that the panes fit without adjustments or cutting. See Figure 26-3 for an example of a finished window frame.

Figure 26-3
Completed window frame.

If you want to have double-hung windows in the rough window opening, you can make two of the individual window units. When you install or hang the windows, you must allow the upper meeting rail and lower meeting rail to overlap by the thickness of one of the rails. This overlap is to keep wind and rain and insects from finding access between the window units.

When double-hanging, you must off-set one of the windows so that the units have room to slide up and down alongside each other without hitting one another. You do this with a series of upper-stop and lower-stop pieces. These are simply strips of wood that are installed in front of and behind the two window units. One of these stops, the back one, is to keep the top sash from falling out into the yard. The front one is to keep the bottom sash from toppling into the room. A narrow strip (one-fourth inch) between the sashes keeps the sashes from bumping each other.

How to keep the windows up is the next matter of interest. In the old days counter-weight systems were used. In this system, weights were hung inside the wall adjacent to the windows, and when the windows were pulled up, the weights descended via a rope and pulley wheel. To get the window back down, you had to pull hard enough so that the force overpowered the weights and the force of gravity. When the windows were back in position, they remained there because there was no momentum to overcome.

In more recent days, builders have employed a system of springs built into the side of the stiles. This spring causes friction or pressure to be exerted sideways, and this pressure, like the friction which is generated by the hands of a rock climber, keeps the window in place.

You must be satisfied with a much simpler method. You can do it one of two ways. The first is the simple method of using a 1″ by 1″ stick kept inside the window, just behind the lower sash. When you raise the window sash, you stand the stick up under the side of the bottom rail and against the window trim.

The second method is to drill a series of small holes. The first hole extends through the lower meeting rail and halfway into the upper meeting rail. When the window is down, insert a nail hacksawed to length so that only the head of the nail is visible. The window cannot be opened by an intruder unless he or she breaks the window, reaches inside, and extracts the nail. Or unless he manages to insert the blade of a hacksaw between the upper meeting rail and lower meeting rail and then saws the nail into pieces. In either event you are likely to hear the noise if you are at home. If you aren't at home, it doesn't matter how much noise the intruder makes, so he can break a window.

Five or six inches from the top of the lower meeting rail, drill another hole. Then raise the window to the desired height and stick the drill bit into the existing hole. Drill a hole into the upper stile until the bit is halfway through the stile.

When you want to raise the window partially, you can do so and keep it in position by inserting the nail through the hole in the lower stile and part-way into the upper stile. The window may then be left open, for instance, five inches. This space is too small for an intruder to crawl through, and the nail is too high for him to reach through the window and pull out the nail.

Thus you can sleep and enjoy fresh air without the fear of an intruder's gaining entry via the window. You can also leave the window in this position during most rain showers and not have to worry about rain getting into the house, unless the wind is blowing briskly.

You can use the same principle and drill holes so that the upper window may be lowered five or six inches and then held in place by the inserted nail. This opening also provides greater security from burglars or intruders.

If you want to have only one window sash but would still like to be able to open the window, you can hang the window sash on hinges and open the window whenever it is convenient to do so. When you want to feel more secure, you can close the window and lock it with a latch or bolt. Either of these two simple devices is very reliable, and an intruder will again have to break the window in order to gain entry into your house.

If you prefer, you can hinge the window at the top and allow it to swing outward. A small metal rod or length of wood will hold the window out from the wall and permit fresh air but no rain or intruders to enter, unless the intruder breaks the wood or pries the metal rod loose.

The disadvantage to this type of window opening is that you cannot install traditional screens because the window would hit the screen as it swings out. You can, of course, build an offset screen, but this is considerable trouble and the appearance is not appealing to most people.

Another method used by some people is to swing the window open from the top. This method discourages intruders, but rain is funneled into the house. Again, screens are difficult, unless you install the screens inside the window, but this means that the screens must be hinged or easily removed if you wish to get to the window.

All things considered, the one-sash window system with the hinges located so that the window may be swung open to the inside of the room is the preferred approach. You can make the window small enough, if it is to be used in a kitchen or bathroom, so that it can be installed over a sink. The smallness of the sash also is a deterrent to intruders, who may find great difficulty in wriggling through such a small opening.

You can also make the window tall and narrow, or short and long. This design is also conducive to security.

If you wish to create a more Alpine look, you can take the basic window approach and divide it into four pane areas. Then, after the mullion and horizontal bar have been installed, you can add diagonal strips of wood that create a diamond inside the square. Run the strips of wood from the center of the window at the mullion down to the horizontal bar, then down in the opposite direction to the bottom rail, then up to the opposite horizontal bar, and up again to the starting point. Four strips of wood, which can be glued to the mullion, bottom rail, and stiles, can be cut and installed quickly and easily. The result is attractive and eye-catching.

Finally, if you want more security, you can install a system of bars between the screen and the sash. The problem with these bars is that you are locking yourself in while you are locking other people out. In the event of an emergency, you may be trapped inside the house.

There is, of course, the Williams security system which involves bars and also provides an easy escape in case of a fire or other emergency. This method, like almost all of the other devices described in this book, is an original idea that I conceived while building our own house.

Here's how to do it. When you leave your rough window openings, allow an extra five inches for the security system. Now cut a five-by-eight-inch piece that will fit into the top or bottom of the rough window opening. Lay the five-by-eight narrow edge up, and mark a line two inches from the left edge as you face it.

Saw along the line and cut down until you are five inches deep. Then lay the timber on its side and mark another line that crosses the timber just above where the five-inch cut was made.

Cut along this line until you intersect with the previous cut. You can now remove the three-by-five-inch block of wood and set it aside temporarily. Drill holes down into the top or wide side of the timber. Space the holes six inches apart, or whatever width you would like your bars to be spaced. The holes will be only two inches deep before the bit penetrates the area where you sawed the cut-out.

Use a level to get the exact placement, and drill three or four holes (for whatever number of bars you have) in either the top or bottom log in the rough window opening. Use the space where you did *not* install the timber. Drill the holes four or five inches deep.

Now insert the bars into the holes opposite the timber. Slide the bars up until the other end can be inserted into the holes in the timber. You will notice that the bars will then fall down into the space created by the cut-out, and that the bars can be removed easily.

If you can do it, so can an intruder. That is why you must replace the cut-out section. Once the bars are in place, push them up into the log until you slide the cut-out into position. Then let the bars again fall until they hit the cut-out. Now they cannot be removed.

But if you slide the cut-out from inside the timber, the bars can again fall deep enough into the cut-out space that they can be removed from the upper holes.

Why can't a burglar slide out the cut-out? When you have done the installation described above, drill three holes one-fourth-inch wide along the inside edge of the timber. Let the drill bit sink into the top edge of the timber, much the way that the nail in the window lock works. Cut off three spikes and drop them into the holes. Ream out the holes so that the spikes will sink fairly easily up to their heads.

If you need to exit by the window, simply lift out the spikes that give the appearance of having been driven into the wood. Then slide out the cut-out and remove the bars.

You can even, if you wish, drive the spikes into the wood half an inch or so. If an intruder tries, he cannot pull out the spikes. Neither can you, unless you leave a crowbar concealed inside a bookcase or other hidden area nearby.

The illusion of the secure bar system is effective enough that the intruder isn't at all likely to try to remove the spikes. Trust me. It works, unless the burglar has read this book. But even if he has, there are many variations on this type of security system, and you can modify it to suit your own needs. The burglar will never know, unless *you* write a book about how you built your house.

Next, drill quarter-inch holes into the front part of the timber. Drill a hole two inches from the outside edge and every foot or so. Now drop back and drill another series of holes which are aligned perfectly with the first holes.

Set the timber into the rough window opening and let the cut-out section face into the room. Sink spikes into the timber once it is positioned exactly in the rough opening. You can install it, as indicated earlier, in either the top or bottom of the rough window opening.

Chapter Twenty Seven:
Window Installation

Now that you have made windows, it's time to frame them, or, more properly, trim them. You have already left the rough window opening, and now it is time to install them.

This is not a particularly difficult task, but there are quite a few things which can go wrong — expensively so. Some of the larger windows, if you buy them, cost several hundred dollars, and if you should let one fall, you could easily ruin the entire assembly.

As with nearly everything connected with building, there are easy ways and hard ways to install windows, just as there are the accepted methods and the radical solutions to typical problems. When we built our house, there were three of us working, and because there were no other people around to help, I had to find ways to do nearly everything unassisted at times and with the help of my wife and son at times.

Here's how we installed our windows, and you can do the same.

When you have built your windows, you have only the sashes and little else. You now need to frame the windows before you can think about installing them.

This is little more than simply building a box around the window sashes. In this series of suggestions, I will use only the most common words so that there is little chance of a serious misunderstanding.

Start by cutting two boards one inch thick and eight inches wide. If your rough opening will handle thicker boards and if you can lift them, you can cut these boards two inches thick and eight inches wide. The height is that of your windows plus the thickness of two of the boards.

I am assuming that you have not done any of the framing work at this point. Lay the first board down, with the side up that you intend to be installed facing the window sashes. Decide where you want your windows to sit in relation to the thickness of the walls. Do you want them flush with the inside edges of the logs in the house? Do you want them recessed? If flush, choose one edge of the board that will be the inside edge of the framing. That

is, the edge that will be nearer you when you are inside the house.

Cut and nail in a 1″ by 2″ unit of lumber that you can nail down along the inside edge of the board you have just placed on the work surface. Use small finish nails to hold the strip in place. Now set the bottom sash in place and line up the inside edge with the strip you have just nailed in place. Allow one-eighth of an inch clearance so the window can move freely. Now nail a second strip behind the sash, so that the sash is positioned between the two strips.

Pause to consider several factors before you proceed too far and too fast. Before you proceed toward installation, you need to determine the exact size, and select the materials you want in your house, if you have not already done so.

Remember that you can buy windows in a wide range of styles and sizes. You can get them in all-wood, all-vinyl, a mixture of wood and vinyl, and other materials.

There are advantages and disadvantages to each type and/or style. Larger windows let in more light and also allow for more heat and cooling loss. Smaller windows admit less light, allow less loss, and are more of a deterrent against criminal entry. Smaller windows cost less but admit less fresh air, if you don't want to run the cooling system.

All-wood windows are not as bad for creating condensation and fogging, but are more subject to decay; on the other hand, they are usually less expensive to buy and less trouble to install.

You can buy clear glass, frosted glass, stained glass, and double-paned glass. The latter is very efficient for controlling heat and cooling loss.

Before you select windows, consult with a dealer to get a price list as well as a list of styles and variations. Ask him about the major advantages and problems experienced with the windows in question. He will likely be very open and honest with you, because he knows that he could lose you as a customer if he gives you bad advice. And after you have looked to your heart's content, go home and start to build your own windows, as described in the previous chapter.

At this point you cannot readily make any serious changes in window sizes except to down-size. You can do this without much problem, but the result is often less than satisfactory.

For now, complete the framing. You were in the process of nailing in strips to keep your sashes in position. Run these strips up both boards and across the top and bottom boards, which you will cut just as you cut the side pieces. With the sashes safely enclosed inside the framing, you are now ready to install. To do so you can follow the few suggestions listed below.

First, use some type of device that will guarantee you that all of your windows of the same size and on the same wall will be perfectly aligned. While discrepancies may not be apparent from inside the house, the problems are very visible from the street.

You can use a simple measuring tape. Measure from the top of the subflooring to the point where the top of the window will stop. Mark that point. Then, while you are working, you can make sure that the window top will conform to that point.

Mark all other windows on that wall in a similar manner. You can then know for certain that you have good alignment if all of the window tops conform to the marks.

You can also use a 2″ x 4″ to measure window height. Mark the timber for one window and compare all other windows to the mark, raising or lowering as required within the extra space afforded by the too-large rough opening.

Before you attempt to install a window, measure the window carefully and write down the height and width. Then measure the rough opening to be certain that the window will comfortably fit inside the space.

If you realize that you will have several inches of space left over when the window is installed, you can add extra boards on each side of the window. Each board will reduce the space by one and one-half inches to two inches.

If you have only a small amount of space between window frame and rough opening, a 1″ x 4″ board on each side or on one side only may fill the space. Remember to install the board on the same side of

each window, if you choose to use this approach, so that outside symmetry is retained.

Check the rough opening for plumb and level. If you need to do so, make minor adjustments by installing shims, wedges, or blocking to get the right reading. Once the frame is inside the rough opening, you can maneuver it to a limited extent only, but enough so that you can assure yourself that it is plumb and level.

Correct any problems with vertical and horizontal position. Use shims and wedges to raise one corner to the desired level.

When the rough opening is correct, nail a temporary 1″ x 4″ board across the outside of the window rough opening. You may need to tack a small block on each end of the 1″ x 4″ to be sure that the window assembly does not touch the board.

Lift the window assembly and set it into the opening. If you lose your grip, the window cannot fall to the outside because of the restraining board. Handle windows with great care and do not subject them to tension. If a window is installed under stress, you may crack a pane. Panes may, in fact, crack several days after installation, as stress places a greater and greater burden on the fragile glass.

If you bought windows with the outside casing already in place, you will need to install the window from the outside for greater ease in handling. In this case, the restraining board should be nailed across the window opening on the inside.

If you are working upstairs, you can turn the window assembly and push it through the rough opening, and then turn the assembly in mid-air and set it back into position. This is easy if you are using small windows, and much more difficult if you are using double-window assemblies.

With the window in the opening, check it on all sides for fit, and then use a level to check vertical and horizontal readings. Any discrepancies should be corrected at this time.

Make sure that the window assembly gives you a correct reading vertically and horizontally and from front to back. You may need to attach shims or blocking at several locations in order to get the exact reading you need.

When you have the correct position, drive one nail in each of the four sides. Do not sink the nails in all the way, but leave enough of the head sticking out that you can extract the nails if you need to do so.

With the assembly partially installed, unlock the sashes and slide the windows up and down or from side to side to see that the sashes move freely and easily. If a window sash moved without trouble on the floor but is now tight, your wedging or blocking is too tight and you need to remove it and re-install it to allow more freedom of movement.

If the entire window unit works as it should, drive the rest of the nails and install the window permanently. Move then to the next unit and repeat the process.

If you are installing windows above girders where there will be no permanent flooring, you may need to build a temporary floor or scaffolding. You can do this by laying three 2″ x 10″ boards from girder to girder and then laying panels of plywood across the boards.

Nail the boards to the girders. Then nail the plywood to the boards. You need to use nails that are strong enough and long enough to keep the plywood and boards from sliding.

Hoist the window assemblies to the temporary flooring and take measures to protect the windows from falling. You can again use the boards across the rough openings, unless you have to push the window assembly through the opening in order to turn it and pull it back into its correct position.

You can lower the top sash and run a heavy rope through the framing of the window before you start to seat the window. Tie the other end of the rope to a point inside the house and allow very little slack. You need just enough to allow you to turn the window outside.

If you lose your grip, the window will not fall all the way to the ground. Such a fall would destroy it completely and break not only panes but the framing assembly as well.

When you turn the window (with assembled casing) out the window opening, you will need to hang on to the window with great effort. Although the assembly does not weigh a great deal, the position is awkward and difficult.

You and your helpers (do not try this unassisted) can turn the window to its proper position and then pull it into the rough opening. Set the bottom of the assembly into the rough opening first. Then, with the top pulled nearly in place, untie and remove the rope.

Pull the window assembly into position and secure it with temporary nails until you are certain the fit is correct and that the sashes move as they should. Check vertical and horizontal readings again, and the readings from front to back. When you are satisfied, nail the assembly into place permanently.

You have two primary ways in which to install windows into concrete block walls. The first method is to use slotted blocks for all rough openings (which are not rough in the usual sense, but are an almost exact fit, so you need to know your window sizes when you build the wall for the basement or for the upper level, if you plan to have a block house). These blocks have slots that must be aligned up and down the sides of the rough opening.

The window assembly you buy will have a blade or edge that fits into the slots. You must lift the window above the opening and align the blade and slots and then slide the window down and into position.

The second way is to build the rough opening and then install lintels above the openings. When you are ready for the windows you can build in the framing. You can start by installing framing timbers at the top and bottom of the opening. Then measure the space, mark and cut the side boards, and install them.

The cement blocks present slight nailing difficulties. You can buy steel or masonry nails that will easily penetrate the blocks. The problem is that the heads of the nails have a strong tendency to break and fly off at great speed. These flying heads can cause serious and permanent injury to eyes, and you should wear protective glasses at all times when driving such nails.

The reason for starting with the top and bottom pieces of the window framing is so that the top piece, if the nails should loosen, cannot fall because of the support offered by the side timbers. You can also use screws and anchor bolts to install the framing timbers.

If you use screws, use flat-headed screws so that there won't be an irregular surface to the framing. Drive the screws into the wood until the heads are seated flat against the wood.

Chapter Twenty Eight: Making Doors

By making your own windows, you save an enormous amount of money. You can now save even more by making your own doors. Keep in mind as you consider door construction that you will need a front and back door, at the very least, and you will want one door each for bathrooms, bedrooms and perhaps other rooms.

We have 14 doors in our house, and if each door would have cost only $50 to purchase, we had a potential savings of $700 in doors alone. But how much does it cost to make your own doors, in terms of money and time?

You can make an exceptional door within two hours, perhaps much sooner, and for a total cost, including door knob and hinges, of about $5. At the price mentioned above (have you priced doors lately? This price stated here is a real bargain!) you could save $45 on each door. If the door requires two hours, you are then averaging $22.50 per hour for your work — in savings.

The easiest door to make is a simple Z-frame. This is the door you often see in many rustic buildings and in highly costly modern versions of log houses. The door consists of several boards laid side by side with a timber installed at the top, another at the bottom, and a diagonal timber connecting the top and bottom timbers.

When you construct the door, I suggest that you cut the lumber well in advance and let it air-dry for as long as possible before you start to work. You will need about six timbers that are 2″ x 6″ for the door itself, another long timber for the diagonal unit, and two shorter ones for the top and bottom pieces.

If you can find a damaged tree or one that needs to be cut for whatever reason, and if you can find such a tree that is at least 12 inches in diameter up to a height of seven feet, you can cut virtually all the wood you need from that one tree.

Cut the log to the correct height, which should be about 80 inches for the typical door. Then slab-cut the first side. Now measure the width of the flat surface. If the width will give you at least six good inches, you can cut 6″ x 6″ timbers from the tree section. If you can get eight-inch or even ten-inch timbers, so much the better, as long as you can cut the timbers straight and true.

When you decide upon the width of timbers you can cut from the tree, mark two chalk lines, one on each side of the good wood. Chalk the line as close to the outer edge as you can, without reaching over into the bark area. Slab-cut along the two marks. You are now left with a log that has three flat sides and one bark side. Lay the log flat on one of the cut sides. You can now begin to slice off the timbers for the door.

The door itself will be 30 inches wide, or 32 inches, if you prefer a wider door. When you cut the needed timbers, double-check them for trueness. Stand the timbers on edge and sight down the length of the board or timber. If there is a significant curve, you may wish to discard the piece or save it for later use.

Now lay the timber flat and hold a chalk line from the top corner to the bottom corner. If the line conforms to the edge of the board from top to bottom, the board is superb. If there is wood showing under the line, you need to chalk the board and trim off any excess wood. Do this on both sides of each board.

When all of your boards or timbers are true, you can assemble them. There are two basic ways. The first is to cut the cross pieces, which should be the exact width of the door. Be sure you have a perfectly square cut on both ends of every timber. Or you can install the timbers, chalk a line, and then cut all the timbers at one time, as long as all the timbers are at least as long as the height of the door.

Start by laying the top piece on a flat work surface. Then align one of the long timbers with the cross piece. Let the long timber reach all the way to the top of the cross piece. Be sure that the outside edge of the long timber is aligned with the edge of the cross piece. Now attach the two timbers either by using nails, screws, or bolts.

My personal preference is bolts, by far. If the wood is still somewhat green, nails will eventually work free. Screws may also work loose when the timbers dry. Bolts will hold despite any and every condition of the timbers, short of a catastrophe. About all that can go wrong is that the wood may shrink and the bolts will loosen slightly, but a wrench will take care of that problem if it should occur.

To install bolts, lay a tape measure across the top of the timber and mark for two bolts spaced at an equal distance from the edge and top of the timber. Drill holes the size of the bolts through both timbers. Use bolts no smaller than one-fourth inch. Use a washer and nut to tighten the bolt.

Before you bolt too many pieces in place, determine which side of the door is to be inside the room. If you plan to secure the room, you will want the bolt heads on the outside of the door. Otherwise, an intruder could use a wrench and gain access to the room without making a sound.

There is another method of strengthening a door. This is the installation of a threaded rod through the door timbers at three points from top to bottom. If you plan to do this, stand the first timber on edge and drill a hole all the way through the width of the timber. Then use a larger bit and drill a larger hole for countersinking a small washer and nut.

Now lay the timber flat and place the second timber beside it and even with it at top and bottom. Run the drill through the hole and into the second timber a half-inch or so. Do this at both top and bottom. Now stand the second timber on edge and drill the rest of the way through.

With each succeeding timber, run the drill through the hole in the previous timber and mark the next timber. Then when all the drilling is done you will have the holes all aligned for the threaded rod.

When you are ready, align the timbers and run the threaded rod through the entire series of timbers. When you are ready, put the washer and nut on one end of each rod. There should be a rod at the top (six inches to a foot from the actual top), another in the center, and a third six inches to a foot from the bottom.

When all timbers have been aligned and the rod extends through all of them, install the washers and nuts at the other end of the rods. Tighten securely by using a ratchet and socket on each end. Snug-tighten the three rods, then return to the top and tighten each of the rods slightly more, and repeat this procedure several times until all of the nuts are securely tight.

Now install the top and bottom units, and then lay the longer unit (the diagonal piece) across the two top and bottom pieces and mark the cut line. You will want the diagonal unit to fit perfectly between the inside edges of the top and bottom pieces. See Figure 28-1.

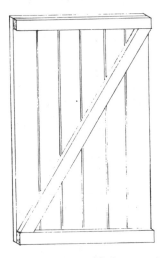

Figure 28-1
Complete Z door.

You now have a completed door.

A second and very easy way to make your own door is to cut several tongue-and-groove timbers and then fit the tongues and grooves together. You can still, if you wish, use the threaded rod for extra strength. If you drill tongue-and-groove timbers, start the drill bit inside the groove, not on the tongue.

You can buy 2″ x 6″ tongue-and-groove timbers, or you can cut your own in a rustic fashion. This means that you can stand a board or timber on edge and chalk two lines down the length of the timber, each line one-fourth inch from the outside edges. Now use the tip of the saw bar and cut down half an inch on each side. What is left in the center is the tongue.

Warning: this is not very easy to do. But do not be discouraged if you do not succeed immediately. You can do it with a little practice and patience.

On the other edge of that same timber, chalk the lines again as before, but this time use the tip of the bar to cut out the wood between the two lines. You will need to make several cuts before the timber is ready.

A third method is to use the splint-and-groove method. You may recall that in this process you make two grooves, each one-fourth inch in width and one inch in depth, down the center of both edges of a timber. Then you cut a spline that is one-fourth inch thick, and press one edge of the spline into one groove. Then position the next timber atop the spline and press downward until the two timbers are seated over the spline. The spline is not seen when the fit is properly accomplished.

A third way is to use the shiplap method. This is done by chalking a line half an inch from the edge of a board and cutting a groove halfway through the thickness of the timber. Then stand the timber on edge and cut down the edge until you have freed the cut-out.

Do this on the opposite side of the next timber, and when the two are fitted together, the two pieces will lap together. By doing this, no cracks will show between timbers. Figure 28-2 shows an end view of such a door.

The final type of door described in this chapter is the panel door, which is by far the most difficult and the most time-consuming. The panel door is one with thick borders and thick pieces down the center of the door and across the center, and with thinner materials inside the thicker borders.

Start by cutting timbers five inches wide and two inches thick. You will need two long timbers for the sides of the door, two shorter ones for the top and bottom, and a still shorter but wider one for the center of the door.

When you have the timbers cut, stand each timber in turn on edge and saw an inch-deep groove one-fourth inch wide down the exact center of the timber. If you wish to use thicker panels, you can make the groove half an inch wide.

Groove the inside edge of all timbers, as shown in Figure 28-3. On the widest timber to be used in the middle of the door, groove both sides.

You can fasten the top left and bottom left corners by cutting a ship-lap cut on the side timber and on the top and bottom timbers, or you can cut a tongue into the top and bottom timbers and fasten them in this fashion. When the units are ready to assemble, glue the tongues, if any, and connect the units.

You can start the center part of this door in the middle and work your way out. By this I mean that you will need to install the center piece first. Be sure that the center piece is sufficiently long to reach from one of the border timbers to the other and still have enough length to allow a tongue on each end to extend into the groove on the inside of the outside timbers.

One way to install the center piece is to install the two side panels and then gently drive the thicker center panel, which has already been grooved, over the edges of the side panels, as shown in Figure 28-4.

To cut the tongue, you will need to chalk a line, as before, along the outside edges of the piece, and cut down from the end of the timber to a point one inch from the end of the timber. Do this on both sides, and then carefully cut off the outside part of the timber until the cut-out can be removed.

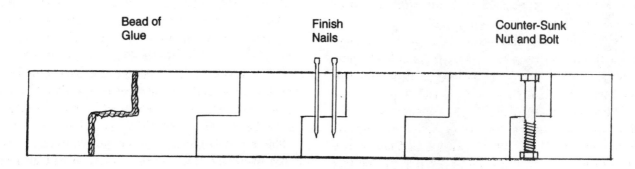

Figure 28-2
End or top view of shiplap door.

Do this on both ends of the timber. When it is ready, slide the tongue on each end into the groove of the outside timbers. You can have one thick panel in the exact center, or you can place it two-thirds of the way to the bottom, or you can have a wide timber at the one-third and at the two-thirds points.

Figure 28-3
Grooving the thick borders of door.

Figure 28-4
Installing the center piece of panel door.

Do not fasten the center pieces yet. Just be sure that you have a good fit. The next step is to cut the vertical timbers that reach from the top to the center pieces, between center pieces, and from the bottom timber to the center piece. These should be six to eight inches wide, grooved on the two long sides, and with a tongue on top and bottom. When these are cut, slip them into position to test for fit, and then slide them back an inch or two.

Now cut the panels, which should be as thick as the grooves you made in the border timbers. These panels will now fit into the groove in the upper left corner, between the center pieces, and in the lower left corner. After you have them in place and check to see that they will fit perfectly or at least acceptably, remove them, spread some wood glue on the parts that will be inserted into the grooves, and put them back in place. Push the other members firmly into position and allow the glue to start to dry while you deal with other matters.

Set the vertical pieces in place, fitting them to the panels, into the horizontal piece or pieces, and into the top and bottom members. Now cut the panels for the right side and insert them and glue them into place as you did before.

You are now ready to install the outside timber for the right side of the door. Lay the timber beside the door assembly and slide the timber so that the tongues on the pieces all fit into the groove on the outside timber. When you are satisfied that the fit is a good one, remove the timber, glue the tongues as before, and slide the entire assembly together.

You can also use wood pegs driven into pre-drilled holes. For added strength, you can apply glue to the pegs before setting them in place. See Figure 28-5.

If you have trouble pulling the pieces tightly together, you can wrap a cord around the entire assembly, and then insert a stick and twist it to tighten the entire assembly evenly and effectively.

The finished product can be attractive, strong, and useful, as well as highly economical. In fact, you can make one of the most expensive parts of your house one of the cheapest. See Figure 28-6.

This type of door can be made for less than one dollar, but it takes three or four hours of steady work to create it. The finished product can be a thing of beauty.

There are many variations on any of the door styles suggested here, and you are encouraged to use your imagination and ingenuity to devise your own creations.

The next chapter is on hanging doors and installing locks.

Figure 28-5
Installing pegs to hold door corners.

Figure 28-6
The finished door, made at a cost of less than $1.

Chapter Twenty Nine:
Hanging Doors

When you framed the exterior walls, you left rough openings for doors and windows. You also left rough openings for interior doors. It is now time to complete the basic framing and to install doors.

Without windows and doors installed, your house admits too much moisture for the welfare of the structure. Absence of doors and windows is also an invitation to thieves and vandals.

Start with the door frames. The frame consists of the door itself in many instances, and the frame elements consisting of side jambs, head jamb, and the spreader, which will be removed when the door is installed. Pre-framed doors come with the door already installed. All you need to do is set the assembly in the rough opening and install the frame. Everything is ready for use.

You can also buy the components of the frame and assemble them yourself, or you can cut your own. The door frames for the outside door openings are already determined by the log walls, but interior doors can be framed easily. When you cut the side jambs, which are the framing members that run up the sides of door openings, make the side jambs slightly taller than the door itself. This extra length is to allow for slight adjustments in the installation of the frame.

You can cut the side jambs by sawing a basic one-inch board as wide as the doorway itself. Often this width is the 3.5 inches or so for the studding, plus the thickness of the wall covering. If you cut your own studs, the studs will be four inches wide. The wall coverings are one inch thick, so add two inches, one for each wall, to the thickness. The side jambs, then, will need to be six inches wide. See Figure 29-1 for a sketch of a door frame.

At the top of the side jambs and an inch or so below the actual end of the board there is a squared groove which is cut half an inch or so deep. This so-called rabbet cut is for the head jamb to fit into. See Figure 29-2. To cut the rabbet, lay the jamb stock on a work

surface and mark the one-inch or two-inch thickness of the head jamb. Because you are cutting your own jambs, you might want to make all members two inches thick, if the rough opening will permit the extra space requirement. If not, you can cut one-inch thick jambs.

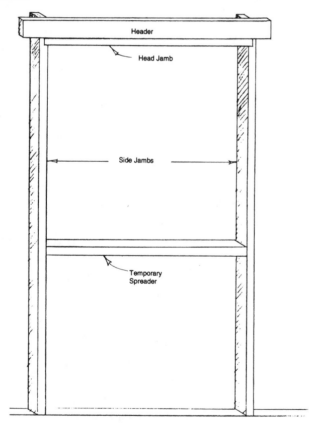

Figure 29-1
A typical door frame, including the side jambs and head jamb.

With the thickness of the head jamb marked by two lines across the board, use the tip of the chain saw bar and make the first groove cut just alongside the first line and between the two lines. You can actually take off the line with the cut.

Now move over one-fourth inch and saw another one-inch groove just beside the first one. Then move over another one-fourth inch and keep moving over until you have grooved out the area between the two lines. Do this for both boards, and the rabbet cuts are completed. You are now ready to install the side jambs.

The side jambs are nothing more than the framing to which the door and latches are attached. The head jamb is the piece that fills the space at the top of the doorway. The spreader is only a temporary piece that keeps the frame separated exactly the right amount so that the door will fit well once the frame is installed. This spreader can actually be a length of wood nailed temporarily across the framing composed of side jambs and head jamb. Nail the length of wood at the bottom of the frame so that while you are positioning the frame you will not inadvertently let the opening become too wide or too narrow.

To assemble, slip one end of the head jamb into the rabbet cut of one of the side jambs. You can stand the head jamb piece on one end and prop the side jamb in position so that you can nail through the back of the side jamb and into the end of the head jamb. Use small nails, because no real holding power is needed except to keep the jambs from separating.

Turn the assembly over so that the side jamb is now on the floor and the head jamb (free end) is pointing upward. Set the other side jamb onto the head-jamb end so that the end of the head jamb fits into the rabbet cut. Nail the two jambs together as you did before.

The spreader is the final part of the assembly. Measure the exact distance between the side jambs at the top, just below the head jamb. Cut a length of lumber (a one-by-four-inch piece is excellent) the exact length of the measurement.

You can insert the spreader into the space at the bottom of the frame assembly, between the two side jambs, and use a very small finish nail driven through

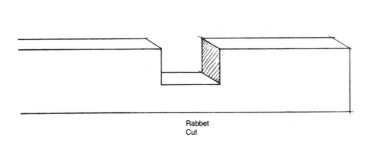

Figure 29-2
A basic rabbet cut.

the backside of the side jambs and into the end of the spreader. You can also cut the spreader an inch longer than is needed and tack it to the side of the jambs.

The first method is better because there are no nail holes left to show when the door frame is completed. You can set the frame inside the rough door opening and install the spreader when the blocking is done.

If you want to tack the spreader in place, as first suggested, the door molding will cover small nail holes. You cannot pull out the nail used to hold the spreader in place, so you will need to tap it back into the wood as far as it will go and leave it there. It will not be seen if you position it in the proper location.

Decide which way you want your door to swing. Usually it is better if a hallway door opens into the bedrooms rather than into the hallway, but closet doors must open into the hallway.

You also need to decide whether the door will be mounted on the left or right side of the opening. A convenient way to swing a door is so that it will open against a wall and form a 90-degree angle with the doorway. Usually, light switches are placed on the wall just inside the doorway, and you do not want to have to enter the room and reach behind the door to switch on a light switch.

When you are ready to install the door frame assembly, first measure to make certain that you have a frame in which your door will fit snugly but not too tightly. Then set the frame into the rough opening.

Here you will need blocking. The blocking is only short lengths of 2″ x 4″ or 1″ x 4″ which fit behind the frame to assure that the jambs are fitted perfectly. If your frame fits exactly, or so close that no blocking is necessary, disregard this part of the job.

Use blocking on all sides of the frame if there is too much open space beside, below, or above the frame. Usually the horns (the protrusions above the head jamb) will eliminate the need for blocking at the top.

When you install the framing, use a level on all jambs as you add the wedges or blocking behind the framing. The head jamb should be perfectly level. The side jambs should be perfectly vertical.

If there is a problem, use a square to see which corner is not squared. All corners should form exact right angles.

If your side jambs are too long, they must be cut. To determine the amount to cut off, measure from the bottom side of the head jamb toward the floor. Measure the exact length of the door plus whatever clearance space is needed.

You do not have your finish flooring installed yet, so you must allow for the flooring or the carpet. You will also need to allow for the cold air return space under interior doors.

If you are installing an exterior door, you will need to allow for the threshold. The measurements for the outside doors should be as exact as possible in order to get the best fitting to prevent heat and cooling loss. Usually a three-sixteenths-inch clearing is all that is needed.

If you plan to run carpet or finish flooring under the interior doors, fit small wedges or blocks of stock the same thickness as the flooring or carpet will be, and stand the door frame on these wedges. You will remove these and slip the finish flooring or carpet under the framing later.

When you have the right measurements and the jambs are all level or vertical, set the level on the outside edge of each jamb to be certain that the frame is not leaning. It is possible to have a frame perfectly vertical on the inside reading, and off the vertical reading on the outside jamb edge.

You will need to nail the framing into place. Usually, you will use long finish nails that will reach through the wedges or blocking and into the studding. If you must use extra-thick wedges, you can nail the wedge to the studding and then nail the framing to the wedge.

Do not try to conserve scrap wood when you are choosing wedges and blocking. The blocking should be as wide as the door framing and should be a foot or so in length. If you need a one-inch board for a wedge or block, there is nothing wrong with nailing in a full-length board.

Hang the door when the frame is acceptable. Determine first which side of the door is the hinge stile and which is the lock or latch stile. Remember that the term "stile" was used with reference to window construction, and the relationship to doors is exactly

what it is to windows. When this decision is made, install the hinges on the door and then on the door frame (side jamb) on the hinge stile.

If hinges are to be inset, lay the hinge at the proper locations (measure from the top down and from the bottom up) and draw a pencil line around the entire hinge section. If you do not have specifications on placement, let the top of the upper hinge and the bottom of the lower hinge fall at seven and one-half inches from the top and bottom of the side jamb.

With the hinge outlined, use a chisel and hammer and cut out a section of wood from the edge of the door the exact thickness of the hinge. Set the hinge in the cutout to be sure that you have a good, even seat.

You can buy a router that is electrically powered and ideally suited for this work, or you can do the work with a chisel. A router is expensive and not often needed, so the chisel might be the best solution for you. If you use a chisel carefully, you can do a very neat job of cutting gains (the spaces to permit hinges to be seated).

To use a chisel to cut gains, set the chisel on the pencil mark you made so that the bevel side of the chisel is facing the inside portion of the cutout. Strike the chisel lightly with a hammer until you have cut into the wood one-eighth of an inch.

Continue doing this until you have made the initial cut all the way around the hinge outline. When you have done so, turn the chisel so that the bevel side is facing outward and tilt the chisel to a 45-degree angle and place the blade two inches from the pencil outline mark at either the top or bottom of the outline.

Tap the chisel with a hammer until the blade bites into the wood very shallowly. When the bite occurs you can flatten the angle of the chisel to the wood even more and tap lightly until the thin sliver of wood is cut away.

Be very careful when the chisel blade is near the pencil outline. You do not want to cut past the outline mark and deface the door.

When all gains are cut, install the hinges. Be sure that the heads of mortise pins are up. Otherwise they will fall out once the door is hung.

You will probably use a loose-pin-butt mortise hinge. This is the type with two rectangular leaves that pivot on a pin. The hinges can be separated simply by pulling out the pin. The hinge assembly is then mortised or cut into the jamb and door so that there will be no gap when the door is closed.

Without the mortise cuts, the door would be separated from the jamb by the double thickness of the hinges when the door is closed. The look is unsightly and allows great heat or cooling loss.

When the hinge cut-out is finished, mount the hinge into the door stile or edge. With the hinge in place, set a nail point into the holes and drive the nail into the wood an inch or so at each hole.

The nail hole makes a good pilot hole for the screws. Such a starter hole allows you to start the screws straight and evenly. Sink all screws fully so that no part of the head extends past the hinge.

Install the bottom hinge in the same fashion. If you are installing or hanging an exterior door, you will want to use a third hinge in the middle of the door.

When you have the door hinges installed, fasten the hinge leaves for the jamb. You will need to be certain that the way you install the hinges will allow the door to open fully.

Fit the two leaves of each hinge together to see that the hinge sections will lie flat against each other. You will see that in one position the hinges will not close completely, and this means that your door will not close completely if you install the hinges in this manner.

Do not be concerned at this point about the remainder of the door and its trim work. That part of your work will be discussed fully in Chapter Thirty Four.

You may wish to install locks on exterior doors at this point. You can choose from single-cylinder or double-cylinder locks in the deadbolt category.

The essential difference is that single-cylinder locks can be opened from the inside without a key. Double-cylinder locks require a key on both sides of the door.

Your choice will depend upon your personal circumstances. For most people, it is convenient to use double-cylinder locks. The reasoning is that if a burglar succeeds in breaking into the house via a window, he will not be able to leave by the door and will not be able to carry out large items that will not pass through the window.

The disadvantage is that if there is an emergency, members of the family cannot open the door without a key. Some people have found that it is convenient to leave a key inside the door when they are at home and to remove the keys when they plan to be away from the house for several hours.

To install a double-cylinder deadbolt lock, open the door to a comfortable working position and first determine the location of the lock. Thirty-six inches from the floor is often a suitable height.

Mark the point. Then use a quick square or similar tool and mark lightly across the point. Make the line two inches or so in length.

You will need to drill a hole (usually about two inches wide) in the door. Check your lock installation instructions for the exact specifications.

To bore the hole you can buy a very inexpensive attachment for your electric drill. This attachment holds blades that will cut circles of various sizes.

Set the template (the paper pattern included with your lock set) on the door so that the horizontal line conforms with the line you made at 36 inches. At the center of the circle on the template use a pencil to mark your starting point. You will need to push hard enough on the pencil to mark through the paper.

Set the point of the blade attachment on the dot and start to cut. Hold the drill as nearly perfectly horizontal as you can. Drill until only the point of the attachment emerges from the other side.

Remove the saw from the cut and move to the other side of the door. Start the point again in the hole just made. Drill from the second side until the new cut reaches the cut from the first side. Remove the core of wood and you will have a neat round hole for lock installation.

If you continue to cut all the way through on the first effort, where the saw emerges the wood will splinter and leave an untidy and unsightly appearance. If you saw from both sides, there will be no splintering.

Set the template in position again and note that on the edge of the door there is another point to be marked. Use the pencil as before and mark the cut.

Change the size of the blade in the saw attachment. You will need a one-inch blade this time (but check the installation directions to be certain).

Cut the second hole so that it intersects with the two-inch hole. Hold the drill in a horizontal position so that the hole will not be slanted.

You will need to outline the bolt-holder rectangle with a pencil, and cut out a gain so that the holder can be flush with the door edge surface when the holder is installed. You have a very narrow space in which to work, so be very careful not to damage the part of the door that shows.

Insert the bolt assembly into the one-inch hole. Then slide the lock assembly into the two-inch hole from the outside of the door. You will notice two cylindrical parts of the lock extending several inches from the outside casing. Insert these cylinders so that they go through the holes in the bolt assembly.

On the inside of the door you will insert the second half of the lock assembly. This time you will use long screws that will fit into the cylinders which are inserted into the bolt assembly.

Installing these slender screws can be difficult. It is easier to start one screw only slightly and leave some working room so that you can seat the other screw.

When both screws are seated, tighten them to a good snug fit. Try your key in the lock to be certain that you can operate the mechanism from both sides of the door.

When the lock is installed, you can install the remainder of the assembly into the side jamb. You will need to drill a hole (about one inch in diameter) for the bolt to enter before you install the open rectangle to hold the bolt.

This major task has now been completed, and you can later add the threshold and the door facing and trim.

Chapter Thirty:
Installing Cabinets

You can make your own cabinets if you wish to devote the time, money, and energy required to do so. Some builders insist that this is a type of false economy unless you have the time, equipment, and expertise to do the work. My feeling is that you have the right and the reasons to make up your own mind.

You can buy your cabinets ready-made for a reasonably low price. By the time you figure in your materials, your time, and the travel to buy the materials, you have a considerable amount of money tied up in the work. Cabinet materials are very expensive, unless you want to use one of the basic plywood exteriors, which can yield a respectable cabinet. You may also want to try your hand at starting from scratch and making your own.

If you try, and if your results are pleasing, you have saved money, and your personal satisfaction is perhaps worth as much as the money involved. A few basic guidelines should be observed in virtually all types of cabinet work.

Units that sit on the floor, sometimes called the base units, are typically three feet high. You can modify this height for your own needs, if you are extremely short or tall, but keep in mind that any extreme heights may interfere with selling the house if you decide to relocate later.

Before starting to work, check with local building supply houses to get prices of materials. Each panel is expensive, and you need to plan your work carefully before you begin cutting. The old adage about measuring twice and cutting once is especially relevant here.

Of the two ways to construct cabinets, one is preferable to many carpenters. Although some like to construct the units by building them into the wall, it is sometimes easier to build the units in the middle of the floor and then hang them when they are completed. Any modifications you need to make can be done more easily with the unit on the floor than with it hanging from the wall.

Make your base for all units first . Use sound, new, and straight 2″ x 4″s to frame the base, which should be two feet wide. That is, the units should extend from the wall into the room space for a distance of two feet. When you choose to cut your own materials, again try to cut the lumber far in advance of the time you will need it, so that it can dry out as fully as possible.

Assuming the unit will be eight feet long, lay out two good and straight 2″ x 4″s and place them so that it is two feet from the outside edge of one 2″ x 4″ to the outside edge of the other. You may even want to trim the size of the frame materials and use 2″ x 2″s or 2″ x 3″s. The less weight, the easier mounting the cabinets will be.

Measure and cut lengths of 2″ x 4″ to fit exactly between the two lengths already placed. Nail one of the short 2″ x 4″s between the two eight-foot (or whatever length you need to use for your cabinets) lengths at each end. Nail in at least two other lengths, evenly dividing the space between the two ends of the frame.

You can now construct another framework just like the first, except that the top members of the framing can be 2″ x 2″s rather than 2″ x 4″s. When this is completed you will have a second frame the same size as the first.

Cut additional 2″ x 2″ lengths to fit at the corners of the two frames. You can install them inside the four corners if you wish. They should be three feet long and they should be nailed in place in a true vertical position.

Measure, mark, and cut the end units. These should be three feet high and 27 inches long (with the extra three inches to allow toe-space under the cabinets). The end pieces should be cut out on the lower outside corner so that the toe space will be four inches high and three inches wide.

Nail the end pieces in place on both ends of the framework. If one end is to be positioned against a wall, you can use less attractive wood for this work. You can also use thinner and less attractive wood for the back side of the cabinets.

Once the ends are in place, measure, mark, and cut the bottom pieces. These should be just the right size to fit against the end pieces, but the corners will need to be notched so that they will fit around the corner posts.

Upright lengths should be installed wherever doors will mount and wherever doors will meet or close on the front side of the cabinet. On the back side, install matching uprights spaced exactly as the front ones are.

You must realize that your wood sections should be as wide as possible and as smooth and true as possible. Because you will be using short lengths of wood, you can use stumps of huge trees where you needed to cut the tree earlier. If you find uprooted trees that are still vital, these trees yield exceptional trunks or stumps that are perfect for cabinet work.

Refer to the chapter on making doors to see how you can cut a groove in a post or unit of stock that runs vertically down the center of an expanse of cabinet space. You can do the same thing with cabinet work. Cut the groove no more than one-half inch from the outside edge of the post, and then cut very thin and very wide short boards that will fit like the door panels into the space afforded by the grooves.

You can cut quarter-inch stock if you will mark carefully and saw even more carefully. If you prefer to increase the size to three-eighths of an inch or even half an inch, do so. You can also make a framing of thin strips that are glued to the inside of the wood for the doors. These strips (1.5″ by 1.5″ stock) should be placed so that they fit as precisely as possible inside the door opening. You can also cut the door size slightly larger than the opening and mount the hinges on the outside of the door space, rather than inside the framing. This makes an easier fitting and results in a neater look.

What kind of wood makes the best panels for cabinets? Oak, of course, is superb. But you can use maple, fir, pine, and even poplar for this work.

Remember that when you cut grooves, you must groove the top, bottom, and side posts or units. And you will need to install extra posts, because you will

probably not find raw wood wide enough for the panel to cover the entire side of a cabinet.

When the uprights you have cut are in place, determine the height of shelves, if any, and cut 2″ x 2″ lengths to run from front to back to match the locations of the uprights, including the corner posts. You can toe-nail these support units or use corner braces to hold them in place.

You can now cut and install the shelf for the base units. Mark on the wall and floor where the unit will be placed. Leave enough space for the carousel unit to be installed in corners.

Frame and complete the other units that will form the right-angle cabinets for the room. Construct them as you did the first unit. When the second unit is completed to the same point as the first one, position it along the wall in its permanent place. The front edge of the two end pieces should not be closer than one foot to 15 inches. The space in the corner is reserved for the carousel unit.

Measure diagonally across the floor from one front edge to the other and from the front edges to the back edges. Cut a framing member to reach diagonally across the space where the two front edges are located.

Complete the framing for the carousel unit as you did the other units. The major difference is that the framing will have five sides rather than four. The fifth side is the short diagonal running from the two front edges.

Measure and cut out the floor or bottom of the carousel unit. Nail it in place atop the framing members.

When all base units are completed to this stage, measure and cut the tops from ordinary stock. You can use plywood if you want a quick solution to the problem, or you can cut your own wide boards (making these an inch thick for greater support and strength). On the front, cut out the stock for the drawers. Mark and cut out rectangles slightly larger than the drawers will be.

From the facing between drawers run a drawer guide from the facing to the back of the framing. This guide is installed so that it will be at the height of the bottom of the drawer. If you need to do so, install a length of 2″ x 2″ or similar stock along the back of the framing to hold the back end of the drawer guide.

You can make a drawer guide by nailing a 1″ x 2″ length of wood on top of a 1″ x 3″ length of similar stock. Center the 1″ x 2″ length so that a right angle is formed by the sides of the two units. Do this on both sides of the drawer, and the drawer will be guided between the two guides.

The left side of the assembly will be the right guide for the first drawer, and it will also serve as the left guide for the drawer to the right of the first one. Check to see that the top unit aligns with the two drawers. You will need a guide on each side of all the drawers.

When the framing is completed, you can cut and install the finish facing for the cabinets. When you are cutting this facing, if you are using a circular saw, remember to cut while the facing stock is laid face down. The splintering will be on the back side rather than the front if you cut in this manner.

Sand the edges until they are perfectly smooth. Install by using tiny color-matched nails or by using wood glue. The glue leaves a very smooth and uninterrupted surface.

When you attach doors, one common method is to cut the door two inches wider and taller than the door opening. Use offset hinges on the doors and when they are closed the outside edge and the top and bottom edges will lap the door opening rather than fit inside the door space.

When you make drawers you can install roller assemblies for smoother and easier operation. If you do not wish to go to this trouble and expense you can construct a simple drawer and slide it along the guide surfaces.

To make the simplest type of drawer, do not buy special equipment to use for rabbet cuts or dados. Use ordinary stock materials and assemble them in the following manner.

Use a board four or five inches wide (depending upon the size of drawer you need to make) and three-fourths of an inch thick up to one inch thick. Cut the board the proper length, so that it is at least an inch and not more than two inches wider than the drawer opening.

Cut similar boards for the sides of the drawer. These boards should be no thicker than one-half inch. Attach these to the outside board by using small finish nails or wood glue. You can also use very small bracket braces installed inside the drawer.

Cut the end piece and attach it to the ends of the side pieces. Let the end piece lap the entire thickness of the side pieces. Use finish nails or wood glue — or both — to fasten the end pieces.

Now add the bottom piece. For the bottom use thin plywood or unscored paneling. This need not be more than three-eighths of an inch thick.

For best results, cut a groove on the inside of the side pieces and the outside piece. You can use a circular-saw set for a very shallow cut. Use a thin chisel blade or even a srewdriver blade to remove the wood from the cut. You will need to make two shallow cuts three-eighths of an inch thick on all three pieces. The cuts need to be at the same height on all pieces.

When the bottom piece is cut, insert it into the grooves before the end piece is attached. Then let the end piece set on top of the bottom section. Add a drawer pull to the assembly and the drawer is completed.

Construct the wall units for the cabinets in the same manner. The difference is that you will not use any stock larger than 2″ x 2″; 1″ x 2″ stock will usually work well.

When the units are completed, you can add the facing immediately, or you can wait until the units are hung before adding facing. It is easier to do the final work while the units are off the wall and in a more comfortable work position.

Now you are ready to hang the cabinets. This is reputed to be very difficult, but in reality it is quite simple and very easy to handle.

Whether you make them or buy them, you can hang cabinents and save that part of the money. Some cabinet-makers will not install cabinets on log walls or other uneven surfaces. They also point out that if the studding is not really solid, the nails or screws might not hold, and the cabinets could fall.

If you have used good studding, you should have no difficulty in securing the cabinets. Your major problem is to lift and hold the cabinets at the proper height, if the cabinets are mounted at eye level and above.

When we called a cabinet maker to give us an estimate on our cabinets, the man told us in no uncertain terms that he would not even consider doing the cabinet work for a log house. The walls are never totally smooth and plumb, he said, and it was nearly impossible to hang the cabinets securely and straight.

So we decided, in our ignorance, to do the work ourselves. We assumed that we could figure out a very easy way to complete the cabinet work and hang the finished product without a great deal of trouble and work.

We were in for a surprise. The very first method we devised worked so well we never had one split second's worth of failure or even frustration. The job went smoother than we could have ever dreamed.

You can install shelves by attaching a small support piece on each side of the cabinet. This can be as small as one-half inch by one inch, with the broad side attached flush against the wall or side of the cabinet. The shelves then sit on the support pieces on each side of the cabinet. You can use tiny nails or wood glue to hold the shelves in place.

When the cabinets are completed, you should mount the higher ones first. You do not want to work over the lower cabinets and risk damaging them, nor do you want to experience the difficulty of trying to work at arm's length.

There are two simple ways of mounting the cabinets to the wall. First, determine the proper height. You must mount the cabinets at least 24 inches above the kitchen range burners for safety. Mount the cabinets low enough that you can reach them without difficulty and high enough to look attractive. When you install the sink, be sure to seal around it. You can use one of the caulking guns to waterproof the installation.

If you choose to use plywood for the cabinet construction, you can build the basic frame, including drawer runners, from rough lumber. See Figure 30-1. If you wish, you can build the entire cabinet from plywood, after the framing is completed, and then you can stain it. Figure 30-2 shows a rough plywood cabinet.

Figure 30-2
Raw plywood cabinet construction.

If you get incredibly ambitious, you can cut doors from blocks of oak wood, as shown in Figure 30-3. When you add stain, handles, and hinges, you will have a very presentable kitchen, such as the one shown in Figure 30-4.

Figure 30-1
Rough lumber framing for cabinets.

Figure 30-3
Cutting cabinet doors from oak stump block.

To mount the cabinets, you will need a power drill and some screwdriver attachments. You will also need three-inch screws with flat heads.

Set up supports to hold the cabinets in place once you lift them. Do not try to hold the cabinets and drill at the same time.

Set the cabinets on a foundation composed of stacked building blocks with boards across them or something similar. With the cabinets in place, drill a hole through the back and into the studding behind the cabinets.

You may have to measure to find the studding. The first hole should be three-fourths of the way to the top of the cabinet. When it is made, move to the same height and find the next stud.

Use a level to be certain that the cabinet is sitting in the exact position it needs to be in. Do not worry much about the vertical position of the front at this point. Lay the level in the bottom of the cabinets so that you can see the bubble as you work. You can get an exact level reading with little difficulty.

Figure 30-4
Finished cabinet installation.

When the holes are all made, use the power drill with a screwdriver blade installed in the chuck to drive the screws quickly while you maintain the level position of the cabinets. Sink the screws until they are almost completely driven. Then use a level to determine the exact reading up and down the front of the cabinets.

When you are satisfied, sink the screws completely until they pull the cabinet unit tightly against the wall. Now remove the support system and use the level once again to double-check the position of the cabinet.

When you are satisfied, install the remainder of the screws. Use screws in every stud no more than eight inches apart up and down the studding.

When all the wall units are installed, move the base units into position. Use a level to get the proper reading from front to back and from side to side. If you must do so, use shims under the framing to get level readings.

Use screws again to attach the units to the studding. Drill holes into the studs and then use screws that, as above, are slightly larger than the pilot holes drilled.

The second method of installation is to lay the units atop a piece of plywood and then mark around the outside edges of the cabinet so that when you cut along the lines the plywood is exactly the same size as the unit. If you wish, you can cut inside the lines slightly to make the plywood a little smaller than the cabinet so that the plywood is not visible.

Mount the plywood, after you have cut it to conform to the exact outside dimensions of the cabinets, on the wall by using either 16d nails or three-inch screws, or both. Use the level to determine the exact position of the plywood.

When the plywood is mounted, use your level to guarantee that the plywood is level horizontally and vertically, and then raise the cabinets as you did before and simply align the cabinets with the plywood. Then, attach the cabinets to the plywood. By doing it in this fashion you do not have to worry about hitting studding. The plywood is securely mounted, and if you attach the cabinets to the plywood securely, your work is done properly.

All that remains is cutting out for the sink and attaching the cabinet work surface. To do the sink marking easily, turn the sink upside down and mark around it, once the sink has been positioned properly. Then you cut half an inch inside the markings so that the lip of the sink will hang from the plywood.

Drill holes for the sink connection. You can use a circle-saw attachment that can be installed in the chuck of your power drill.

To install the laminated cover of the work surface, you need to lay the cover in position and mark the underside where it hangs over the edge of the cabinets. Turn the laminated cover over and cut along the mark. This material is very hard to cut, and you may need to use a jig saw or a hacksaw to make the cuts.

When the cuts are made, place the covering back in position to make sure that you still have a correct fit.

You can let it extend over the outside edge slightly, no more than one-eighth inch.

Use a brush to cover the top surface of the plywood and the bottom surface of the covering. When you start to install the laminate, it will adhere instantly to the plywood, so you cannot place it and then try to adjust it. You must position it exactly the first time.

Start by lowering the back part of the cabinet covering to the plywood. Hold the covering so that it will not sag and touch anywhere else. Lower slowly from both ends. When proper contact is made, slowly lower the front part of the covering until it is positioned flatly across the entire surface.

Later, you can cut thin strips to fit under the slight lip you left extending past the edge of the plywood. The strip will create an even corner. Install it exactly as you did the top covering.

You are now ready to let the laminate set up while you work on other projects in the house. How much can you save by making your own cabinets?

From $3,000 to $8,000, generally.

If you want to install makeshift cabinets in the corners of rooms, you can do so by cutting and installing 2″ x 2″ stock from the corner outward on the wall at a height of three feet. The stock must extend from the corner in both directions. Then move up two feet and do the same. Keep climbing until you reach the ceiling. Divide the distance into equal gradations for a better appearance. Then cut boards, starting with right-angle cuts, to fit into the corners. Succeeding pieces will also have to be angled to fit.

Then, if you wish, build cabinets under the shelves. You will then have a rustic and attractive corner storage area that is pleasing both in utility and looks.

Chapter Thirty One:
Stairway Construction

The first step in building stairs is the decision as to where to locate the stairway. In the rough plans suggested earlier in this book it was recommended that the stairs to the basement and to the upstairs or third level should be located in the center of the house.

The purpose for this location is that heat convection from the basement (where, in this house, the wood stove is located) will bring warm air up the stairs and help reduce the cost of heating the house. Another reason is that the house plan requires that the stairs be located either in the center of the house or at the end of the hallway. This location is also very handy for all parts of the house.

The hallway space is needed for closets and bathroom, and the center of the house location is the handiest one for this particular house plan. You can adapt the plans to your own needs, or you can use different plans altogether.

This particular house plan has three sets of flights or stairs, actually: one from basement to first floor; another to the second floor or third level; and third, a set of "disappearing" steps into the attic. All three are necessary for the floor plan used.

You can buy sets of stairs or staircases from some lumber or building supply houses. Prices vary from several hundred dollars to as much as the cost of a new automobile. We priced stairways and learned that the one-flight stairway would cost us $25,000. We returned home immediately and set out to build our own. Our stairs, we found, while not elaborate, could be built for less than $50.

Far less. In fact, our stairway was constructed for around $15 at the most — plus, as always, your time and lots and lots of sweat equity.

Stairways can be focal points of great beauty, or they can simply be utilitarian. A third possibility also exists: you can have stairs that are physically attractive as well as highly functional.

If you construct your own stairway from materials at hand, you can have sturdy yet simple stairs. Do not expect to build highly fashionable stairs without years of experience and very expensive materials.

At this point in your work you should not plan to complete the finished stairs. Much work remains, and you will have a number of workers in to complete electrical or plumbing work. Finished treads will be dirtied and scratched badly. So plan to use only basic steps until you reach the finish carpentry stages of your house.

Several terms need to be added to your vocabulary at this point. The length of the stairs in linear feet is called the total run of the stairs.

This means the distance from the foot or base of the stairs to the wall or point on the floor directly below the top of the stairs. A flight of stairs may have a total run of 10 and one-half feet but the staircase itself may be 14 feet long. The difference in the two lengths is accounted for by the angle of the rise of the stairway. See Figure 31-1.

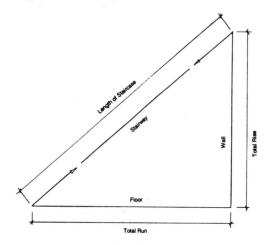

Figure 31-1
Simple diagram of a stairway.

The total rise of stairs is the distance in feet from the floor of one room (at the bottom) to the floor of the room above. The distance is to the top of the finish floor rather than from subfloor to subfloor.

The long timbers that are cut out to hold the treads and risers are called the stringers, or carriage. The steps of the staircase are called the treads, and the boards used at the back of the treads are called risers. See Figure 31-2.

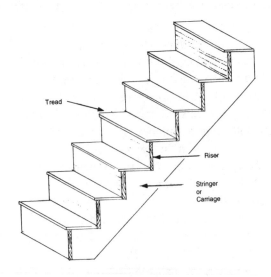

Figure 31-2
Stringer or carriage diagram.

The unit run is the width of a horizontal plane of the treads. The unit rise is the height of each riser, or the height in inches from one tread to the next. See Figure 31-3.

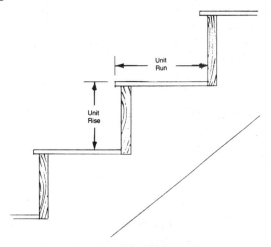

Figure 31-3
Unit rise and unit run.

As with all other parts of the house, stairs are subject to building-code regulations. The code requires a certain amount of head room, and some codes dictate the need for railings or rails and balusters. Some codes similarly control the angle of the stairs.

Stairs that have treads which are too narrow can be very dangerous. Stairs that are too steep or have risers which are too high can be equally dangerous. Code regulations are to protect you from your own careless mistakes or your lack of awareness of the potential dangers involved in certain types of construction.

There are several designs for stairs, but the simplest of these is the straight run. This is the stairway that leads in a direct line from one level of the house to another. I strongly recommend this approach. The spiral staircases are gorgeous, but they require tons of work and expensive materials.

And I don't know how to build them.

You have some flexibility in determining the width of treads or the height of risers. A general rule is that the treads for most residences are from nine to 12 inches wide. The average height of risers is about seven inches. The actual dimensions of treads and risers are largely dictated by the degree of the slope or incline of the stairs.

One important element of stairway construction is that all treads should be the same width, just as all risers should be the same or very nearly the same height. Any significant variation can cause accidents.

Start your stairway work, after all decisions on location and design have been settled, by removing the panels of subflooring (if any) in the location. The space occupied by the single panel of subflooring will give you four feet of working room, less the space occupied by double headers and spacers.

The finished stairway should be at least three feet wide. This space will permit ample room for persons using the stairs and for workers or others to carry equipment and items of furniture up or down the stairs.

You may need to remove two panels or one and one-half panels of subflooring in order to have enough room for the stairway. When the necessary subflooring has been removed, your first step is to install headers at both ends of the rough stairway opening.

Double the headers at both ends. At the same time, double the floor joists on both sides to give maximum strength for the stairs. Add bracing or bridging at the back of the headers as needed. See Figure 31-4.

To calculate the length of the stringers or carriage, you have a choice of mathematical operations. Decide first how high, roughly, your risers will be. Assume that you want risers seven inches high.

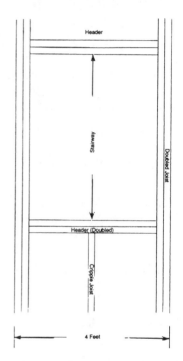

Figure 31-4
Joist layout of stairway well.

Next, determine the width of the treads, not including the nosers. Assume that you need treads ten inches wide.

You now know that your total unit rise and total unit run will equal 17 inches or nearly so. Assume also that the total rise of the stairs is eight feet and 10 inches. This gives you a total of 106 inches of total rise.

Divide the total rise by the unit rise. This is 106 inches divided by seven, or, rounded off, 15. This figure gives you the number of risers.

Now divide the total rise (in inches) by the number of risers in order to arrive at the exact height of each riser. You started with seven inches as the basic riser height, and now the exact height is available for you: in this case it remains the same.

Now use the architectural ruling that the total inches of unit rise and unit run should be 17 and one-half inches. Your answer is 10.5 or ten and one-half

inches. You now have not only your working width of treads but the exact width.

Your total run will equal the unit run of a tread (ten and one-half inches) times the number of treads you will use in the stairway. If you plan to use fifteen treads, your total run will then be 157 and one-half inches or 13 feet and three inches.

Next, drop a plumb bob from the head of the stairway well and mark the spot. Measure off the length of the total run and mark the point. This is the anchor point for the stairs.

You are now ready to cut the stringers, which are made from 2″ x 12″ stock for maximum strength. Before you cut the stringers, make another quick check. You are about to cut two (four, if you count doubling them) boards that required considerable time to cut and required considerable wood, and if you cut them wrong you have wasted a considerable amount of money.

You can return to the ancient Pythagorean Theorem for finding the length of the hypotenuse of a triangle. Square the length of both known sides and then add the two figures. Then find the square root of the sum, which is the length of the stringers.

As an easy pattern problem, assume that the total rise is nine feet, which, squared, is 81. Now suppose that the total run is 13.5 feet which, squared, is 182.25.

Now add the two sums: $182.25 + 81 = 263.25$. The square root of that figure is roughly but close enough: 16.4 feet.

Cut one timber at 16 feet and 3 inches. You will need to make a cut for a vertical or plumb cut at the top and for a horizontal cut at the bottom so that the board will sit well in the allotted space.

You can make the cuts while you lay off the stringers. This is a very crucial step and must be done very carefully.

To lay off the stringers, lay the board flat on the work surface and locate your carpenter's square. Hold the square so that the heel points toward your chest and the tongue is in your left hand and the blade in your right hand.

Lay the framing square on the board so that the tongue (the shorter side) is set on the unit run. The longer side, or the blade, should be set on the unit rise.

What this means is that you should hold the square so that the number corresponding to the unit run (ten and one-half inches) should be even with the edge of the board that is away from you. The other setting, the unit rise, is seven inches or seven and one-half inches, depending upon your final decision. See Figure 31-5.

Mark along the side of the square nearer to you. These two marks represent the first tread (the longer mark), and the other represents the first riser.

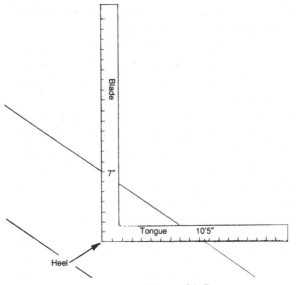

Figure 31-5
Square used to lay off stringers.

If you measure to a point exactly seven and one-half inches below the tread mark (do this at both ends of the mark), and then use the square to connect the marks, you have the cut line for the bottom of the board or the seat line for the floor.

Now set the square so that the tongue is set on ten and one-half inches and the blade is set on seven inches (or seven and one-half inches, depending upon your final choice). Mark as you did before.

Continue in exactly the same manner to mark or lay off the entire stringer, all the way to the top. At the top, do as you did at the bottom, and you have the cut line for the fit of the top end of the stringer into the header.

Make the top and bottom cuts and stand the board into its final position to see if the fits at top and bottom are correct. If they are not, make whatever minor adjustments are necessary. If they are correct, take the board down and cut out for the risers and treads.

Once again, stand the cut board (now a stringer or carriage) in place. Use a level to determine that the tread cutouts are perfectly level or horizontal.

When you are assured that everything is acceptable, cut the other three boards, using the first one as a pattern for all three of the remaining boards. You can now nail two boards together and install the doubled stringer in place.

If you intend to use the doubled stringer against the wall, on the outside of the stringer nail a 2″ x 4″ that runs the entire length of the stringer. Position the 2″ x 4″ so that it is aligned with the bottom edge of the stringers.

This 2″ x 4″ is your spacer. It is used to allow you enough space between the stringer and wall for you to install whatever wall coverings you intend to use.

To install the stringers, hold the first one in position and nail it to the header at the top of the stairs. You will need to toe-nail on both sides of the stringer. Nail (again toe-nailing) the stringer to the wall studding at every point where the stringer crosses a stud. You will actually need to toe-nail the spacer to the studding or use very long nails that will reach all the way through the doubled stringer and spacer.

Set the opposite stringer in position. Fasten it to the header at the top of the stairs as you did before. Measure to see that the two stringers are exactly the same distance from the wall at the bottom of the stairs.

You can now nail temporary treads across the stairway. Use two-by-fours placed side by side, if you wish. You can also use short lengths of boards that are strong enough to support the weight of workmen carrying lumber and other materials.

For extra support you can cut a fifth board and install it in the middle of the stairway. You will now have the treads well supported on both ends and in the middle.

At this point you can use the rough stairway, although you do not have railing installed yet. For a temporary rail, nail short blocks of wood to the wall studding and then nail a 2″ x 4″ which is stood on edge to the blocks.

To get the proper positioning, measure from the first tread to a point 36 inches up the stud. Do the same at the last tread. Then snap a chalk line between the two marks.

You can nail the 2″ x 4″ directly to the studding if you wish. This is purely a temporary railing, and will be taken down when the finish work is being done.

In the plans suggested in this book, your stairway out of the basement to the first floor ends at the opening to the hallway. The suggested plans call for you to round the corner and move to the front wall. Measure off the proper distance from the wall to the beginning of the second stairway. This distance will be your landing space.

You can now climb to the upstairs area and install the header for the stairway, if it has not yet been prepared. You did not subfloor this area, so no panels will need to be removed.

You can measure, if you wish, from the header to the floor and be doubly certain of the length of these stringers. Be sure to measure from the bottom edge of the header to the floor.

Double-check by using the mathematical computation for the hypotenuse of the triangle formed by the floor, the total rise to the header, and the unknown length of the stringer. Calculate it as you did for the basement.

When you are ready, divide as before and determine the number of risers needed. Check to see that the combined length of the unit rise and unit run equals 17 and one-half inches.

Use the framing square as you did before and mark off the stringers, cut them out, and install them as you did earlier. Use doubled stringers and one in the center for extra support.

When the stringers are anchored to the subflooring and to the headers, as well as to the studding on one side (after first nailing on the spacer to permit wall covering later), you are ready to install temporary treads.

When the temporary treads are in place, you can add the supports for the stairway. Use 2″ x 6″ stock for these supports, and install pairs of supports at three equally spaced locations along the stairway risers.

Angle cut the 2″ x 6″ timbers at the top. Square-cut the timbers at the bottom. You can cut a slightly longer timber than you need and stand it in place, letting it extend past the bottom edge of the stringer.

Use a level to be sure that the support timber is perfectly vertical. When it is in the perfect position, mark along the bottom of the stringer and onto the

side of the timber. Cut along the line, then use the first timber for a pattern and cut a second one.

Stand the first timber on the square-cut end and move it into position so that it fits perfectly against the bottom slope of the stringer. Nail the support to the stringer.

Toe-nail the support to the subflooring. If you are working in the basement, you cannot nail to the floor. Instead, you need to install the second support and let the straight-cut end rest on the basement floor.

All wood in contact with concrete should be treated wood. When the two supports are in place, measure the distance from the inside of one support to the inside edge of the other.

Cut a length of treated 2″ x 4″ and lay it between the two supports. Nail the timber in place by driving nails through the outside edge of the support and into the end of the spacer. At the other end you will need to toe-nail into the top edge of the spacer and into the bottom end of the support against the wall.

Your rough stairways are now completed.

The finish treads can be installed as soon as the wear-and-tear on the stairways has been completed. If you want a railing and baluster system composed of 2″ x 4″ stock, it is very easy to have such a system for only a dollar or two.

First, buy wood glue if you don't have a supply. Then buy some dowels an inch in diameter. Then cut a series of long and perfectly straight 2″ x 4″s from the best wood you can find. These 2″ x 4″s should, if possible, reach all the way from the top of the stairway to the bottom.

When you have the rail, cut it to length and install it by first setting up posts at the top and bottom of the stairway. The posts can be made of two 2″ x 4″s fastened together and installed. At the bottom of the stairs on the first (or bottom) tread, have the assembled posts ready and then drill two one-inch holes in the bottom of the 2″ x 4″s. The holes should be at least three inches deep. Then cut two dowels four inches long. Three inches will be inserted into the bottom of the posts, and the other inch will be inserted into holes to be drilled into the bottom tread.

Coat the ends of the four-inch dowel sections with wood glue and push them into the drilled holes. Now mark the locations for the holes in the treads.

If you want a really easy way of locating the holes, use pliers to snip the heads off of two small finish nails, and drive one of the nails about an inch into the center of each of the dowels. Now stand the post where you want it to be located and lay a block of wood over the top of the posts. Hit the block of wood with a hammer hard enough to drive the ends of the cut nails into the wood of the tread.

Now remove the posts, and you can see the holes. Drill so that the tiny holes are at the center of the hole you drill.

Insert the dowels into the holes but do not glue or fasten in any way. Simply stand the posts there while you construct the top posts in the same manner, and drill the holes and insert the dowels.

Stand the top posts in the holes. Now hook a chalk line at the desired height of the top post (about three feet generally, but tailor the height of the rail to your own needs) and pull the line to the bottom post. Stretch the line across the side of the posts. Snap the line and you have the angle of the posts.

Cut at the angle, and then glue the bottom part of the dowels to install the posts permanently. Then construct a third post assembly for the center part of the rail and stand it in place, chalk the line, and then cut and install that post in its permanent position.

Lay the railing (which can be a 2″ x 4″ placed flat across the tops of the posts) in position and cut a series of shorter 2″ x 4″s to be used as balusters. Stand the 2″ x 4″s atop the treads and hold them (use a level to be certain) vertically against the side of the railing. Mark under the rail and across the side of the balusters. You can then cut and install balusters exactly as you did the posts. Use dowels to help secure the balusters into the treads, but use finish nails

to drive down through the rail and into the slant cut of the balusters. You can also use wood glue for extra security. See Figure 31-6 for a portion of a stairway constructed in this fashion.

Figure 31-6
Portion of completed stairway.

Later, you will wish to put a railing around the sitting area. Set up the railing and balusters exactly as you did the stairway rail and balusters. At corners, double the 2″ x 4″s for added strength. Be sure to use the dowels. These add greatly to the lasting power and strength of the rails.

Finally, if you want only the simplest stairway possible, cut two long pine logs and square them or cut them into long rectangular shapes. I recommend using 8″ x 10″s for this work. Angle-cut the bottom so that the cut will fit neatly onto the floor, and angle the top so that it will seat against the header or joists at the top of the stairway.

Then, with the two runners or stringers in place, determine where you want the steps to be located. It is a good idea to space the stringers at least 36 to 40 inches apart. When you have chosen the tread locations, use a level to mark horizontal cuts on the stringers.

Then use the chain saw to cut back into the stringer five inches or so. Make two parallel cuts two inches or three inches apart. Then use a chisel to chip out wood from between the two cuts.

When you are ready, cut three-inch-thick treads and slip these into the cut-outs. You can glue these into place. If you prefer, you can set the treads between the stringers. Cut the treads so that they fit exactly between the stringers.

Then cut ledger strips to install horizontally on the inside of the stringers. Use bolts to hold these ledgers in place. Then set the treads onto the ledgers and nail them in place.

Chapter Thirty Two:
Building Book Cases

Many homes have very few books, so a coffee table or bedside table will accommodate the scarce volumes; other families, on the other hand, have hundreds of books and need broad expanses of book cases to hold their literary treasures. Such families might wish to use an inexpensive wall covering, such as cement block or wallboard, and then cover the entire wall with book cases.

If you are among those families needing lots of shelf space, the following pages might be of interest and help. Many do-it-yourselfers stay away from complete wall book cases because of the expense and the time needed to construct the shelves. The truth is that such full-wall book cases are not at all difficult to build, and they are not expensive to construct.

You will need the following materials and tools. First, you must have wide and smooth and straight boards, preferably an inch thick and dry. You will also need a saw, a square, some screws and nails, a tape measure, and very little else. Don't think you must have perfect boards, however; the books themselves will conceal minor imperfections.

You will have to decide what to do about wall receptacles and light switches. These are not major problems. You can simply enclose them in the book case area and even construct a small compartment for the switch and receptacles.

When you are planning the book cases, plan to cover the entire wall, from floor to ceiling. It is easier to cover the wall completely than it is to interrupt the flow of the work.

You will find that if you build the book cases on the floor inside the room, you will not be able to stand the cases into their final positions. You are better off to build them in the place they will occupy.

Start by installing one end of the cases in a corner so that the board will rest against the adjacent wall. Many people use lumber that is 1″ x 12″ or at the least 1″ x 10″. This can be a very costly mistake in

terms of wood and effort and time. Most books are not that large. You will find that a shelf eight or even seven inches wide will hold nearly all the books on the market today, and that eight-inch shelving lumber can be bought for far less than 12-inch boards, or sawed with far less effort.

As an example of size, a volume of *Encyclopedia Britannica* is 11 inches high and only 8.5 inches wide. So a nine-inch board will hold a very large book. Only special books will be larger than the encyclopedia volumes.

There is also a way that you can use six-inch boards and make a book case large enough to hold the *Encyclopedia Britannica* and similarly oversized books. You simply install the first boards an inch or two from the wall. The space behind the shelves can be used for extending the books beyond the edge of the shelf, if necessary.

By the same token, a five-inch board can be used to hold books that are eight inches wide. Let the book rest on the five-inch board and the final three inches can extend past the back edge of the shelf. The weight and width of the book will keep it from toppling, even if there were room for it to fall or tilt.

When you saw book shelving, use poplar, fir, pine, or other woods that are easy to work. Oak is beautiful, but is often in short supply.

When you put up your first board, measure from the ceiling to the floor and cut the board one full inch shorter than the actual distance or length. Stand the board in place against the wall adjacent to the one where the book cases will be built. Let the board stand two inches from the actual corner. Fasten the board to the wall by driving nails or screws into the studding in the corner where the partition wall was formed when the house was framed.

Do the same in the opposite corner. Leave the board one inch too short again.

When both boards are installed, measure from wall to wall and cut a board to that length. Slip the board over the top of the boards which are already installed in the corners.

You cannot nail the top board in place, so you will need to use corner braces. Use two of the one-inch braces to fasten the top board to the side board. You can also use screws or nails to fasten the top board to the ceiling joists so that the book case, when filled with books or other display items, cannot topple or be pulled over. See Figure 32-1.

Figure 32-1
Using brackets to attach top shelf.

You need to keep the bottom shelf off the floor at least three inches. The thickness of a 2″ x 4″ from the lumber yard stood on edge is almost perfect, so you can cut enough lengths of eight-inch 2″ x 4″ sections to reach, when spaced two feet apart, across the whole floor along the wall. See Figure 32-2.

Cut another board long enough to fit between the two end boards, and lay it across the on-edge 2″ x 4″s. Use one-inch corner braces to attach the bottom board to the end boards. You can use nails to attach the bottom board to the upright 2″ x 4″ sections.

Next, install upright boards spaced 24 to 36 inches apart, to suit your own needs. Run these boards from the top to bottom boards and fasten them with corner braces and screws.

You need to decide now how high you want the individual shelves to be. You can buy shelf fasteners or shelf holders and leave the spacing decision until you need to use the shelves.

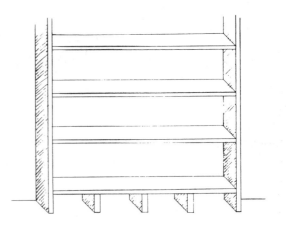

Figure 32-2
Using blocks to hold bookcase off the floor.

These shelf holders are strips of aluminum with slits for shelf brackets. You can fasten the aluminum strips up and down the upright boards. Use two strips on each board, and locate the strips about two inches from the edge of each board. You can use screws or nails to hold the aluminum strips in place.

Fasten the brackets onto the bottom of the shelves and then insert the free end of the brackets into the spaces in the metal strips you have already installed. By using this manner of installing the shelves you can move shelves as you wish without trouble or tools.

A good idea is to set up the shelves at varying heights so that you can use the shelves for video tapes, books of varying sizes, coffee-table books, and sets of encyclopedias. The one-inch-thick shelving boards will be strong enough to hold a two-foot to three-foot shelf of books.

If you make the shelves all the same width, you can move any or all of the shelves interchangeably across the entire room. This will give you much greater flexibility and utility from the book cases. You can even install the shelves on ledger strips cut to a one-by-one-inch dimension and attached to the upright boards by nails or screws. The shelves themselves may be set upon the ledger strips and not nailed or fastened at all. The weight of the books will hold the shelves in place.

Be sure to make use of the space above doorways in the room. Let the top board, installed against the ceiling, reach over the doorway and into the corner. The top shelf itself can run across the door casing, and you will be able to make full use of every inch of space in the wall.

Even the space behind the door can be used. Run boards up and down the wall and against the door facing. You can install shelves four to six inches long, and use them to store paperback books or less expensive or not-so-showy items.

Where there are switches or receptacles, install the full-length upright boards so that they run close to the switch or receptacle boxes. Then install short upright boards six inches from the full-length boards on the other side of the switches or receptacles. When you need to use the plugs, you can run the cord into the small cubicle for convenient use.

If it is not convenient for you to buy the aluminum strips, you can install the shelves quickly and easily by using short shelf-holder strips that you can cut from scrap wood, as suggested above. Earlier it was mentioned that you might have foot-long ends of boards left over from another job. You can now make use of the scrap lumber.

Use a C-clamp to hold the foot-long lumber steadily so you can saw it. Use a circular saw or chain saw to saw off strips one and one-half inches wide. Shorten these strips to the six or seven inches needed.

Use an electric drill and small drill bit and drill two holes in each strip. One hole should be a third of the way from the end, and the other should be two-thirds of the way to the end.

Measure up from the top edge of the bottom board to the point representing the height of the shelves you want. Assume that you want the shelf to be ten inches high. Mark the point on both of the upright boards, and use your square to mark a level line from the front to the back of the upright board.

Use a screwdriver to start screws one and one-half inches long through the holes you have drilled. When the screws are through the narrow shelf holders, position the strip along the marked line and fasten it to the upright board.

Do this on both sides. Then cut a board to the proper length and insert it between the upright boards. Let it lie across the shelf holders you have installed.

You can use a very small finish nail to fasten the shelf to the shelf-holder strip, or you can drill a small hole and use small screws, one in each end of the shelf, to hold the shelf in place. Install the holder strips for all of the shelves you need. When you want to change the height of a shelf, you can remove the

screws holding the holder strips and re-position the shelves to the location you need.

You will find that you cannot use full-height books under the strips of wood. Use this space for shorter books, and use the space in the middle for taller books.

Another method of holding shelves in place is yet another way to make use of scrap lumber. If you have short lengths of boards that are six or seven inches wide, cut the scraps to the proper length for shelf height and then fasten the scrap lengths to the side of the upright boards.

Use one length on each side. Fasten these with screws that are short enough that they will not reach all the way through the two boards. Two screws per board will suffice.

Now lay the shelf on top of the ends of the boards you have just installed. You can use small finish nails, screws, or corner braces to hold the shelves in place.

If you do not want to cover a complete wall with shelves, you might wish to cover the space between the windows or between window and door in a room. If there is a small alcove that has no particular use, you can install shelves and convert the alcove into a book case or novelty case.

You can also use the same basic plan and install shelves to hold a VCR, stereo equipment, tape decks, or television sets. The space not occupied by the equipment can be used to hold records, tapes, and similar items.

If you have a desk along one wall, you can install shelves above the desk so that the space on the upper part of the wall will not be lost or wasted. Because of the suspended weight of shelves filled with books, you will want to incorporate extra holding power.

Use a full-width shelf board across the back of the shelf assembly. The board will fasten to the back edge of all of the upright boards, and in turn will be attached to the wall studs so that the book case will be supported by the board, ceiling joists, and studding.

You can build a small and very simple desk by using upright sections of plywood with a longer panel segment stretched across the tops of the plywood in upright positions. Use a section of plywood 30 inches wide, and later you will fasten this to the wall in a corner. Cut another segment the same size and set it aside for the moment, along with the first piece.

Now cut a length of plywood 40 inches long and 30 inches wide, and install it to cover the section already fastened to the wall and the second piece you cut and set aside. Use a fourth piece to form the back of the desk. This piece needs to be 40 inches long and 30 inches high.

Use wood glue and nails or screws to unite and hold this assembly. Now set the assembly into a corner and fasten one of the panels to the wall in the corner. The remainder of the desk will extend along the wall.

You can now build book cases or shelves from the free side of the desk to the wall. The plywood on top of the desk can be double-thick if there will be a great deal of weight on it.

You will now have a very simple and inexpensive desk area that will work well for holding a computer or typewriter. If you wish, you can run a full eight-foot length of plywood along the wall and use another section of plywood to act as a support for the extended desk surface.

This surface can hold a printer, pen sets, desk calendars, and similar items. You can also use the basic ideas presented here to build a number of other wall covering items that can be very functional and inexpensive.

If you want to build a very small desk-top bookcase, saw two boards eight inches to one foot high, depending upon the kind of books to be held. If the books are dictionaries or reference works of various types, make the boards ten to 12 inches high. The boards should be at least six to seven inches wide.

One inch from the bottom of each board, use a square as a guide and mark a light line across the board. Drill a one-inch hole two inches from each side of the board. Do the same with the other board.

Now use two lengths of dowel one inch in diameter, and insert these dowels through the holes. The dowels should be at least a foot long, if you have several books to shelve. You can use longer ones if you have more books, but if the books are heavy you might want to use three holes in each board and three dowels for greater strength.

Situate the book shelf so that the bottom edge of the two boards is in contact with a smooth surface. The dowels will hold the two boards upright. If you have a wide shelf of books, slide the boards further to the outside. If you remove some of the books, simply slide the boards toward the inside.

The book case will work if there is only one book in it, or, for that matter, if it is empty. Or it will hold as many as you can put in it without running out of dowel length.

Be sure to drill holes into the boards, rather than attempting to cut small squares and use squared strips of wood. The boards will not be held firmly by square strips, but the round ones work well.

The cost of a desk-top book case is typically less than half a dollar. The time required to construct the book case is roughly 30 minutes at the most.

Chapter Thirty Three: Chinking and Insulation

No matter how well you work and how careful you are with tiny details, your house will still not be completely satisfactory until you have done all you can, within reason, to establish the best possible climate control. This means, briefly, the installation of chinking and insulation.

You should understand from the outset that it is physically impossible to stop the passage of hot or cold air or temperatures through materials used in building. The best you can do is slow down the passage of the heat or cold.

If you think about it, you will realize that a wall 20 feet thick would eventually allow the heat or cold inside to pass through the walls, or heat or cold from the outside would in time permeate the walls and reach the interior. Insulation is a highly effective means of keeping your heated or cool air inside, and chinking can be a marvelous aid to insulation.

Start with chinking. You may use several methods of stopping up cracks and air passages between logs. No matter how carefully you try to fit logs, there will be at least small cracks, and in most cases the cracks will be an inch wide or even greater.

Your job is to stop up the cracks on both the inside and the outside of the house. Several materials are available to you: these include mortar, mud, a mixture of mud and sawdust, or one of the newer commercial chinking compounds that include a vinyl base which allows the chinking to expand or contract as the house heats and cools.

The best bet, of course, is the commercial compound, but these materials can be very expensive. Before you decide on one, shop around and find the best bargains you can find. We had planned to use a mixture of mortar and sawdust, until one of the manufacturers we contacted agreed to give us an incredible price on one of their unpopular chinking colors.

The color of chinking is another matter. You can buy chinking to match logs, your drapes, or virtually anything else. The compound that we bought, the one that no one else would buy, was, in fact, exactly the color we would have chosen even if we had been forced to pay the full price. Besides, if you can get a great buy on even purple chinking, a couple of dollars worth of paint may convert the color to one that you like.

But if you plan to buy chinking, at least choose a color that you can live with comfortably. It is often economically unrealistic to buy a color and then paint over it.

Before you start to chink, there are several matters you need to take care of first. Your initial step is to work at the largest cracks, because these will naturally admit the greatest amount of cold or hot air, as well as insects and even mice and small snakes.

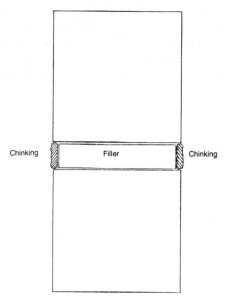

Figure 33-1
Filler between logs and chinking on edges.

Start by measuring the width of the crack, and if you can do so, locate a thin board and force it into the crack for as snug of a fit as you can manage. Do not let the board reach all the way to the outside edge, either inside or outside the house. Rather, let the board come to within a half-inch or so of the outside surface of the logs. See Figure 33-1.

Be certain that the fit is a snug one. Choose a board section that is almost too tight and tap it with a hammer until it has been forced into the crack. It does not matter how long the board or filler material is. If the crack between logs is 20 feet long, you can use two, three, or even ten filler sections. Once these are installed, you can apply chinking over the exposed edges. This will be discussed in more detail later.

If the cracks are V-shaped, cut filler sections that have an acute triangular shape. Then insert the sharpest angle into the crack and let the widest surface stop a quarter-inch inside the crack. If you need to do so, you can use tiny finish nails to hold the filler in place. See Figure 33-2.

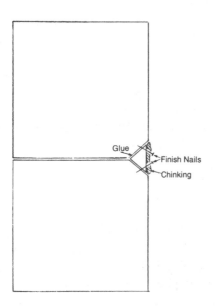

Figure 33-2
Using glue and finish nails to install filling.

If filler is not readily available, you can install small sections of commercial insulation into the cracks. Fill the cracks completely, but do not pack the insulation tightly. If you do so, you will lose the effect of the insulation, which is based in large part upon the dead air held inside the material.

Go around all of the exterior walls in the house and fill the cracks, both inside and outside. Only when this is done should you open the container of chinking compound.

If you have bought commercial chinking, you may find that it has separated slightly. If so, use a small trowel to stir the compound until it is mixed well.

To apply the chinking, dip the back side of the trowel into the compound and lift a small bead of compound. Press the bead of compound into the crack, apply gentle pressure, and move the trowel as you do so to get the best covering you can. The ideal thickness of the chinking is one-fourth inch. If it is thicker, it is a waste of expensive material. If thinner, it may separate and the wood will show through.

Do not smear the chinking compound on the outside surfaces of the logs. When this material dries, it is almost impossible to remove. Work along one full length of a crack. Fill the crack as needed from one end to the other. Then, before the chinking can start to set up, fill a small bucket with water, dip your trowel into the water, and use the back side of the wet trowel to smooth the surface of the chinking.

The principle is very much the same as that used in pargeting a wall with mortar. Keep wetting the trowel and smoothing until the chinking compound is as smooth as you can get it. Then move to another crack.

When you must stop for a lunch break or for the day, be sure to close the chinking container so that it is sealed as tight as you can get it. When the chinking starts to dry out, it becomes stiff and impossible to spread. You will simply have to discard it. But if you keep it tightly closed when you are not working, it will remain mallable and easy-to-spread for months.

When you have stopped up all of the cracks in the walls, fill the cracks, if any, where the subflooring meets the walls. Fill all the cracks along window and door frames. Do not neglect any areas where air can pass through. Concentrate more thoroughly on the side of the house from which your worst weather comes.

If even the tiniest hairline cracks are not filled, blowing rain will be forced through the logs, and cold winter air will find its way into the house and make the house more difficult and expensive to heat.

When you have completed the work, seal and set aside at least a part of a container of compound for later use. No matter how carefully you covered the cracks, there will be places where the chinking compound cracks apart. When this happens, return to the compound you kept and re-chink in these small areas.

If you choose to use mortar or a mixture of sawdust and mortar, install the filler as before and apply mortar with a trowel. Pack the mortar into the cracks tightly and then smooth the bead while the mortar is plastic. If you wish, you can drive small nails into the cracks, but leave half an inch of the nails sticking out and then mortar around them, which will help to keep the mortar from falling out if it cracks. See Figure 33-3.

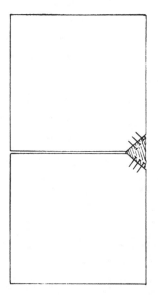

Figure 33-3
Using mortar and nails as chinking method.

You are now ready to start on insulation. You need not install insulation inside the interior walls, of course, but you will want to install at least six inches of insulation in the ceiling, particularly if you have a cathedral ceiling.

Consider the cathedral ceiling for a moment. If you have a large house, one side of the roof will be 20 feet from peak to eaves. If the house is 52 feet long, you will have 1,040 square feet of roof exposed to the weather. You will have enormous heat loss from inside the house, unless you insulate heavily. To check this for yourself, notice the roof of your neighbors' houses on the morning of a heavy frost or if there is a snowfall.

You will see that the frost melts off the roof of one house within minutes, while other houses may remain frost-covered or snow-covered for hours. Snow may remain on the roof all day or for days at a time.

The houses with the fastest melt-off are those with the poorest insulation and the greatest heat loss. These are also the houses with the greatest heating bills.

The same holds true for air-conditioning. In many parts of the country it costs as much to cool as it does to heat, and you have an escape of dollars in proportion to the amount of air passage you have through the roof or walls.

Earlier we noted that you had 1,040 square feet of roof space. This is, of course, for only one side. The entire roof has 2,080 square feet.

Earlier I suggested that you install ceiling and insulation for the cathedral ceiling at the same time. The logic behind this is simple. On top of the girders you will need to lay sheets of plywood over 2″ x 10″ timbers to provide you with a temporary floor surface, and atop the temporary surface you will need to set up ladders or scaffolding.

This procedure requires considerable time and effort. You will not want to set up the scaffolding for the insulation, then take down the scaffolding and move it, only to replace it when you work on the ceiling. Eliminate this time- and energy-consuming double-handling of scaffolding.

Start at the bottom: where the roof joins the walls, begin installing insulation. You will notice that on the rolls of insulation there is a paper backing. This backing should face the interior of the room.

You will also notice that there are flaps or tabs that extend from the sides of the backing. The backing is spread so that the flaps will cover the bottom edges of the rafters. You can then staple the flaps to the rafters to hold the insulation in place.

Insulation, which is made of fiberglass, can cause extreme burning and itching when it comes into contact with your skin, so wear gloves and long sleeves when you work. When the day's work is finished, wash the clothing separately from your better garments.

The fiberglass can also cause great irritation to your eyes, so please wear protective glasses. Another precaution: breathing the tiny fiberglass particles can cause bronchitis and other respiratory difficulties, so you are advised to wear a mask while working. Stop and take fresh-air breaks at regular intervals.

If you are using 12-foot ceiling covering, insulate a 12-foot section and then start nailing up ceiling tongue-and-groove boards. Work until you have gone as far as you can go before you move the scaffolding, until you have finished insulating the entire lower portion of the ceiling.

Keep installing insulation and ceiling boards. Take both of the materials up at the same time, until you have reached the peak or are up to the collar bracing.

Collar bracing is essential for maximum roof strength, and if you haven't installed the braces at this point, it is time to do it, particularly before you install ceiling boards too high. Remember that the collar bracing is a timber (2″ x 6″, 2″ x 8″, or similar-sized and -strength materials) that is nailed to the rafters in order to provide the greater strength needed to keep the rafters from sinking and pushing outward on the walls.

When you nail up collar bracing, use a level and tape. Measure carefully so that each and every brace is exactly the same distance from the peak. The bottom edges of all braces should be perfectly horizontal from side to side and from brace to brace.

Remember that you will be nailing boards to the bottom edge of the braces, and if the braces are not straight, then your ceiling cannot be straight. Take a few more minutes to install the braces correctly, and save yourself a great deal of trouble a short distance down the road. See Figure 33-4.

Figure 33-4
Installing boards across collar bracing.

When you reach the collar bracing, you will need to fit the tongue-and-groove boards at right angles. This can be difficult unless you follow a couple of very basic suggestions.

As you prepare to nail up your final board before you stop the slanted climb and start the vertical installation, you will have the tongue of each board facing upward. If you will saw off the tongue of the final board, you can then saw a 45-degree angle on the groove edge of the next board, and the two surfaces will fit together neatly. See Figure 33-5.

Continue across the collar bracing until you reach the other side, where you stopped earlier. Here you will need to do the same thing: trim off the tongue and angle-cut the groove side of the final board.

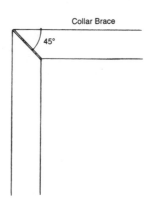

Figure 33-5
Starting boards across bottom edge of collar bracing.

But if you do not have room for a full board, you simply measure from the final board on the incline to the edge of the last board installed. Then chalk a line and angle-cut the final board to fit.

Your only problem is that the one thin board may look out of place. You can prevent this from happening if you will measure the width of several boards and write down that measurement someplace where you will not lose it. Assume that you will lay 16 boards side by side and insert tongues into grooves, just as you plan to install the boards. Assume that your finish width of each board is 4.5 inches. When you multiply 16 times 4.5 you have a total of 72 inches. This means that your collar bracing timbers should be 72 inches long, plus the lap area on each side of the rafter. If you feel more confident by doing so, nail up a collar brace with just enough nails that the brace will remain in place while you measure across the horizontal area.

If you don't have exactly 72 inches, adjust the brace up or down slightly until the distance is exact. Then nail in all the braces at that location, and you will have little difficulty in installing the ceiling boards across that area.

Chapter Thirty Four:
Finishing Touches

One of the undeniable aspects of house building is that the nearer you come to completion, the less it seems that you will ever be finished with the house. This is not meant to be discouraging, but there are literally dozens of small touch-up or finish-up jobs that must or at least should be done.

None of these jobs are demanding in terms of money, energy, or time, and none can be spared or delayed without remorse. You may, like so many people, decide that you will go ahead and move in, and in your abundant spare time you will take care of all the detail work that has thus far gone unfinished.

Sure, and you will win the lottery that same day. Experience has shown me and thousands like me that once we move into the house, we find that we are so tired of the work that we simply must have a vacation, if only to devote time to other chores that have been neglected. And three years later these small jobs have still not been done.

My wife was in the process of compounding sheet rock we used in the basement, and I offered to bet her six months of free dish washing that the job would not be completed a year from the date she started it. She completed all but about two square feet and then we accepted a writing assignment in New Mexico. We returned in 1991, and after five years the area has still not been compounded.

So plan to finish as much of the house as your finances and time will permit. But if economy forces you to move into the house, make a concentrated effort to get the small jobs done. Following, you will find a short list of assignments that you can complete in a day or so, or much less, in some cases.

Fascia and Soffit

You have doubtless noticed that on the traditional house the rafter ends or tails are boxed in with either wide boards or panels of plywood. This boxing is done for looks and to keep birds and other pests away from the rafter ends. It is also done to weather-proof the house even more. This work area will only be called the soffit from this point on.

You recall that you spaced your rafters 16 inches on center, and if you buy a panel of plywood you will be able to cover several of the rafter ends with it. So don't buy a large amount of plywood until you have checked to see how far one panel will go.

Start by measuring the distance from the outside wall at the highest point (where it joins the rafters) to the ends of the rafters. This will perhaps be one foot exactly. This means that you will be able to rip the plywood into four eight-foot strips and thus be able to cover a large number of rafters with the one panel. You can cover, in fact, seven rafters with one strip. (Or eight, if you count the first rafter. In other words, you can cover 96 inches of length with the first strip.)

If your house is 52 feet long, you will need 6.5 strips of plywood to cover the rafter ends. So one and one-half panels will cover one side of the house. And three panels will cover the entire house eaves, both front and back.

Then you will need to cover the actual end edges of the rafters, and you will need strips of about 12 inches to allow you to cover rafter ends as well as roof sheathing. This means that you can get four strips from one panel of plywood, so you will need a total of about eight panels to allow you a little extra in case you cut incorrectly or you have a flaw in the plywood. Naturally, you will need more if you have wider eaves.

To install soffit, mark and cut the plywood and simply hold it in place while you drive small nails (eight or 10d) up through the plywood and into the under-side of the rafters. Use at least three or four nails to each rafter. If you use ring-shanked nails, they will be less likely to pull out. See Figure 34-1.

If you choose to cut your own boards, you will need two six-inch boards as straight and smooth and uniformly thick as you can cut them. Nail these in place side by side.

Figure 34-1
Nailing up soffit.

Do the same for the actual ends of the rafters. It is a good idea to hold a plywood strip or board in place and mark along the bottom corner of the rafters. Then connect the marks with a chalk line and saw along the line.

Sealing the Logs

Once soffit is installed, you may wish to seal the logs with a special spray that generally water-proofs and insect-proofs the logs. You can buy a small garden sprayer and then simply spray the logs from a distance of about three feet or less away. In fact, if you keep the nozzle or spray tip within one foot of the logs, you can get a deep, full covering of the logs. Let the spray fill the cracks, and saturate the tiny cracks around windows and doors.

Omit nothing that is wood and exposed to the weather. Insects love wood, and you will find that some of them will try to bore into the wood itself, and woodpeckers will come in search of the insects, and you will start to see slight areas of damage. If you spray carefully, wait two or three days and spray again, and even add a third

coating, your wood will stay sound and insect-free for a long, long time.

Several years later, you may want to repeat the process. You will find that the spray will prevent the wood from fading or darkening into an unwanted shade.

Bleaching Wood

For the inside of your house, if you want the wood to return to its original shade or color, you can buy five-gallon cans of restorer (and perhaps it is on sale in smaller amounts). Brush on the restorer, which goes by several descriptions, and the process begins immediately. Within a period of a day or so the wood will be noticeably light, and in a remarkably short time it will return to its original color and will look the way it did when you first cut and installed the logs.

You can also use a commercial bleach, such as Clorox, either in a half-and-half bleach-and-water mixture or at full strength. We found that while a brush worked fine, we learned that a coarse cloth wadded tightly and with the tip of the wad saturated in the bleach worked wonderfully. We held the wadded cloth and pushed against the wood with gentle pressure until we were certain that the bleach had permeated the entire surface of the wood. The action began instantly, and within an hour the wood had been restored to the appearance we wanted.

Protecting Floors

If you want your finish floors to remain bright and shiny, you will need to apply two or three coats of a polyurethane covering. You can buy the covering in five-gallon cans, and we invested in a pan and roller apparatus. An entire floor in a large room can be done within about five to ten minutes.

That is, it can be done if the room is empty. If it already has the furniture in it, you will have to carry out the furniture and then leave it in the hallway or adjoining room while the first coat dries completely, which takes about one full day. So if you apply three coats you will need to allow about three days for total drying — if the weather is warm and clear. If the weather is cool and wet, drying takes a much longer time and the covering should not be attempted in such weather unless you have a form of climate control, such as a heating system that dehumidifies.

When you work with any of the sprays or bleaches, by all means have the room well ventilated, and never work around open flames. Do not smoke or allow anyone else to smoke during the work process. Keep all containers tightly sealed and out of the reach of children at all times.

Filling Spike Holes

When you spiked the logs into place, you were advised to drill a hole through the side of the log at the end, and then drive and countersink a spike into the hole. This is a necessary part of solidifying the walls, but you will also have a hole left after the spike has been countersunk. The holes in the tops of the logs will be covered by other logs, but the end holes will remain open. And they become a favorite spot for bumblebees, spiders, and other unwanted pests. Once you have completed work on the walls, go back to the holes and fill them with either wood putty or, if you want to save more money, with a stiff mixture of sawdust and wood glue.

Another reason for filling the holes is that during driving rains there will be moisture accumulations inside the holes, and the standing water or constant dampness will result in decay and the weakening of wood. Filling the holes takes a very short time, so do not neglect this simple but important chore.

Shutters

Once the house is livable, you will want to start protecting it and your valuables and your family from two-legged intruders. On the lower floors you will of necessity have windows that are easily accessible to burglars or other intruders. In our house we made two-by-six-foot wood shutters that were bolted together. We drilled holes in cross pieces at the top and bottom, and used round-headed bolts that cannot be grasped with pliers or wrench. The washers and nuts were located on the inside of the room.

To install the shutters, we drilled holes into the masonry blocks and installed anchors. Then we used butterfly hinges and sank the holding screws into the anchors. When the shutter is closed, the screws cannot be reached or, for that matter, seen. On the inside we used a simple slide-bolt lock that cannot be opened from the outside. The pins in the hinges are, of course, inside the room.

Insurance

This is not something you can make, but you should be aware that you can purchase construction or builder's insurance to protect your work and property while you are away from it. This insurance covers theft, fire, storm damage, and other actions that can reduce your hard work to a pile of ashes or rubble.

When you purchase an insurance policy of this type, it can be converted without difficulty to regular home insurance as soon as your power is turned on or you move in. At this point your clothes, guns, cameras, and other property will also be covered.

Incidentally, when you buy insurance, ask pointed and very specific questions about what is and isn't covered. Ask whether the policy will offer replacement value for damaged or lost items. You may have bought a camera for $150, but you may not be able to replace that same type of camera for less than $750.

Ask, too, about violent weather coverage. Be aware that during the flooding in Georgia, the earthquakes in San Francisco, and the Mississippi Valley flooding, as many as 75% of the victims did not get any benefits, or they received only very limited benefits. In our case, we had been insured by the same company for more than two decades, and we did not receive one cent when a tornado destroyed our house.

Once you get your answers, either tape record them (after having the agent identify himself by name and as authorized agent for the company, and by dating the tape and by having witnesses present) or have the agent or a company official write an official letter stating exactly what they told you. Then rent a safety-deposit box and store the letters and master tape in it. Make copies of the tape and give one to the agent and another to a trusted and reliable friend.

Alarm System

Once you are far enough along to do so, if you plan to have an alarm system installed, this is the time to do it. Talk with several companies, and be certain that whatever system you buy has constant 24-hour monitoring. Don't settle for the cheaper systems that simply trigger an alarm when an intruder enters.

What good is the alarm if the neighbors won't call the police or fire department or you, if you are at work? While this isn't a part of construction, a good alarm system is a vital part of a safe and sound house.

So these few suggestions might serve as guidelines. You will want a system that has distinct modes for night, away, and at home. The system should be equipped with an emergency alarm that summons an ambulance or fire truck, and it should have a heat detector, smoke detector, and motion detector. It should also detect loud noises or breaking glass.

Two of the fine points of such a system are that if the power is off, a battery unit will operate the system for at least several hours, and that if someone cuts the telephone line, the alarm is sent in. Many systems work in a basic fashion: you arm the system when you go to bed, leave home, or plan to be at home but perhaps are working in a remote part of the house so that you might not be able to hear the sound of an intruder entering the house.

You arm the system by entering a four-digit code (known only to you and to the top level of the monitoring company and to those select people you inform) and push either "away" or "night" or another option. Then you lock the door and leave. When you return you unlock the door, enter the four-digit code, and press "Off."

Many systems have a hostage code which permits you to turn off the alarm but which also sends the silent message to the monitoring station, which in turn sends help to your house. If an intruder should happen to accost you at gunpoint in your yard and force you to take him into the house and then to turn off the system, he has no way of knowing whether you did in fact disarm the system or sent in the silent alarm.

You can pay from around $3,000 for such a system, plus a monthly monitoring fee.

Eaves Completion

When the walls are completed, you still have the task of filling in the space between the peak of the house and the top of the log walls. You can do this work by sawing logs the same size as the first ones installed, with each log being cut at an angle on the ends and each one becoming shorter than the previous.

Warning: you are now working very high, and it is extremely difficult to hoist huge logs to such heights. There is physical danger in addition to the difficulty. So you have a second option.

This option is to use siding panels. The siding is much lighter than logs, and the work goes much faster.

To install siding panels, you will nail the panels to the studs you erect from the top log to the rafters on the extreme end of the house.

The siding panels are extremely difficult to hold, so to make the job easier you can drive three or four nails partway in and leave the heads sticking out far enough that the nails will hold the panels so that you can nail them in position while they rest on the nails. You can also drive three or four nails partially into the stud at the side of the panel so that the panel cannot slip sideways while you are working.

When you reach the point that it is hard to hoist the panels and wrestle them into position, you can complete the job from the inside of the house. Do this as you would do the dormers or even roof sheathing by nailing 2″ x 4″s onto the inside of the panel.

Measure off the exact locations of the studs, and position the 2″ x 4″s along the stud line. Lay the panel upside down, so that the outside of the panel faces upward. Then position the 2″ x 4″s along the line you have marked.

If you have trouble seeing the mark under the panel, mark the location on the bottom and top edge of the panel, and then make sure that the marks align with the 2″ x 4″. Then drive ring-shanked nails down through the panel and into the 2″ x 4″s. Place nails only six or eight inches apart.

Then, and this is the difficult part, drive a spike three-fourths of the way into the rafter and above the location of the panel installation. Loop a rope over the spike and bring both ends of the rope inside the work area. Tie one end around the panel and fasten the other end to a girder or other stable part of the house. Pull the end of the rope, before you tie it, until it is nearly taut with the panel standing on its bottom edge. Leave only enough slack so that you can maneuver the panel outside the studding and then position it. See Figure 34-2.

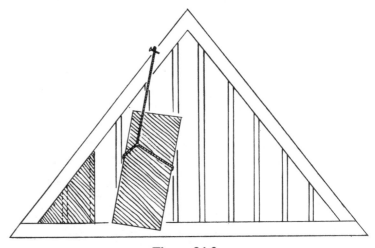

Figure 34-2
Using rope to hold panel while it is installed.

Push the panel between the studs, and while the rather heavy panel is suspended from the spike, turn the panel and swing it into position. Now pull the 2″ x 4″s tightly against the studs, and then drive through the 2″ x 4″s and into the studs.

Once these and other finishing touches are completed, you can turn your attention to the process of building a deck, which is the topic of Chapter Thirty Five.

Chapter Thirty Five:
Deck Construction

The question of whether to add a deck or not is not only a matter of economy and/or aesthetics; it is also a matter of both safety and convenience. It can also be a necessity.

Many (or most) insurance companies and building inspectors insist on a front and rear exit from the upstairs or ground floor levels. You may already have a basement door that opens to the front of the house; if so, you probably will not need an exit from the ground floor level of the house. But, even so, there is a severe safety factor.

When we were building our house, many friends and strangers came by to visit, to see what progress we were making, and in almost every instance these visitors wanted a tour of the house. And, almost without exception, at least one member of each party opened the front door on the upper floor and started to step out onto the ground. In their tour of the house, they became slightly disoriented and thought they were back on the ground floor. If they had stepped out and had fallen to the concrete patio below, they could have been seriously injured or even killed.

Consider aesthetics or beauty for a moment. Look at the photo of the front of the house before the deck was added (Figure 35-1). The house front, while not yet completed, is plain and even austere. Now turn to Figure 35-8 and compare the appearance of the house with

that shown in Figure 35-1. They are hard to recognize as even the same structure.

From an economic standpoint, we could have built a small deck, perhaps 10´ x 10´ (and considered doing so), but we reasoned that the extra expense could easily be justified if we built a deck that reached across the entire front of the house.

The deck we built is 52 feet long and 10 feet wide, a total of 520 square feet. Such a deck can be built, by using a chain saw to cut the timbers, for slightly more than $60, including the cement blocks, mortar, framing, and railing. If you buy your lumber but do your own work, the total price of a deck like ours is slightly less than $800. If you hire someone to build it, the price will be about $4,500 or more.

When you are ready to start building, your first step, once you decide on dimensions, is to dig and pour footings. In our case the footings had already been poured (in the form of a paved patio) and we built piers atop the patio concrete.

Your piers may be wood posts, bricks, or cement blocks. You can even pour concrete piers, but this is exacting and rather expensive work. My suggestion is cement blocks, which can later be veneered with bricks or stone.

To construct piers for a deck, first determine how many piers you will need. For a 52-foot deck, you will need six piers on the front and on the back. In addition to the piers at

Figure 35-1
The log house without the deck is roomy and comfortable, but the absence of a deck detracts from the looks of the entire house.

each end, you will need four inside piers, all spaced evenly apart.

Start by marking off the exact size and location of the piers to be built against the basement wall. Be sure that the piers clear windows and doorways properly. Next, determine the height of the piers.

A cement block is eight inches high. Eleven of these will give you a height of 88 inches, plus 9½ inches for the floor framing and headers, and another inch for the flooring. The total height will be 98.5 inches.

The proper height for your deck depends upon the height of the door opening. You do want the deck to be slightly lower than the floors inside the house.

When you start to build the piers, mix mortar as detailed in Chapter Eight. Consult that chapter also for information on how to lay cement blocks. Before you lay a bed for the first block, use a sprayer or squirt bottle and moisten the concrete and the surface of the cement blocks against which you will lay the blocks for your piers.

Figure 35-2
*Keep blocks in perfect alignment
so that the deck floor will be level.*

Start laying the blocks for the first pier. Use a drop cloth or plastic to cover the patio so that you will not mar the surface by dropping mortar on it. Lay a bed of mortar around the outline of the first cement block, and then lay the block length-wise so that the long side butts against the basement wall.

Be sure to check that each block is level from side to side and from front to back. When you have laid four or five blocks, start another pier. Use a line level to see that the blocks are constantly even as the pier climbs. When you have laid five blocks on each pier, lay a 2″ x 4″ or 2″ x 6″ across the top of the blocks, and then lay a level on top of the timber, as shown in Figure 35-2.

Start other piers and bring them up together with the others. You may want to add four blocks or so to a pier, then change locations and lay blocks at another pier to be sure that you do not allow the piers to climb out of alignment.

Do not be content to check only the nearest piers. Run a line level from the first to the last piers, and fasten the line securely. Then make certain that all blocks along the line are at the same height.

As the piers grow, stop and fill the cores of the blocks with concrete or metal rods. Cement blocks have great strength when it comes to supporting weights, but they can be pushed over easily if they are not supported from within.

If you used bricks to fill in over the window lintels, you may wish to parget (or cover with mortar or stucco) when the piers reach their ultimate height.

When the parget process is completed (See the chapter on masonry for discussion of parget work), you need to start framing the deck. One of the first steps is to bolt the header (treated lumber) to the side of the house or to the basement wall.

One of the easiest ways to do this is to use an electric drill with a foot-long masonry bit. Before drilling, use a line level to determine the exact points where the bolts should be drilled, and then drill a hole completely through the concrete blocks along the top course. Use bolts ¾″ that are long enough to reach completely through the blocks. The bolts must be eight inches long (for the block), plus another two inches in length for the header timber.

When the hole is drilled, drill matching holes through the header timber, and insert the bolt through the header and through the cement block. Leave the rounded head of the bolt on the outside of the header.

This is also a good time to cut and nail in place the ledger plate that is fastened to the bottom of the header, and which is used later as a support for framing timbers. See Figure 35-3 for the locations of header or framing timber, bolts, and ledger plate.

Now complete the framing of the deck. Start by running 2″ x 10″ timbers around the entire outside of the deck area. Position the timbers so that the first timber reaches from the first outside corner to a point halfway across the second pier. Let the end of the timber reach the outside edge of the corner pier.

Next, measure and cut a timber to reach from the inside edge of the timber you've just positioned to the inside edge of the timber that is bolted to the concrete blocks. Nail through the outside edge of the timber, and then toe-nail it to the timber which is bolted to the house.

Figure 35-3
Note bolts fastening framing timber to cement blocks.
At lower right ledge plate section can be seen.

Cut an inside timber to butt against the end timber you've just installed. This timber can be shorter or longer than the outside timber, but the two should not be the same length. Keep the framing timbers staggered so that there will not be weaknesses in construction

caused by too many framing members ending at the same place.

Install joists between the header timbers. Use 16-inch on-center locations for the joists. On each end, cut out a square for the space needed by the ledger plate.

When all of the joists are installed along the entire length of the deck framing, you are ready to install the decking or flooring boards. Unless the deck is to be covered or enclosed later, you may wish to leave a small amount of space between the decking boards to allow moisture accumulations to drain freely. One simple method of spacing boards uniformly is to position them so that you can drop the pointed end of a 16d nail through the crack, but the head will not pass through the opening. Another easy way is to use the point of a crowbar to provide the needed space. See Figure 35-4.

Figure 35-4
Pry boards apart, if needed, while someone drives nails through boards and into joists.

Figure 35-4 shows joist placement, the position of decking boards crossing the joists, and the use of a crowbar point to provide the needed space between boards.

When you install decking, you should stagger the decking ends just as you staggered the joist ends. By doing so you greatly increase the strength of the deck. To install decking without cutting every other timber, buy it in lengths that will span joists exactly. The length should be divisible by 16. Ten-foot boards work well for this type of construction, as do 12-foot and 16-foot boards.

Start by running the outside (or inside) board the full length of the deck. Then cut a board in half and install it alongside the first board. Then use a full-length board alternating with a half-long board for the remainder of the distance along the deck surface area. After you cut the half-length boards for the first installations, you will not have to cut boards again until you reach the end of the deck area.

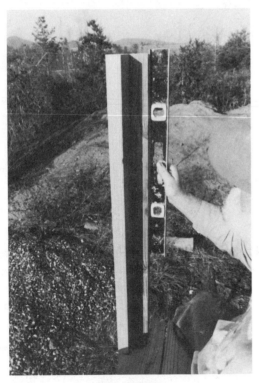

Figure 35-5
Right-angle structure of corner deck post. The third member of the assembly fits inside the angle.

When the deck flooring is installed, you are ready to put up posts for the railing. Start at an outside corner and, after determining how high you want the railing to be (three feet or forty inches is a good protective

height), add the width of the header timber to the length of the post. If the railing post is 40 inches high, and if the header is ten inches wide (actually, 9½ inches, unless you cut your own), you will need two posts that are 49½ inches long. You will also need a third post timber that is 40 inches long (or whatever height you chose) to complete the corner post.

Nail the two post timbers together by standing one timber on its edge and laying the second timber atop the top edge of the standing timber. The outside post timbers will then be connected at right angles. See Figure 35-5.

If the outside decking board fits flush with the edge of the piers, you can install the assembly just as it is. If you have a slight overhang, mark and cut out a space just large enough to permit the 2″ x 4″ to fit inside it. When the assembly is nailed in place, use the third post timber to fit inside the right angle so that you will have the corner post supported by the extension on the front and the one on the outside, as well as by the post member on the inside.

Nail the other corner posts in place, and then install the inside posts by cutting one post member 49½ inches long and one 40 inches long. Cut just enough space out from the overhang to permit the outside post member to fasten directly to the header timber.

Set the posts in place eight to ten feet apart, whatever is a handy fraction of your deck length. If the deck is 60 feet long, ten-foot spacing is ideal. If the deck is 45 feet long, a spacing of 7.5 feet is ideal. Be sure to use a level so that all of the posts will be vertical or plumb.

When all of the posts are installed, you can nail up the top rails. When you do so, measure from the outside edge of the corner post to a point halfway across the top edge of the second post. You will need to leave nailing room atop each post.

Keep the railing as smooth, level, and neat as you can. Do not permit one post, for instance, to be even a fraction of an inch too high or too low.

When the entire top rail is in place, you are ready for the bottom rail and the balusters. There are several ways that the bottom rail and balusters can be installed, but two primary ways work well (and one way works better than the other — for us, at least).

The first way is to cut two short lengths of 2″ x 4″ and use them as your guides. Measure and cut the bottom part of the rail and then position the 2″ x 4″ lengths, standing on edge, against the posts. Toe-nail the bottom rail member into the side of the post, and then remove the 2″ x 4″ sections. Then cut the balusters to length and install them. Space them properly.

The two slight problems with the first method are that often the 2″ x 4″ sections will become wedged under the bottom rail and are difficult to remove, and that the baluster lengths must be cut exactly to size, or else they will be too loose or will not fit at all between the rails and must be re-cut.

The method which we found to be very satisfactory was to assemble the railing section first and then fit it into the system. If you wish to try this very easy method, which works beautifully, start by measuring and cutting a timber that fits exactly between the two posts. Then measure and mark off the space you want between the balusters.

This measuring and marking can be tricky. Remember that the first balusters will not be located on the ends of the bottom rail because the posts will serve as balusters in these positions. So you will need to determine the spacing of only the interior balusters.

Assume that your entire section is ten feet long. Mark off the bottom rail by first determining the exact center, which is at five feet. Then divide the halves, which gives you 2.5 feet. Now divide the fourths and the eighths. These two locations will be, respectively, at 1.25 feet and .62 feet.

In other words, your balusters should be 7.5 inches apart. So measure from the end to a point 7.5 inches away, and mark the spot. Then move to 15 inches and mark again. Mark at 22.5″, 30″, 37.5″, 45″, 52.5″, 60″, 67.5″, 75″, 82.5″, 90″, 97.5″, 105″, and 112.5″. Remember that you will not install balusters at either end, so in one section you will have 15 balusters.

The above designations are all based on ten-foot sections with balusters spaced at 7.5 inches. You may choose whatever spacing and section lengths that are appropriate for you. Whatever you choose, all you need to do is find the center point and then divide the halves into fourths and the fourths, if necessary, into eighths. Install balusters on-center at each mark.

Start by nailing in the balusters for each end, remembering not to install one on the very end but at the first marking from each end. Turn the section upside-down so that you can nail through the bottom of the rail and into the ends of the balusters.

When all of the balusters are installed, carry the section to the rail position and slip it into place. The

baluster tops will still be loose at this time, as shown in Figure 35-6.

Figure 35-6
When bottom rail sections are in position,
move top ends of balusters into rough position.

Now use a level (See Figure 35-7) to align the balusters perfectly, and then drive 16d nails down through the top of the rail and into the top end of the balusters. If you use a level to plumb the balusters, they will be spaced perfectly at the top as well as at the bottom, and you need not worry about marking the positions on the top rail.

It is a good idea to cut and install short blocks of 2″ x 4″ timbers at the mid-points of the sections. This block is to keep the sections from sagging, particularly if the timbers have not dried completely.

Finally, note the dramatic difference seen in the two appearances of the house as a result of the addition of the deck. Figure 35-8 shows the house with the installed deck. Turn back to Figure 35-1 to see the contrast. Even if the deck is built at the full price of about $800, this is a small price to pay for such a vast improvement in looks. And in the bargain you get a huge space for cookouts, sitting, entertaining, and other delights.

Figure 35-7
Using a level to align balusters; install balusters by driving nails through top rail and into ends of balusters.

Figure 35-8
Completed deck creates marked improvement over the house without decking.
Compare with Figure 35-1.

Chapter Thirty Six:
Confidence Boosting Projects

All right! At this time it's permissible for you to admit that you are scared witless over the formidable task of building a house with a chain saw. You have heard of people who did so, but when you investigated more carefully you learned that the people either bought their lumber and simply used the chain-saw to cut the lumber to length, or they cut down trees and had lumber sawed from the logs, or they had an expensive chain-saw mill or portable sawmill on their property, or they were people with a lifetime of chain-saw experience.

Whatever their status, they had so much previous knowledge or such superior equipment that you felt that there was no way you could compete with them in order to build a house. In fact, you would feel ashamed of what you finally produced.

And you had severe doubts that the house featured in this book was built for less than $15,000. And you'd be right.

It wasn't. The house shown here was built for far, far less than the figure given. But we had advantages you may not have, and we had access to some excellent bargains. Let me explain this matter for a moment.

The total cost of our house includes the house itself, the chain saw (which cost us $400), furniture, light fixtures, and a hospital bill for a broken leg I suffered in a freak accident along the way. I had once planned to build a small house and to build the furniture as well for about $500, but this house would have been merely a weekend cabin consisting of only two rooms and a sleeping loft, plus rustic furniture.

Yet, any way you count it, $500 for a cabin isn't a great deal of money.

Our walls, one of the most expensive parts of building any house, cost $132.64. This was the figure for the interior and the exterior walls, because one wall serves both purposes. And lest you doubt that we could do this, and, more importantly, that you could and can do it, keep in mind that the figure given includes chain-saw chains, repairs, gas and oil for the saw, and even the cost of driving the family truck to and from the store or hardware store in order to buy needed materials.

If we reduce it to the cost of the actual log-milling only, the cost of the walls would be less than $75.

We laid hundreds of cement blocks, and the cost of these blocks was one of our major expenses, because we could not come up with a way of avoiding the expense, except by using field stone.

Let me assure you that if two conditions had been different, we would have used field stone. First, you will recall that a tornado had destroyed our house and our insurance company did not pay one cent to us. We lost house, furniture, clothing, personal effects, cameras, guns, and everything else we owned. We were homeless, and we desperately needed a house we could call our own.

For these reasons, we were in a great hurry, and we could not afford the time to hunt for stones we could use in our foundation walls. Another reason was that all of our trees had been uprooted by the storm, and all of our stones were under the giant piles of debris. But rest assured that if these factors had not been present, we could have and we would have built foundation walls of field stones. And we'd have saved a huge part of our expense.

We could not find a way to cut back on the cost of roofing, but this was not terribly expensive. We could have cut our own wood shingles (and we did so for some of our outbuildings) but the code would not let us use wood shingles on our dwelling, even if we had been willing to do so, and we weren't.

But rest assured that if we had been permitted the luxury of plenty of time, we could have built our house for far less than the cover price of $15,000. And we have proof.

We built a two-car garage for $24. We built a tractor barn for $30. And we recently built a three-car garage for $450, and the vast majority of this cost went for plywood sheathing and shingles. If we had the time to cut our own sheathing boards, as we did on other buildings, we'd have built the three-car garage for about $85, and that includes everything.

Now, you need to develop confidence. Anybody with reasonably good health and strength and coordination can do what we did, and if you have any hesitation, start by cutting some damaged trees (never good, vital trees if you can possibly avoid it!) that are small enough for you to work with comfortably.

Get a good chain saw if you don't already have one. Don't buy a small, cheap rig. Get a super saw, and then practice cutting square logs, boards, and smaller units of lumber. And don't feel defeated if your first efforts are not exceptional.

Once I had gained confidence, one of my first projects was to cut a picture frame. The frame cost less than ten cents and was, to me, a success. Keep in mind that this experiment occurred before the tornado, and when the storm hit, I had considerably more experience at chain-sawing lumber. Try your hand at simple projects, unless you are in a real rush. Even if you are, remember that haste indeed makes waste.

After the picture frame, I tried a basic bench, and then decided to add a picnic table and another bench. See Figure 36-1 for the picnic table.

Next, you may want to try your hand at cutting wood for a swing. My efforts were not complicated. I simply cut two long framing pieces (1″ x 3″ stock) and five short framing pieces from the same stock. Then I cut ten one-by-two strips for the seat.

You can add the frame for the back of the swing. Then you can complete the remainder of the swing, as shown in Figure 36-2.

As you build confidence, you can build a frame for the swing and enjoy outdoor enjoyment while you work on your house.

It's time to get even more ambitious. This time, cut a series of eight-foot studs. You will need two dozen or more of them. Cut corner posts. You will need four of these. You will also need rafters. Remember that when you are cutting a series of rafters from one log, leave part of the cut unfinished so that the log will stand steadily while you work.

Assemble the frame of the garage, which is what you are now building. When the complete frame is finished, cut shingles. You can use an old block of wood from a stump for this work.

Nail up the wood shingles by first nailing a row laid side by side from the nailers to the edge of the eaves.

Then install another row to cover the spaces between shingles. Keep rising higher and higher with the shingles, as shown in Figure 36-3, and when you are finished, you will have a superb two-car garage that will have cost you about $28.75.

The garage cost $24, and the house beside it, which is a two-story structure of 4,000 square feet, cost a little less than $12,000. The total price also included the well, a septic tank, and 24 acres of land, which was purchased, admittedly, at a terrific bargain price.

Next, try a small utility shed, built entirely of logs and shingles. The shed shown here is large enough to store a garden tractor, a riding lawn mower, a tiller, a mulcher, and a large supply of tools, fertilizer, seeds, and sprayers.

It cost $32.40 to build, and the vast majority of that money went for hinges and locks. The actual log structure itself cost less than $10.

Start by building a foundation wall of used cement blocks. These can be laid just as you would lay any other masonry blocks. Then cut full-length logs and stack them. Logs this short can be easily lifted into place by two people.

Use logs which are generally unfit for use in the house. At the corners, use short logs to provide a rough door opening.

Shingle the roof as you did before, by cutting your own wood shingles. Then build double doors of 2″ x 6″ lumber, like those shown in Figure 36-4. All that is left, then, is to install the final board for the door (omitted from the picture to show how the doors were constructed), and to enclose the front and rear spaces under the roof peak.

You are now ready to build the house of your dreams at a cost you never thought possible. Good luck, and great building! When you get discouraged, look at the cover of this book and remember that if you keep on working well, you can have a house of this sort, or even a better one, for less than the cost of a new car — and even less than the cost of a late-model used car!

Figure 36-1
Benches and picnic table.

Figure 36-2
The completed swing.

Figure 36-3
Garage nearing completion.

Figure 36-4
Nearly finished utility shed.

YOU WILL ALSO WANT TO READ:

☐ **17079 TRAVEL-TRAILER HOMESTEADING UNDER $5,000,** *by Brian Kelling.* Tired of paying rent? Need privacy away from nosy neighbors? This book will show how a modest financial investment can enable you to place a travel-trailer or other RV on a suitable piece of land and make the necessary improvements for a comfortable home in which to live! This book covers the cost breakdown, tools needed, how to select the land and travel-trailer or RV, and how to install a septic system, as well as water, power (including solar panels), heat and refrigeration systems. Introduction by Bill Kaysing. *1995, 5½ x 8½, 80 pp, illustrated, indexed, soft cover. $8.00.*

☐ **17040 SHELTERS, SHACKS AND SHANTIES,** *by D.C. Beard.* A fascinating book with over 300 pen and ink illustrations and step-by-step instructions for building various types of shelters. Fallen tree shelters; Indian wickiups; Sod houses; Elevated shacks and shanties; Tree houses; Caches; Railroad ties shacks; Pole houses; Log cabins; And many more. One of the great classics of outdoor lore. *1914, 5 x 7, 259 pp, illustrated, soft cover. $9.95.*

☐ **17054 HOW TO BUY LAND CHEAP, 5th Edition,** *by Edward Preston.* This is the bible of bargain-basement land buying. Revised and updated 5th edition shows you step-by-step how to find cheap land, evaluating it, bidding on it and closing the deal. New addresses and sample letters to help you get results. You can buy land for less than the cost of a night out — and this book shows you how. *1996, 5th Edition, 5½ x 8½, 136 pp, illustrated, soft cover. $14.95.*

☐ **14116 BUILDING WITH JUNK, And Other Good Stuff,** *by Jim Broadstreet.* A complete guide to building and remodeling using recycled materials. Millions of dollars worth of building materials are thrown away every day. This book shows how find, store and use this good stuff. Covers floors, ceilings, walls, foundations, roofs, plumbing, wiring, utilities, windows, doors, cabinetry, trim, insulation, appliances, furniture — even solar power! *1990, 8½ x 11, 174 pp, illustrated, hard cover. $19.95.*

☐ **14177 THE WILD & FREE COOKBOOK, with a Special Roadkill Section,** *by Tom Squier.* Why pay top dollar for grocery-store food, when you can dine at no cost by foraging and hunting? Wild game, free of the steroids and additives found in commercial meat, is better for you, and many weeds and wild plants are more nutritious than the domestic fruits and vegetables found in the supermarket. Authored by a former Special Forces survival school instructor, this cookbook is chockfull of easy-to-read recipes that will enable you to turn wild and free food (including roadkill!) into gourmet meals. *1996, 7¼ x 11½, 306 pp, illustrated, indexed, soft cover. $19.95.*

☐ **14178 COMMUNITY TECHNOLOGY,** *by Karl Hess, with an Introduction by Carol Moore.* In the 1970s, the late Karl Hess participated in a five-year social experiment in Washington, DC's Adam-Morgan neighborhood. Hess and several thousand others labored to make their neighborhood as self-sufficient as possible, turning to such innovative techniques as raising fish in basements, growing crops on rooftops and in vacant lots, installing self-contained bacteriological toilets, and planning a methanol plant to convert garbage to fuel. There was a newsletter and weekly community meetings, giving Hess and others a taste of participatory government that changed their lives forever. *1979, 5½ x 8½, 120 pp, soft cover. $9.95.*

And much, much more. We offer the very finest in controversial and unusual books — a complete catalog is sent FREE with every book order. If you would like to order the catalog separately, please see our ad on the next page.

• •

LOG96

LOOMPANICS UNLIMITED
PO BOX 1197
PORT TOWNSEND, WA 98368

Please send me the books I have checked above. I am enclosing $ which includes $4.95 for shipping and handling of orders totaling $20. Please include an extra $1 for each additional $20 ordered. *Washington residents please include 7.9% for sales tax.*

NAME_____

ADDRESS _____

CITY/STATE/ZIP _____

We accept Visa and MasterCard. To place a credit card order *only*, call 1-800-380-2230,
8am to 4pm, PST, Monday through Friday.